JOURNEY INTO OUR HERITAGE

The Story of the Jewish People in the Canadian West

Harry Gutkin

LESTER
&ORPEN
DENNYS
PUBLISHERS

The publisher wishes to thank the Multicultural Program, Government of Canada, for its support in the publication of this book.

Canadian Cataloguing in Publication Data

Gutkin, Harry, 1915-
    Journey into our heritage

Based on the national exhibition of the same name, 1976-77.

Bibliography: p.
Includes index.
ISBN 0-919630-08-1

1. Jews in the Prairie Provinces — History.
I. Jewish Historical Society of Western Canada.
II. Title.

FC3250.J5G87   971.2′004′924   C79-094566-5
F1060.97.J5G87

Design: Jack Steiner
Production: Verbatim
Typesettting: Alpha Graphics Limited
Printing: The Bryant Press Limited

Printed in Canada

JOURNEY INTO OUR HERITAGE

For my wife, Mildred,
who made this journey possible

CONTENTS

ACKNOWLEDGMENTS

Primary acknowledgments in the genesis of this book must go to the Jewish Historical Society of Western Canada, which functions as the repository for documents, photographs, and artifacts pertaining to the Jewish community in the west. With the co-operation of the executive director, Dorothy Hershfield, the Society's valuable archives and research facilities were entirely at my disposal.

Much of the material on the European experience comes to the Historical Society from the YIVO Institute for Jewish Research of New York, from the Central Archives of the History of the Jewish People in Jerusalem, and from Yad Vashem, the museum of the Holocaust, also in Jerusalem. Cyril Leonoff, archivist for the Jewish Historical Society of British Columbia, has been instrumental over the years in furnishing much of the collected material on his province. In addition, the research for this book was greatly assisted by the co-operation of the provincial archives of Manitoba, Saskatchewan, and Alberta; the Glenbow Foundation of Calgary; the Public Archives of Canada; and the archives of the Canadian Pacific Railways.

The immediate forerunner of this book is the travelling exhibit on the growth of the western Canadian Jewish community which was produced under my direction in 1976. Also called "Journey Into Our Heritage," this is the third and most ambitious of such exhibits prepared by the Jewish Historical Society of Western Canada as part of its ongoing program, and selected portions of the material on display are incorporated into the present book. Among all the people whose efforts went into the preparation of the first and second exhibits, acknowledgment is due Abraham J. Arnold, the first executive secretary of the Jewish Historical Society, for his work on these earlier exhibits specifically, for his contribution to the organization of the Society, and for his pioneering stimulation of interest in local Jewish history. Funding for the Society's work is provided in part by the Canadian Jewish Congress, by the Winnipeg Jewish Community Council, and by the Department of Cultural Affairs, Province of Manitoba. The travelling exhibit has also received generous support from the Department of the Secretary of State and the National Museums of Canada. Sol Kanee, the treasurer of the World Jewish Congress, has been among the Society's most perceptive supporters; we owe him a particular debt of gratitude for spearheading the necessary drive for private funds to send the travelling exhibit on tour.

For the 1972 exhibit of "Journey Into Our Heritage," co-sponsored with the Manitoba Museum of Man and Nature, the Canadian Broadcasting Corporation filmed twenty-four interviews with representative members of the community. Three of those interviews—with Paul Berger, Rabbi Peretz Weizman, and John Hirsch—were then restructured into a film on the Holocaust called *It Must Be Told*, which I edited and co-produced and which is still in wide circulation. The three participants have kindly given permission for portions of their stories to appear in Chapter 10, "The Valley of the Shadow."

A deep-felt tribute must be paid to my publishers' late partner, Eve Orpen, whose encouragement in the first stages of our discussions, just before her untimely death, was profoundly appreciated. I am greatly honoured that she took a personal interest in this book, and can only hope that the finished work will justify her confidence.

The complex task of research and writing has been made easier by the very able assistance of Esther Nisenholt, the archivist for the Jewish Historical Society, who helped with the selection of photographs and documents, provided the research for caption copy, read the manuscript with knowledgeable attention, and was a source of additional insights and information. That she also assisted efficiently in the voluminous correspondence contributed greatly to the book's orderly progress towards completion. When the manuscript was in its final stages, David Rome, the historian and archivist of the Canadian Jewish Congress, Montreal, generously lent his scholarship to many clarifications of both fact and interpretation.

The most widespread expression of thanks must be extended to all the anonymous individuals, families, and organizations who have contributed to the archives of the Jewish Historical Society of Western Canada. Because of their sense of history, the Society is able to assemble an ample record of Jewish life in western Canada. Every possible effort has been made to trace the owners of copyright materials in this book, but in some instances identification has proved impossible, and we do not have names and sources for all the photographs shown. Information leading to more complete acknowledgements would be very welcome and will be included in subsequent editions of *Journey Into Our Heritage*. In the meantime, my apologies for any omissions.

The final acknowledgement must go to my wife, Mildred, who collaborated with me from the beginning, discussing and evaluating each chapter and section, and demanding an uncompromising integrity of content and style, and who scrupulously re-read and edited the entire manuscript.

FOREWORD

This book invites its readers to take a journey into the development of the Jewish community of Western Canada, and an even longer journey back into the traditions and experiences that have shaped that community. It is about the life of a people: what they looked like, their homes, their work, their schools, their places of worship, their organizations and community involvement. It is a story of their achievements and their failures, and of the events, large and small, that have determined the pattern of their existence.

The arrival of Jewish settlers in the Canadian west can be divided into three major periods: from the beginning of the first mass immigration from eastern Europe, in 1882, to 1920, after World War I and the Russian Revolution; from 1920 to the start of World War II; and from 1945 onward. Why they came and how they came is part of the history of the Jews; these facts and figures, photos and stories, reflect one particular segment of the multiplicity that is now Canada. Canada drew its people from every ethnic background and all parts of the world with the same promise of greater well-being, of freedom from want and fear, of a secure and tranquil future, and all the newcomers endured much the same trauma of uprooting, arrival, and acclimatization. The Jewish immigrant experience in the prairie provinces and British Columbia is a microcosm of ethnic settlement in the west, mirroring the essential immigrant experience everywhere.

For many of the people who arrived in Halifax or Quebec in the early immigration days, whether they stayed in the east or moved farther into the sparsely populated west was largely a matter of chance. Some, of course, came to friends or relatives in one part of the country or another, or were attracted by specific job opportunities or by the offer of free land. Many simply stopped wherever their money ran out. "My wife's father was poor," one native-born westerner now explains. "He only had enough money to take him to Montreal. But my father was much better off. He managed to get all the way to Regina, so that's where I grew up." East or west, the Jews of Canada are one community, with the same values embodied in much the same institutions.

The actual span of Jewish history in the west is no more than one hundred years, so that many people today can still re-create the pioneer past out of the tales of their parents and grandparents. It is such stories that have been recorded in this book. Family albums have supplied many of the photographs, setting down for all time the daily life of a people in the particular look of each individual, the unique style of each family. These images acquire new significance when placed together, and the treasured mementos of each family take their place in the rich pattern of a common heritage.

Many of these photographs were taken by amateurs with the simplest equipment, but their awkward, often accidental effects are eloquent of time and place. Others, artfully arranged by professional photographers, speak with even greater clarity of the aspirations of their subjects. For an immigrant family the signal of newly achieved security was customarily the family portrait, parents and children posed in their very best clothes, to be sent back home to impress the less fortunate relatives left behind. As often as not, the proud silk top hat on a sitter's head and the shiny gold chain across his vest were supplied for the occasion by the photographer. Sometimes the stratagem did not quite succeed. A Winnipeg woman remembers being taken for a group portrait in 1935, at the lowest ebb of the depression, because her father felt it important to reassure his mother back in Poland that the family was doing well. The photographer arranged the hand-me-down clothes with elegant precision and touched up the scuffs on the worn boots, but something must have caught the sharp eye of the old grandmother. "I see, my son," she wrote, thanking him for the picture, "that you aren't exactly gathering gold in the streets of your Winnipeg."

Yet gold of a sort was to be found here — for the community as a whole, and for most of the individuals of that community — in the flourishing vigour of a new life-style. The journey towards that achievement has been long and arduous, and some of its stages are not pleasant to remember. But the heritage of the pioneer generations has been passed on to their descendants. In retracing their steps we come to know ourselves better.

THE SOURCE

1. THE JOURNEY BEGINS

In the ancient regions of the Middle East, sacred myth dissolves into history. The Biblical tales of exile and endless wandering are rooted in reality. Jewish migrations moved outward from the Biblical homeland with the ebb and flow of empires—Egyptian, Phoenician, Babylonian, Assyrian, Greek, and Roman. There were Jewish settlements in Europe as far back as the time of the Second Temple in 70 A.D. When the Arabs carried the Moslem faith abroad during the seventh century, Babylonian Jews moved into Palestine and North Africa, and then into parts of western Europe. There Jewish life prospered during the Middle Ages. It is thought that settlements also existed in parts of eastern Europe, which later became Russia, but that these were wiped out by Mongol invaders in the thirteenth century.

The Crusades, beginning in 1096, brought about a disintegration of the Jewish presence in western Europe, as popular wrath against the remote "infidel" in the Holy Land was turned against the Jew nearer home. In the economic and religious turmoil which swept Europe in the next four hundred years and more, Jews were banished from England and France, from the German states, from Spain and Portugal, in an uneven pattern of persecution and toleration. Jews were officially deprived of citizenship in the Holy Roman Empire in 1343, although in the absence of a strong central authority many managed to escape expulsion. England expelled its Jews in 1290, and some of them took shelter in France. By 1306, however, Philip the Fair of France had found it expedient to seize Jewish property, driving his Jewish subjects to Spain and Portugal. There they enjoyed a splendid "Golden Age," almost two centuries of economic and cultural growth, until the flames of the Inquisition sent them forth once more. At that point Venice and Amsterdam accepted the aliens, and France briefly opened its doors again, suspending momentarily the consistently repressive stand of the Roman Catholic Church. In England, it was the Puritans under Cromwell, with their particular interest in the Old Testament, who sanctioned the return of the "people of Israel" in 1649, while in France, more than a century later, the French Revolution finally brought full emancipation of the Jews.

For the Jews, the primary consequence of all these upheavals was their dispersal in many directions. Some reached the already known New World, where they settled for a time in Brazil, the West Indies, and then North America. Most important, by the sixteenth century the centre of the Jewish world had shifted east of the Rhine, and the east European chapter of Jewish history had begun. For several hundred years, Jewish life and culture flourished in Prussia, Austria, Poland, Lithuania, and finally European Russia, linked by spiritual ties and a common language. In the fifteenth, sixteenth, and seventeenth centuries, relative freedom for Jews within the feudal structure, particularly in Poland, made possible a cultural renaissance like that of the earlier period in Spain.

By the first half of the seventeenth century there were probably fewer than two million Jews in the entire world. A million, at most, lived in Europe, and the rest were settled in North Africa and Asia. Some of the North African and Asian Jews had attained wealth and security through trade and shipping and through influence at court, but the majority were poor craftsmen and small traders, sharing the lot of their Moslem neighbours. In the Ottoman Empire, while Jews sustained a vigorous spiritual life, their economic life was at the mercy of the oriental despots.

In Europe, a further political event served to alter the climate of

THE PALE OF SETTLEMENT IN 1835

Provinces in which settlement in villages was forbidden

Area along the western border where new settlement of Jews was forbidden

★ City forbidden to Jewish settlement

✪ City forbidden to new Jewish settlement

existence for Jews. The year 1772 brought the partition and absorption of Poland by her neighbours, Austria, Prussia, and Russia, with the major Jewish centres coming under the domination of the Russian czars. Here, in eastern Europe and primarily in Russia, the community which produced most of the Jews of western Canada took its definitive shape.

The Endless Ghetto

Russia, it has been said, is the last-born child of European civilization. At the time of the annexation of Poland, and for perhaps a hundred years after, its social structure was still basically feudal, with millions of serfs governed by an unimaginably wealthy nobility and aristocracy, while the development of a bourgeoisie was barely beginning. The newly acquired Polish Jews, with their predominantly middle class occupations, were a visibly alien element.

In 1791 Empress Catherine of Russia decreed the establishment of the "Pale of Settlement," an area consisting of twenty-five provinces along the empire's western borders, from the Baltic to the Black Sea, to which the Jewish population was restricted. Jews were thus barred from residence in ninety percent of Russia, including the great cities of Moscow and St. Petersburg. Permission to live outside the Pale was granted to certain professionals, businessmen, and artisans, whose skills were needed to stimulate the economy, and to students, with the calculated cynical intent that the Russification process would lead to complete assimilation. The fate of Jews discovered outside the Pale without permission depended, as a rule, on the goodwill of the local governor.

Denied access to the influence of the modern world, doubly isolated within a medieval Mother Russia, an extraordinary Jewish society developed in the smaller towns and villages of the Pale, a society that scarcely changed from generation to generation. Millions of east European Jews were born, lived, and died in the *shtetl*, the small town that has come to represent the essential life-style of the east European Jew. That vanished world lives still in the writing of the three great classicists of Yiddish literature—Mendele Mocher Sforim, I. L. Peretz, and Sholem Aleichem—and in the rueful memories handed down to present-day North American Jews by their parents and grandparents. By the end of the nineteenth century, when eastern Europe emerged into the mainstream of European history, the intense spiritual energies that had been generated within the ghetto walls reshaped Jewish life to its modern pattern, swiftly, within the space of a single life-time.

The Towns Where Time Stood Still

Hamlet after hamlet was home to the Jews, scattered across the endless reaches of the Russian hinterland. Often only *grois vie a genetz*, "the size of

The drayman, with wicker basket and wooden cart. Goods were often transported on foot by carriers.

The cobbler. Shoes were mended again and again, shared and handed down.

a yawn," a typical *shtetl* was no more than a jumble of paintless wooden houses with thatched or wooden roofs, weathered into the landscape like the peasant houses scattered all around. Mud or cobblestones paved these narrow, twisting streets, impassable in the spring thaw and after a heavy rain.

The hard-pressed village Jew and his toiling wife brought up their brood in a house with one or two dark and drafty rooms. The floors were of lime-washed earth, the walls sooty—but scrupulously whitewashed each spring in preparation for the Passover. The housewife stirred her pot on the thick-walled clay stove, and the family huddled around at its tasks, mending or reading by the light of a candle or lamp. On a bitter winter night, as the heat from the stove faded to a comforting glow, its flat top became a coveted place to sleep.

Somewhere in the midst of these ramshackle homes was the market place or *yarid*, the town's reason for being. On market days it was filled with livestock, grain, fish, birds, vegetables, and noise, as peasants from miles around exchanged their produce for goods which the Jews either made or imported from the distant city: dry goods, shoes, boots, lamps, oil, sugar, salt—bits of everything and anything.

Shtetl Jews were either tailors, butchers, cap-makers, innkeepers, cobblers, blacksmiths, draymen, water-carriers, dairymen, small shop-keepers, musicians, or simply *luftmentshen*—literally, people who made a living out of air; if a man lacked a trade he picked up what crumbs he could on the fringes of a meagre economy. A *shteckle-draiyer*, his neighbours might call him, a "stick-twirler." (Their descendants added another term to the list of such put-downs in Yiddish: a *Menachem Mendel*, from the archetypal portrait of the *shtetl* ne'er-do-well created by Sholem Aleichem.) Given the value which Jewish society has traditionally placed on piety and

The tailor. A new suit of clothes was an event for customer and tailor alike.

learning, it was not at all uncommon for the woman to be the bread-winner, scraping together a few *kopecks* at a stall in the market-place, while her husband pursued his studies at the house of worship by day and by night. Characteristically, the community supported—at its own level of impoverishment—a large number of learned and near-learned men: rabbis, cantors, *shochtim* or ritual slaughterers, scholars, teachers.

Since Jews were prohibited from owning land, there were relatively few in agriculture. An orchard might be rented from its absentee Russian owners, and the crop sold to a dealer. A particularly lucky individual might manage the flour mill or the timber reserve for the *poretz* or nobleman in the district; these overseers were considered well-to-do. Or a Jew might become a dairyman like Sholem Aleichem's Tevyeh, that endearing char-acter from a nineteenth-century Russian backwater who sprang to fame, a hundred years later, in *Fiddler on the Roof*, on a Broadway that would have been beyond his own wildest imagination. Tevyeh did possess a cow or two, and even a horse and wagon; a less fortunate dairyman simply bought his milk from a farmer and trudged into town with it, carrying two pails balanced on a yoke over his shoulders. In essence, Tevyeh spoke for all his brethren with his ironic and yet devout summing up: "I was, with God's help, a poor man."

Although locked into economic interdependence with the Russians, Ukrainians, or Poles, the Jews were distinctly different in racial origin, religion, and historical background, in habits and customs, in language, and above all in their community life. In small villages and larger towns, surrounded by an illiterate peasant population whose unpredictable vio-lence was a constant threat, the close-knit Jewish community lived within its own laws and attended to its own affairs. Almost every town, even the smallest, had its own Holy Burial Association (*Chevre Kedisheh*) which kept a minute book or *pinkes*, fully recording all statistics. An itinerant *shochet* or ritual slaughterer provided whatever kosher meat there was, and he might also double as a *mohel*, circumcising the baby boys on their eighth day.

In the larger towns, the community council administered all religious and community affairs. It derived its income from a tax on kosher meat, and sometimes depended for additional funds on the goodwill and generosity of the wealthier members of the community. The council maintained the synagogue and paid the salaries of the rabbi, the cantor, the *shochet*, and the *mohel*. It provided for the ritual bath or *mikveh*, used mainly for the obligatory purification rites for females, and frequently maintained a public bath-house as well.

If the town was large enough, it had a loan society (*Gemilut Chasadim*), which by tradition granted loans without interest, in fulfillment of the

In the *shtetl*: mud roads and patchwork houses.

Talmudic injunction to *tzedakah* (charity). Jewish teaching from the earliest times has maintained that the poor are entitled to assistance, that there is an obligation on the community and on the individual to provide such help. A large town, therefore, might maintain a *hegdesh* (poorhouse). In the tiny *shtetl*, *tzedakah* had to be more direct—the passing of a few coins from one hand to another.

Unless the town was wholly Jewish—and some, indeed, were—the small-town Jew generally spoke the dialect of the surrounding peasants, as a matter of necessity. At home, however, his language was *mammeloshen*, the mother tongue: Yiddish. (An offshoot of late medieval German, Yiddish is itself an interesting record of the Jewish odyssey, with its admixture of Hebrew and Slavic vocabulary, and more recently its strong infusion of English.) Hebrew, the language of prayer and study, was reserved for the synagogue, and the man who knew his way among the little black letters on the holy pages was revered above all others. The synagogue was the centre of the universe, a physical refuge in time of attack, a spiritual refuge from the degradation of the workaday world.

Thus the pious Jew, as he had done from time immemorial, obeyed the complex code of religious law that governed his daily existence. He read the Talmud, the collected records of scholarly disputation and of judicial administration of Jewish law going back to 200 A.D. He watched over *kashrut*, the Jewish dietary laws, and was scrupulous in observing the Sabbath and the holidays. He concerned himself with the fate of his brothers, and prayed for the coming of the Messiah.

Especially if he lived in the Russian Ukraine, the *shtetl* Jew might be a disciple of a Chassidic *rebbe*, looking to his master for advice in all matters, both practical and spiritual. Chassidism, a movement of religious revival among Jews, originated in Poland and Lithuania in the early eighteenth century and spread throughout eastern Europe, against the opposition of doctrinaire religious leaders. It stressed the mystical joy of a direct relationship with God, and elevated the common man by insisting on the equality of all men before the Creator. Typically, a Chassidic *tsaddik* (righteous man) acquired renown among the common folk for his transcendent piety and his mysterious contact with other-wordly forces, and gathered around him a "court" of followers, devout believers in both the glory of God and the limitless wisdom of their beloved *rebbe*. The Chassidim vied with each other to recount tales of their master's prowess, and together they celebrated the reciprocal love between God and man in ecstatic song and dance, led to transport by the *rebbe* himself. In its initial stages the movement was specifically anti-intellectual, a rejection of the age-old Jewish preoccupation with education, that seemed to deny heaven to the ignorant, the unlettered. In Russia and Poland, however, Chassidism turned again to study, and schools of higher learning, *yeshivot*, were founded. Several great dynastic families of Chassidic rabbis continue the tradition to the present day.

Foremost among his responsibilities, the pious Jew was acutely aware of his duty to educate his sons. A man who failed in this obligation might well forfeit his place in heaven. Thus, from the age of five or six, or sometimes even earlier, the little boys were sent to the *cheder*, the school in the house of the *melamed*, the tutor. There, under relentless drilling, they learned their letters and their Bible, and then went on to the Talmud, struggling to grasp the subtle distinctions of long-dead generations of commentators. At thirteen they achieved Bar Mitzvah and were deemed ready to assume adult responsibilities. If a youngster really showed promise, he might be sent on to a *yeshiveh*, an advanced school in a larger town, where the community, after a fashion, assumed the obligation of providing board and lodging for the fledgling sage. Otherwise, and when the family's economic needs became overpowering, the boy was probably apprenticed to learn a trade by the time he was fourteen.

A girl picked up what education she could at home. If a father was able, and particularly indulgent, he might pay a teacher to instruct his girls, and

ABOVE
The *shtetl*, or small town. Woodcut by
Solomon Udowin.

ABOVE LEFT
The village synagogue. Woodcut,
artist unknown.

The *cheder*, or religious school, with
the teacher in attendance. These
seven- or eight-year-old boys have
probably been studying the Torah for
several years. Head covering is
obligatory for all males.

he might even allow them to learn a little Russian. In the larger towns, a
girl might be apprenticed to a seamstress by the age of fourteen; or if her
family was too poor to maintain her, she might go into domestic service
even earlier. As time went on, and the ways of the outside world penetrated
the hinterland, boys and girls alike were reluctantly permitted something
of a secular education: a little Russian literature, a little history, some
arithmetic.

The village well. The man in the centre foreground may be a water-carrier, making a living by delivering water by the pail.

For all its seeming changelessness within the remote isolation of czarist Russia, *shtetl* society came finally under the influence of that outside world, yielding to forces that had been set in motion a long time before. The eighteenth century in western Europe was the Age of Enlightenment, a remarkable period of intellectual activity from which stemmed many of the ideas that would reshape man's concept of his role in the world. Germany, at this time, afforded its Jewish citizens open access to the arts and professions, and in this benign climate the Jews themselves experienced their own age of enlightenment, developing a social philosophy for the emancipation of their people. The *Haskalah* (Enlightenment) movement, centring on Moses Mendelssohn, held that the liberation of Jewry from the immemorial hostility of its gentile neighbours could only be achieved by the accommodation of Jews to modern European culture. Jewish religious and social customs, the *Haskalah* taught, must be adapted to conform with those of the surrounding society, and the ancient Hebrew language must become a vehicle for contemporary literary expression, on a par with any other modern language. In this secular, westernized spirit, the *Maskilim*, the advocates of the *Haskalah*, heaped contempt on what they considered the outlandishness of Orthodox Jewish religion, and especially on the unbridled emotionalism of the *Chassidim*, and they directed their reformist zeal against that fortress of Jewish tradition, the eastern European community. Before long, the centre of the *Haskalah* movement was Lithuania, and in particular the city of Vilna.

Magazines and newspapers were founded and books and pamphlets published, to carry the message of enlightenment into the Pale of Settlement. European works of all kinds, from poetry to politics and science, were translated into Hebrew or into the Yiddish vernacular, the better to reach the masses. Secular schools were opened, and women too were encouraged to seek an education. By the early 1840's, most of the larger Jewish communities in the Russian Pale had modern schools. Religious leaders, both dogmatist and Chassidic, fought back fiercely, anathematizing these heretics and all their ways, but the process of secularization could not be halted. It was at this same time, also, that the long-delayed upheaval in Russia's political and social structure began to take shape, so that in the end the integrated, dynamic Jewish community of the *shtetl* was brought down in the same violence that destroyed the entire czarist regime.

From the outset the policies of the Russian czars towards Jews had been provocative, repressive, and unrelenting, feeding on the deep-seated hostility of the peasantry towards the incomprehensible strangers in their midst. But while Jews and all other foreign nationals were denied rights under absolute czarist power, fully ninety percent of native Russians were simply serfs bound to the land, virtually chattels of the aristocratic landowners. Kept illiterate, required to toil endlessly, allowed no more than a meagre subsistence out of the rich crops they produced, the peasants held their remote, high-living masters in awe and reverence, but their frustration erupted frequently in acts of mindless brutality against the alien Jew close at hand. The massively patriarchal Russian church, also demanding total obedience of its worshippers, taught that Jews were the "Christ-killers," so that, especially in the religious fervour of the Easter season, the peasants often attacked Jewish lives and property. The Jew became the scapegoat of the Russian poor, and the lightning rod used by czarist tyranny to divert the peasants' wrath.

By the middle of the nineteenth century, popular movements for reform had begun to take shape, slowly and against savage opposition, repeating the pattern of political change that had swept the rest of Europe almost a century earlier. When the accession of Alexander II in 1855 ushered in a period of relative liberalization, the number of radical intellectuals soared. By 1864 there were rumblings about a Utopian society and talk of workers' co-operatives and women's rights. There was a cry for land for the peasants and freedom for all, and in the cities a growing industrialization went hand in hand with the founding of unions and revolutionary workers' parties.

The little towns deep in the Pale began to hear remotely of factories, theatres, and universities, of the stirring of politics and of movements for human betterment, of poets and writers and novels and daily newspapers. A traveller from distant points was eagerly questioned for news of that far-off world, even though its ways were feared and shunned. A student coming home from the city smuggled in forbidden publications for his friends, and challenged his father's authority. Gradually, one *apikoiris* or free-thinker was joined by another, as young men in the *shtetl* and in the city started to resist being absorbed into their elders' world of daily study and prayer. Some young people were caught up in the fervour of the growing radical movement, only to find that, although revolutionary ideology proclaimed the eradication of antisemitism, the Russian "liberals"

"In The Name of the Czar," a series of drawings on the persecution of the Jews, by Abel Pann (1883-1963). Born in Russia, Pann settled in Palestine in 1913.

ABOVE LEFT
At Two Hours' Notice

ABOVE RIGHT
After the Pogrom

RIGHT
Homeless

The Lame and the Halt

The ultimate insult: a Polish Jew with half his beard cut off by pogromists. Ca. 1918.

still regarded their Jewish comrades with the age-old suspicion and contempt. Other young Jews found a channel for their aspirations in the new spirit of cultural secularism, which centred on the Yiddish language and was given shape and direction by the Bundist movement, the "General Federation of Jewish Workers in Lithuania, Poland, and Russia." Still others were fired by the Zionist movement and the dream of a national home in Palestine. In an incredibly short time all the pent-up energy generated within the Russian Pale had erupted explosively, to the bewilderment and distress of the pious older generation, and many a home was torn apart by dissension.

At the same time that the traditional life-style was being eroded from within, it was also subjected to an intensified assault from without. The assassination of Alexander II, in March 1881, touched off a new wave of legal measures against the Jews. Riots were instigated, and frequently led, by government officials. The peasants, manipulated and inflamed, responded with a series of vicious pogroms across southern Russia: in Elisavetgrad on the night of April 15, then in Kiev, Bialystok, Kharkov, Odessa, Peraislav, and uncounted smaller towns. Konstantin Pobyedonostzev, the Procurator of the Russian Holy Synod and the new czar's chief advisor, charged the Jews with responsibility for Alexander's murder, and proclaimed that one third of the Jews were to be compelled to emigrate, one third forcibly baptized, and the rest reduced to starvation. Beginning with the May Laws of 1882, the noose of residence restrictions set up by the Pale of Settlement was further tightened, banning Jews from all villages and agricultural districts and from some urban areas. Economic hardship in the remaining centres where Jews were permitted was made worse by overcrowding, so that by the end of the century fully half the Jewish population depended to some extent on the charity of the rest.

A quota system for Jews was established in secondary schools, universities, and technical institutes. No Jews were permitted in the civil service, no Jewish doctors or lawyers in state institutions, although compulsory military service, the dreaded *prisiv*, was used deliberately as an instrument of Russification.

The classic charge against Jews of ritual murder reappeared, the accusation that the Jews used Christian blood in their religious services. In the late nineties an elaborate fabrication began to evolve and was soon published, offering fictitious "evidence" of a world-wide Jewish conspiracy. The last day of Easter, 1903, brought the passion of antisemitism to a climax with a virtual bloodbath at Kishinev in the province of Bessarabia: forty-five Jews murdered, six hundred injured, fifteen hundred homes and shops looted or destroyed. Most of the ten thousand left homeless were poor artisans and small shopkeepers.

The Russian chapter of Jewish history was coming to an end in the familiar pattern of exodus, as thousands of Jews began to look for a haven in other countries.

In the thirty-three years between the assassination of Alexander II in 1881 and the outbreak of World War I, one-third of east European Jews left behind their homelands and the dust and bones of their ancestors. Individually at first, and then in larger and larger groups, the more desperate and more adventurous among them began to find their way out, crossing borders by stealth or bribing officials when they could not produce the required exit permit. "Stealing the border" became for many the harrowing initiation into a hoped-for new life, and something approaching the dimensions of an underground railway developed. During the summer of 1881 several thousand refugees poured over the western borders of Russia into Brody in Austrian Galicia, followed by more and more, in an ever-increasing stream. Many remained in the countries of western Europe, others moved towards a more distant promise. Some went to fulfill the ancient prophecy of a return to Jerusalem, and thus played a significant role in the development of present-day Israel. Most of them, two million strong, carried the heritage of their long European past across the Atlantic to the New World.

A Conscience Aroused

Slowly, for news from Russia was long in coming, tales of the Russian persecution began to arouse indignation and a desire to help in many world centres. In France, Victor Hugo and other prominent citizens spearheaded a protest, and the Alliance Israélite Universelle in Paris became the first organization to send a group to Brody to assist the refugees. In England, the drive for relief funds brought together a roster of distinguished men from all walks of life: Cardinal Manning, the Archbishop of Canterbury, the Bishops of London, Gloucester, Manchester and Oxford, the Earl of Shaftesbury, Charles Darwin, Robert Browning, and Matthew Arnold; and on February 2, 1882, the Lord Mayor of London presided over a crowded public meeting at the Mansion House, his official residence. Prominent British Jews, notably the Rothschilds and Herman Landau, the London representative of the Canadian Pacific Railway, marshalled the Jewish community's drive for relief funds, and used their influence in government circles to urge the settlement of the refugees where they might hope to become self-sustaining. In New York the arrival of the first refugees was marked by a huge rally protesting the Russian actions, and the U.S. Congress formally requested that President James Garfield appeal to the czar to protect his Jewish subjects against violence. And in the far-off Canadian outpost of Winnipeg, incorporated as a city just eight years earlier, a forceful editorial appeared in the *Manitoba Free Press*, condemn-

TOP
Nathaniel, the first Lord Rothschild (1812-1870).

ABOVE
Alfred de Rothschild (1842-1918).

BELOW LEFT
The Mansion House, official residence of the Lord Mayor of London.

BELOW RIGHT
Lord Mayor of London, Sir Henry Edmond Knight, 1882.

Sir Alexander T. Galt, Canada's first High Commissioner to Great Britain.

ing the indignity and brutality inflicted on "a peaceful, intelligent, and industrious element of the population."

Among those present at the Mansion House meeting was Sir Alexander T. Galt, Canada's first High Commissioner to Great Britain, who had already written to his Prime Minister, Sir John A. Macdonald, suggesting the possibility of settling in Canada some of the homeless Jews, who were appearing by the thousands in Britain and western Europe. With the Canadian Pacific Railway forging ahead across the Canadian plains, Macdonald perceived a very practical opportunity to introduce stable and productive settlers into these thinly populated regions, and agreed to make land available to the Jews. Simultaneously, a relief committee was formed in Montreal at the instigation of the local branch of the Anglo-Jewish Association, uniting with the Young Men's Hebrew Benevolent Society and the Ladies' Hebrew Benevolent Society to found the Jewish Emigration Aid Society, the first Jewish organization of its kind in Canada. It was dissolved in a few months, leaving the task of caring for the refugees in Montreal in the hands of the Young Men's Hebrew Benevolent Society. A relief committee was also launched by a number of Christian groups, with Archbishop Bond as chairman.

As a result of all these efforts, the first party of Russian Jewish immigrants arrived in Winnipeg on May 26, 1882.

Attitudes

A series of letters concerning the plight of the Jews reflects vividly the complex of motives that prompted Canada's humanitarian gesture in inviting them to its western territories.

A week before the Mansion House meeting, on January 25, 1882, High Commissioner Galt had written privately to Prime Minister Macdonald, informing him of his intention to join the relief committee and broaching a possible Canadian interest:

> The Jewish persecution in Russia has induced me to write Rothschild suggesting that I would like to discuss with him the feasibility of removing the agricultural Jews to Canada. I have only sent my note to-day. It seems not a bad opportunity of interesting the Hebrews in our North West.

A second private letter, the day after the Mansion House protest, elaborates the suggestion with considerable persuasiveness:

Dominion of Canada. Office of the High Commissioner, 9 Victoria
Chambers, London S.W.

3 February, 1882.

My dear Macdonald,

As I mentioned in my last note I have had more or less conference with
the leading Jews in regard to Emigration from Russia to Canada and at their
request I have consented to act on the Mansion House Committee to which
I was nominated at the very influential meeting held on Wednesday.

Into the next century.
Demonstration in London's East End,
1919, against the persecution of Jews
in Poland.

Sir John A. Macdonald, Prime Minister of Canada, 1867-1873 and 1878-1891.

From what I learn these Russian Jews are a superior class of people, partly farmers, but generally trade people. Most of them were well off and though many have been ruined, still my opinion is that a large proportion will still be found with sufficient means to establish themselves in Canada or the United States if Russia will let them go.

I found the American Jews were actively promoting emigration to the United States and I thought what was good for them could not be bad for us.

When the Committee meet I will know what their ideas are and may perhaps be able to suggest some mode by which we may get a share. The Jews are really now so influential in Europe, that there can be no harm in cultivating them.

Galt was exaggerating the extent to which the proposed immigrants might be expected to arrive with financial means. A small number may have been relatively "well off" before the destruction of their Russian or Polish homes, and many were skilled in various trades, but in material goods very few had more than their meagre personal possessions, and the funds raised in Britain were urgently needed to help the Russian Jews make the long voyage across the Atlantic.

Macdonald may have been persuaded by Galt's emphasis on the tactical advantages to be expected from assistance to the Jews, or by his own urgent need for settlers along his new railroad, or by the humanitarian outcry against the persecution of the Jews that swept through Europe and America. At any rate he moved quickly, advising the Marquis of Lorne, Governor General of Canada, on February 20, 1882, that Galt "has been attending to the Jews," and adding, "I hope something will come of this. He will be instructed to act for the Immigration Department, and we are quite ready to assign the Jews lands."

Despite this declaration, however, the Jews who arrived in Winnipeg in May and June found that no land had as yet been provided for them, and repeated representations were made to the Dominion government to fulfill its agreement without further delay. Galt himself wrote again to Macdonald, this time from Montreal, on July 7, 1882:

My dear Macdonald,

I wish you would read the enclosed and determine how far the view of the Jewish Committee can be met.

I think it of great importance, especially in view of my return to London, and future influence with leading Jews there & in Paris, that you should find the means of giving a district for settlement to these people. It cannot fail to have a good effect.

Could you give them the spare Mennonite Townships or if this cannot be done, might not some of the Colonization Companies be called on peremptorily to take this land or *leave* it. It seems absurd to have the whole district covered with bogus applications (in many cases) to the exclusion of bona fide settlers.

The Colonization Companies Galt mentions were privately organized concerns for whom the government had reserved close to three million acres of land, on condition that they bring to Canada the hundreds of thousands of immigrants the new country needed. The scheme was unsuccessful, attracting scarcely twelve hundred settlers. Between 1884 and 1891 the terms of the contracts were re-examined and many of the companies dissolved for their failure to fulfill the agreement.

A rather cynical and derogatory footnote appears in a further private letter from Macdonald to Galt, on February 28, 1882:

> The Old Clo' move is a good one — A sprinkling of Jews in the North West would do good. They would at once go in for peddling & politics and be of much use in the new country as cheap jacks and chapmen.

Macdonald's offhand witticism about the "Old Clo' move" echoes the familiar stereotype of the Jewish peddler; and he evidently realized that the Jews would serve his purposes as they had served many a ruler before, in providing the necessary middle class skills in an economy hungry for expansion. Far different in its tone is the moving appeal addressed to the Marquis of Lorne by John Taylor, the Icelandic agent in Manitoba, reminding the Governor General of another group of hapless Europeans who had prospered under Canada's hospitality:

St. Andrews, Manitoba.

13th February, 1882.

The Marquis of Lorne,
   Governor General of
   The Dominion of Canada.

My Lord,

   I had the honour of addressing Lord Dufferin in 1875 on the subject of the Icelanders who were suffering from the effects of a severe volcanic eruption in that desolate country. The favourable notice taken of my letter by his Lordship has been the means of promoting a desire for emigration, and of delivering some three thousand persons from a condition of helpless and hopeless poverty at home, to the enjoyment of prosperity and even affluence in this favoured country.

   The administration of Lord Dufferin will be always gratefully commemorated by this considerate act.

   Recalling the kind reception of my appeal at that time, I feel encouraged to write to your Lordship in behalf of a class of sufferers in another country from the effects of a more terrible eruption, not however of a physical but of a social nature, — namely of the Jews in Russia and Poland.

Collecting old clothes at a fashionable London residence. The "Old Clo'" peddler was a familiar stereotype of the Jew.

The extensive fertile country now being opened up by the Dominion Government of Canada presents a most desirable refuge for these oppressed and persecuted ones.

Asking your Lordship's favourable consideration of this subject, I would take the liberty of suggesting that under your Lordship's kind influence and patronage, a suitable block of land might be obtained for this purpose from the Dominion Government and placed in the hands of trustees to carry out the benevolent design of providing new homes far removed from the cruelties and atrocities so shamefully perpetrated on this people in the name of religion.

Such a timely measure for the relief of the Jewish refugees, if happily connected with those now being made in England, would be a lasting credit to this country and a bright memorial of your Lordship's distinguished administration.

I have the honour to be,
My Lord,

Your Lordship's most obedient servant

JOHN TAYLOR , Icelandic Agent.

Seen in retrospect, this was a moment in history when official philanthropy coincided with the practical concerns of the benefactors and shaped the lives of generations to come. Icelanders, Jews, Europeans in flight from want and persecution, set sail for Canada in the succeeding years, to endure the grim hardship of passage and settlement and ultimately to flourish, in a country immeasurably enriched by their presence.

They Were Not the First to Come

The Jews who flocked to America in the immigration period of the 1880's were not the first of their people to set foot on this continent, for Jewish ties with the New World date from the earliest period of the European venture across the Atlantic. In Spain at the time of Christopher Columbus, the Inquisition hunted down not only practising Jews, offering them a choice between conversion and death at the stake, but the Marranos as well, the hidden Jews who had ostensibly accepted baptism but practised their religion in secret. So vigilant was the zeal of the Inquisitors that if a man put on fresh clothes on a Friday afternoon, the eve of the Jewish Sabbath, he might come under suspicion of being Jewish. The very year of Columbus' voyage of discovery, 1492, brought an edict from King Ferdinand and Queen Isabella expelling Jews from Spain. Scholars have now generally discounted some intriguing evidence that Columbus himself may have been of Jewish or Marrano origin, but his interpreter, Luis de Torres, and at least one of his patrons, Luis de Santangel, have been identified as Jews. Certainly the discovery of the New World was partly backed by Marranos, perhaps in their need to find a haven from persecution.

As the Spanish and Portuguese colonized parts of South and Central America, small groups of Marranos appeared in the settlements, only to be followed and extirpated by the Inquisition. The first known Jewish community in the western world dates back to 1624, when the Dutch captured Bahia in Brazil from the Portuguese, and a large Marrano group openly declared its Judaism. The next year the city was retaken and the Jews disappeared. After 1630 a more permanent Jewish community was established in Recife, Brazil, also under Dutch occupation. Marranos had lived here in peace for several generations, and Jews now came from other parts of Brazil and neighbouring Spanish colonies, as well as from Holland, Germany, Poland, Hungary, Turkey, and North Africa, and a vigorous economic life developed around the sugar trade. There were two synagogues, and the first Jewish attorney in the New World, Michael Cardoso, is known to have practised here. When the Portuguese recaptured the colony in January 1654, the Jews dispersed, and twenty-three of the refugees landed in New Amsterdam, now Manhattan, to form the nucleus of the first Jewish settlement in North America.

In Canada there were Jews among the earliest fur traders in the vast Indian territory to the west claimed by the Hudson's Bay Company. The first person who was reported to be of Jewish origin and who actually settled in Canada was a young man named Ferdinande Jacobs, who lived in the Manitoba region as a Hudson's Bay Company apprentice in the fur trade. According to records, he was hired on April 20, 1732, and moved up in the ranks of the company to become chief factor, first at Fort Prince of Wales and later at Fort York. The British capture of Canada from the French in 1763 brought a stream of merchants from England, challenging the Hudson's Bay Company monopoly over Canadian wealth. Among these competing independent English and Scottish traders, called the Montreal Peddlers by the embattled company, there were initially five Jews, associated in partnership: Ezekiel Solomons, Chapman Abrahams, Gerson Levy, Benjamin Lyon, and Levy Solomons. (The independent traders were incorporated as the North West Company in 1783, and the two rivals in the fur trade merged as the Hudson's Bay Company in 1821.)

Intriguing though it may be to speculate about the lives of these early Jewish adventurers in the Canadian west, an even more colourful incident is to be found in the annals of French Canada. In 1738, a passenger listed as Jacques La Fargue disembarked at Quebec from the ship *Saint Michel* — and then identified herself to authorities as Esther Brandeau, the twenty-year-old daughter of David Brandeau, a Jewish trader of Bayonne, France. When questioned, she told a wild tale with a rather story-book flavour, of shipwreck some five years earlier while en route from Bayonne to Amsterdam, of her reception in the home of a widow and of her departure two weeks later in boy's disguise, and of her subsequent adventures. She claimed that she had worked as a ship's cook on two different vessels, and

ABOVE
Aaron Hart, born 1724 in London, England, settled in Three Rivers, Quebec.

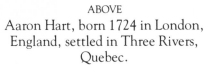

CENTRE
Ezekiel Hart, son of Aaron Hart, was elected to the Legislative Assembly of Lower Canada in 1807, but not allowed to take his seat.

RIGHT
Levy Solomons (d. 1792), a member of the group of independent fur traders known as the "Montreal Peddlers."

also with a tailor; that she had lived in a monastery and with a baker and with an ailing nobleman; and that, just before taking passage for New France, she had been falsely imprisoned as a thief. Asked why she had maintained the boy's disguise, she replied that while in the widow's house she had been forced to eat pork, forbidden to Jews, and had decided not to return to her parents, but rather to enjoy the freedom which Christians enjoy. The authorities were understandably a bit sceptical of her story, but agreed to permit the girl to stay, provided that she receive instruction towards conversion to Christianity (Jews were not allowed to settle in French colonies). Unfortunately, Esther appears to have been an extraordinarily flighty individual, for the good clerics could make no headway with their teaching, and she was sent back to France a year later. Brief though her stay was, she might be considered the second Jewish resident on Canadian soil. In addition, several possibly Jewish names in documents surviving from the New France of about the same time also suggest rather tenuously that other Jews or Marranos may have found their way to this part of the New World in the eighteenth century.

There are, however, some unsubstantiated reports of even earlier arrivals in Canada. For example, Henri de Levy, Duke of Ventadour, Louis XIII's Viceroy of New France from 1625 to 1627, is rumoured to have been of Jewish descent. Interest in this story is heightened by the fact that among the heraldic symbols on his coat of arms were three stars greatly resembling the Star of David. About the same period the first Catholic missionaries were arriving at Port Royal, including a Jesuit named Biart who, it is speculated, was descended from Spanish Marranos. Other possible Marranos were Father Joseph le Caron, who arrived in Quebec in 1615, and Marc Lescarbot, whose *History of New France* was first published in 1609. Lescarbot's writings show that he was fully conversant with the Talmud, and he devoted considerable study to the similarities between Hebrew and Indian languages and customs, in an attempt to demonstrate that the Indians were descendants of the Ten Lost Tribes of Israel; but his rather unusual interest does not, of course, constitute proof of a Jewish origin.

It was during the Seven Years' War, 1756-63, as France fought her losing battle to retain Canada, that the Portuguese-Jewish merchant and banking house of Gradis, in Bordeaux, developed strong trading and shipping ties to Canada. Abraham Gradis, the founder's eldest son, established warehouses in Quebec City, but did not take up residence there.

On the other side of the conflict, British troops received supplies from the New York trading firm of the Frank family, and there were Jews in the British army under General Amherst. Known to be of Jewish origin was Sir Alexander Schomberg, captain of the British frigate *Diana*, one of a fleet which repulsed the French attempt to recapture Quebec in 1760.

Settlers East

After New France was ceded to the British in 1763, many of the Jewish officers and men in the conquering army stayed and settled, and they were joined by others. Aaron Hart and his brother Moses, Samuel and Uriah Judah, Levy and Ezekiel Solomons, members of the Frank family from New York, all appear in the records of this period. Aaron Hart was a commissary officer on the staff of General Amherst during the British attack on Montreal in 1760, and he served as postmaster of Three Rivers from 1763 to 1770. By 1768, the Jews in Montreal, largely of Spanish and Portuguese extraction, founded the very first Jewish congregation in Canada, Shearith Israel. Quebec's Congregation Beth Israel began in 1862, in rented quarters and with a plot of land acquired for a cemetery, but it did not build a permanent home until 1892.

In 1807 Ezekiel Hart, son of Aaron Hart, was elected by a majority vote to the Legislative Assembly of Lower Canada after an explosive campaign during which his opponents made full use of the religious issue. When the Assembly met on January 29, 1808, Hart took his oath "in the Jewish manner," with his head covered and his hand on the Old Testament, rather than on the New as was the custom of his Christian colleagues. His opponents, who were also the political opponents of his friend, the Governor General, Sir James Craig, contended that Hart did not conform to the "true faith of a Christian," and his seat was denied him. In May 1808, the voters again gave Hart a majority, but once again he was refused his rightful seat. Not until June 5, 1832, was the act proclaimed granting Canadian Jews their full rights as British subjects—and even this was some twenty-three years before the Jews of England were permitted to take their seats in the British House of Commons.

The first official count of Jews in Upper and Lower Canada combined, in 1831, listed 107 residents, and the census ten years later recorded only 154, living chiefly in and around Montreal. Most of these early Jewish settlers had come from the eastern American states, and the 1840's brought a number from Great Britain and parts of Europe.

In Upper Canada the presence of a number of Jews in York, now Toronto, as early as 1817 can be surmised from a communication from the then Attorney General to the Government Secretary, Lieut.-Colonel Cameron, pointing out that it was necessary to make an exception in the

82   C. 56-57.   Anno Primo Gulielmi IV.   A. D. 1831.

Public Act.   VIII. And be it further enacted by the authority aforesaid, that this Act shall be taken and deemed to be a public Act, and as such shall be judicially taken notice of by all Judges, Justices of the Peace, and all others whom it shall concern without being specially pleaded.

CAP. LVII.

AN Act to declare persons professing the Jewish Religion intitled to all the rights and privileges of the other subjects of His Majesty in this Province.

31st March, 1831 —Presented for His Majesty's Assent and reserved "for the ' signification of His Majesty's pleasure thereon."
12th April, 1832,—Assented to by His Majesty in His Council.
5th June, 1832,—The Royal Assent signified by the proclamation of His Excellency the Governor in Chief.

Preamble.   **W**HEREAS doubts have arisen whether persons professing the Jewish Religion are by law entitled to many of the privileges enjoyed by the other subjects of His Majesty within this Province: Be it therefore declared and enacted by the King's Most Excellent Majesty, by and with the advice and consent of the Legislative Council and Assembly of the Province of Lower Canada, constituted and assembled by virtue of and under the authority of an Act passed in the Parliament of Great Britain, intituled, "An Act to repeal certain parts of an Act passed in " the fourteenth year of His Majesty's Reign, intituled, "*An Act for making* " *more effectual provision for the Government of the Province of Quebec, in North* " *America,*" and to make further provision for the Government of the said " Province of Quebec in North America." And it is hereby declared and enacted by the authority aforesaid, that all persons professing the Jewish Religion

Persons professing the Jewish Religion to be entitled to all the civil rights of British Subjects.   being natural born British subjects inhabiting and residing in this Province, are entitled and shall be deemed, adjudged and taken to be entitled to the full rights and privileges of the other subjects of His Majesty, his Heirs or Successors, to all intents, constructions and purposes whatsoever. and capable of taking, having or enjoying any office or place of trust whatsoever, within this Province.

Photographic Reproduction of the Act Granting Jews Equal Rights

The Bill of Rights, granting Jews equal rights in the Province of Lower Canada, as presented for approval to His Majesty William IV, King of England.

application of certain civil laws governing the celebration of marriages, insofar as they affected Jews and Quakers. Many of the Jews who settled in York were of Anglo-Jewish origin and had come from Montreal and Quebec, where they had first taken up residence. The first Jew specifically mentioned is in the York town directory for 1833: Arthur Wellington Hart, who was in the insurance business; but in 1846 a religious census revealed that there were only twelve Jews living in York. By 1856 the community was large enough to establish the Sons of Israel Congregation, which held services in a rented room and acquired a plot of land for a cemetery. The Sons of Israel later became the Holy Blossom Temple.

In 1834 L. Joseph had a general store in York, and a William Meyers is mentioned in the directory as Deputy-Secretary Registrar. One year later Goodman and Samuel Benjamin were in the wholesale dry goods business in York, under the name of Benjamin Bros., and during the Mackenzie Rebellion they received a contract from the government to supply the troops with greatcoats. Henry A. Joseph and Judah G. Joseph, who were distantly related, arrived in York in 1838. Judah G. Joseph was an optician and jeweller at 56 King Street East, and was instrumental in laying the foundation for the Toronto Jewish community. Henry A. Joseph engaged in the fur business at 70 Yonge Street. Jacob Maier Hirschfelder was an instructor in Hebrew and other languages at the University of Kings College in 1845.

While there were some Jews living in Halifax in the early 1750's, the entire Maritime Jewish community was still very small until well into the 1880's. The first Jewish settlers in Saint John, New Brunswick, were three brothers-in-law, Nathan Green, Solomon Hart, and Henry Levy, all cigar makers, who arrived there in 1858 from England. When in 1882 Lewis Green, the son of Nathan, married his cousin, a daughter of Solomon Hart, the rabbi who conducted the service had to be brought from Boston. Years later, on January 11, 1899, the first synagogue in the city was consecrated. The dedication ceremony began with a reading from Genesis by Solomon Hart's young grandson, Master S. Hart Green, who later became one of the leading citizens in the distant western city of Winnipeg.

Strong evidence exists that in the nineteenth century there were Jews in Newfoundland's fishing, seal, and coastal shipping trades. An English Jew is said to have lived there in the early 1800's, but an organized community did not develop until after 1900. I. Perlin, who settled in St. John's in 1891, undertook a kind of spontaneous immigrant aid service, meeting the weary Jews who passed through the port. At Passover, in particular, he provided *matzos* (unleavened bread) to Jewish immigrants.

Settlers West

By the middle of the century a Jewish community had appeared on the Pacific coast, largely engaged in supplying provisions for the whaling industry and the exploration for gold. Frank Sylvester was the earliest recorded Jew to arrive in Victoria, in 1858, and many others who were to become prominent citizens, including Selim Franklin, Henry Nathan, and the Oppenheimer brothers, followed in rapid succession. The congregation Emanu-El, erected in Victoria in 1863, was probably the third Jewish house of worship in all of Canada; nine years later, there were one hundred Jews living in the province.

In Manitoba, the earliest permanent settler was Edmond Coblentz, who came and worked as a clerk in Winnipeg in 1877-78, and was later joined by his two brothers, Adolphe and Aachel Benvoir. With the arrival of Reuben Goldstein and Hyman Miller in 1879, and in the following year of George Frankfurter, Louis Wertheim, Philip Brown, David Ripstein, Samuel Ripstein, and Adolph Bieber, what was to become the largest Jewish settlement in the Canadian west was well on its way. This group came mainly from England, Germany, and the United States, and most were merchants of modest means. They established themselves at and around Logan and Main, then the centre of the business area in Winnipeg.

The Coblentz brothers. Left to right: Adolphe, Aachel, and Edmond. Ca. 1877.

A reading of the Henderson Directory of 1880 and 1881 gives some sense of business activity in Winnipeg at the time, and indicates that the very first Jewish arrivals were now settled in various occupations and enterprises:

M. K. Auerbach, book dealer
Abraham Benjamin, clergyman
Isaac Berkman, peddler
Adolphe Bieber, wholesale jeweller
Philip Brown, tailor and clothing
   merchant
D. Cohen, land speculator
Isaac Cohen, second-hand dealer
M. Drozdowitz, clothing merchant
George Frankfurter, dry goods
   merchant
Isaac Goldbloom, peddler
Isaac Goldstein, trader
Max Goldstine, men's clothing
William Harris, salesman for
   Montreal firm
Jacob Kleinber, peddler

Hubert Kohen, salesman (Maxwell
   & Co. Farm Machinery)
Joseph Levine, bartender
Hyman Miller, co-owner Miller &
   Morse, Hardware Co.
David Ripstein, jewellery salesman
Simon Ripstein, jewellery salesman
Hiram Rosenthal, tailor
J. Silverstone, peddler
Mr. Tobias, merchant
Dr. Hiram Vineberg, physician
Louis Vineberg, pawnbroker and
   auctioneer
Victor Victorson, hardware and real
   estate
Harry Weixelbaum, hotel keeper
Louis Wertheim, tobacconist

The Dr. Vineberg listed as a resident of Winnipeg actually practised in

Rhoda Lechtzier and her brothers,
Jack and Harris. Ca. 1900.

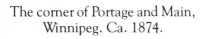

The corner of Portage and Main,
Winnipeg. Ca. 1874.

Portage la Prairie. Many years later, he recorded in a letter to Winnipeg's Jewish newspaper, the *Israelite Press*, that as the only Jew among the five or six physicians in town, he "did not encounter any prejudice whatever," and was later appointed Board of Health Officer.

The first Jewish boy born in Manitoba was William, the son of Adolphe Coblentz and his wife, the former Sarah Weixelbaum. Born January 28, 1879, the child was circumcised by a *mohel* brought all the way from Chicago. Manitoba's first Jewish wedding took place on July 29, 1882, when Annie Feinberg and David Ripstein were united in marriage by the Reverend A. Benjamin, who had arrived from New Orleans a year earlier. Manitoba was also the birthplace of Rhoda Lechtzier, who became Mrs. Maurice Halter; born on April 29, 1883, she was one of the first native-born Jewish girls to survive in the west.

According to the census of 1881 there were thirty-three Jewish families living in Manitoba, twenty-one in Winnipeg and twelve scattered throughout the province. The total Jewish population was about one hundred.

Thus, when the first mass immigration of Jews into Canada began in the 1880's, following the intensification of Russian pogroms and legal persecution, a scattering of small Jewish communities had already formed across the country, and their members had established the beginnings of an economic and social base. This was fortunate, for the newcomers would be in dire need of almost every kind of assistance.

Winnipeg street scene, 1876, showing the city's rapid growth.

THE FIRST IMMIGRATION: 1882-1920

2. STRANGERS IN PRAYER SHAWLS

On May 26, 1882, less than four months after the Mansion House meeting in London, the first of the Jewish immigrants on their way from Russia reached Winnipeg, and were given shelter at the immigration building on Fonseca Street by Mr. Magelsdorff, the assistant immigration agent. They were a small group, the oldest about thirty: three carpenters, a blacksmith, a cabinet-maker, a painter, a dyer, eight farmers, and four women and a child. Waiting for the rest of the contingent to arrive, they busied themselves with cleaning out the immigration sheds. Six days later, on Thursday, June 1, 247 Jewish men, women, and children reached Winnipeg in their long flight from eastern Europe.

Their journey had been horrendous. Most of them had spent two or three weeks on the ocean, crowded into the dehumanizing squalor of a steerage deck, only to be herded through the alarming indignities of immigration clearance at Halifax and sent on by rail into an apparently endless wilderness. Their reception at either Montreal or Toronto can hardly have been reassuring. The Jewish relief organizations were able to accommodate each successive wave of immigrants only long enough to make arrangements for their passage through to their ultimate destination. After some further waiting in Toronto these new settlers had been sent by rail to Sarnia, where they had embarked on the S.S. *Ontario* to cross Lake Huron and Lake Superior to Duluth, and then by rail again, with their boxes and bundles, for the last lap to Winnipeg.

The S. S. *International* at the immigration sheds in Winnipeg. Ca. 1870.

Main Street, Winnipeg, looking
south from William Avenue.
Ca. 1884.

The *Manitoba Free Press* of June 2, 1882, provides a graphic description
of the event:

Supper was furnished them by the Jewish residents of the city, and it was
clear to the spectators who happened to be present that the kindness was
well-timed. The travellers ate as if famished, and their evidently destitute
condition touched the sympathies of those who saw them. Scarcely had
they finished eating when the men were informed that if they liked to go to
work immediately and work all night, they might all do so, and that their
wages would be paid at the rate of 25 cents per hour. This noble offer was
made to them by the firm of Jarvis and Berridge, and the work with which
all immigrants began their experience in Manitoba consisted in unloading
two rafts of lumber which had just been brought down from Emerson by the
S. S. Omega. It is said that the people almost wept when the offer was
interpreted to them. With the promptness of a company of soldiers, they fell
into line and marched to the bank of the Red River, a little south of
Broadway Bridge, where they were soon at work. At a late hour 37 of them
were labouring industriously and showing that they were neither averse nor
unaccustomed to work. They impressed their employers and others who saw
them, very favorably, were regarded as intelligent looking and of good,
strong, physical constitutions, and were
thought to give promise of making
hard-working and valuable settlers
of this new country.

Canadian Pacific Railway passenger
train, at the station in Winnipeg.
Ca. 1884.

Immigrants aboard the *S. S. Pennland*.
Ca. 1893.

Canadian Pacific Railway "Colonist"
sleeping car. Passengers who could
afford the extra comfort of these
accommodations were provided with
blankets and rough pillows.
Ca. 1885.

The *Times* adds:

> They worked like Trojans until 6 a.m., when they retired, having to sleep in
> their clothes on the floor, as their effects had not by that time been removed
> from the station.

The Strangers
Who Would Not Work on Saturday

Winnipeg in 1882 was a small town of seven thousand people, with muddy
streets, wooden sidewalks, and log houses. The resident Jewish community
of some thirty families tried to cope with the 250-odd refugees, but was
overwhelmed by the flood of responsibilities, especially when a further
seventy Russian Jews arrived a short time later. The farm land which had
been promised to the new immigrants was slow in materializing, and the
government had made no other provision for their employment or maintenance. The *Manitoba Free Press* repeatedly criticized Dominion
authorities for ignoring the people they had brought in, as did the Winnipeg city council. Private relief drives were organized, churchmen of
several denominations appealed to their congregations for money and
supplies, and the Bishop of Rupert's Land contributed $100. The estab-
lished Jewish citizens raised a commendable $360 among themselves.
Mattresses and ticking were donated by two dry goods firms, and the
Dominion immigration agent provided some staples: one thousand pounds
of flour, ten pounds of tea, two kegs of syrup, and two hundred pounds of
oatmeal.

Housed in the barely habitable immigration sheds, the newcomers
were often on the brink of despair as they tried to maintain themselves by
what temporary jobs they could get. Even employment brought on problems: every time one of the immigrants went out on a job, someone who
spoke English had to take time off from his own work to interpret the boss's
instructions. With all the difficulties threatening to become unmanageable, Victor Victorson — the hardware merchant and real-estate dealer of
the 1881 Henderson Directory — was put in charge of organizing the care
of the city's unhappy guests, and Louis Wertheim, identified by the *Free
Press* as the "proprietor of the cigar store in Firestine's tonsorial parlour,"
offered to act as treasurer.

The regular provision of three meals a day was quickly organized, and
those who found work were required to pay for their meals at the sheds or to
board elsewhere. True to their offer, Jarvis and Berridge did hire some of the
Jews, for a few hours at a time, to unload the lumber barges arriving at the
docks. In addition, the city employed a number on public works, and a few
more found work at various trades. But it was not nearly enough.

For all the newcomers, the period of acclimatization was extremely

Mr. and Mrs. Mordecai Weidman and two of their children. Studio portrait, 1889. The Weidman brothers and their father were in the first group that arrived in Winnipeg on May 26, 1882, and from 1884 to 1887 they farmed in the Moosomin district. Both returned to Winnipeg to play an important role in business and community life.

difficult. As they struggled with the complexities of a strange language, neither understanding their neighbours nor being understood, they also had to find a place in Winnipeg's rudimentary economy for such skills as they possessed. The better educated found that their scholarly lore was irrelevant in this raw Canadian town. Some of the tradesmen, like the blacksmiths, were in demand, but there were no industries to employ those who had factory experience, and most were glad to get unskilled labourers' jobs digging ditches, building roads, excavating basements, and carrying cement for new buildings. Eventually it was the C.P.R., with its constant need for workers, that provided many of the immigrants with a summer's employment.

Poster, 1890. The busy illustration is characteristic of the advertising of the period. Abraham Lechtzier was one of the founders of the Hebrew Benevolent Society.

The non-Jewish community, still not used to the first few Jews in its midst, showed some predictable hostility. As the aliens' efforts to integrate themselves into the work force proceeded slowly and painfully, they were charged with being lazy because they clung to their religious beliefs and refused to work on the Sabbath. The *Times* launched a vicious attack against the immigrants, calling them idlers and ne'er-do-wells, and demanding that they be deported. The *Manitoba Free Press* labelled the *Times* diatribe as unjustified and motivated solely by prejudice, but was not above a reference to the Jews as "schooled in dependence and beggary," and "so unfit for every class of regular work that nobody will employ them."

Within a few months conditions began to improve somewhat. Victorson found jobs for some of the men, splitting rails for the C.P.R. at Whitemouth, Manitoba; and from July to October 150 Jews went to work laying track to Medicine Hat. Special quarters and food were provided for them and they were excused from work from Friday evening to Saturday at sundown so that they might observe the Sabbath. The High Holidays of 1882 were celebrated by the Jewish labourers in their tents, some forty

miles from Winnipeg. They collected $100 amongst themselves and sent to New York for a *sefer Torah* or scroll of the Law and a *shofar*, the ram's horn used to herald the Jewish New Year and to end the Day of Atonement.

Though the C.P.R. fired the imagination of its promoters and of later generations, the men who actually built the line were generally a rough lot. The night the Jewish immigrant workers arrived at Whitemouth—to be met by a bully of a foreman who underlined his orders with a heavy club—they were attacked by about seventy non-Jewish workers in a raid terrifyingly like an old-country pogrom. Stones and missiles flew, and one of the Jews was severely injured. They tried to take shelter in the railway cars but were driven out, and their kosher food was stolen. A major blood-letting was narrowly averted when an anonymous Swedish machinist persuaded the reluctant Whitemouth hotel-keeper to let the Jews in. Some of the newcomers left for Winnipeg immediately, but the hardy ones clung to their rail-splitting job tenaciously because they needed the work. The *Manitoba Free Press* was indignant: "Lawlessness of this character ought to be suppressed with an iron hand, and it seems, to say the least, shameful that these poor creatures, persecuted out of their country, should meet with treatment so much like that from which they had fled."

Two weeks after the Whitemouth skirmish, another incident took place while Jewish immigrants were laying track for the C.P.R. at Rosser Station in Manitoba. A railway worker attacked Kieva Barsky, hitting him on the head with an iron bar. Unlike his compatriots at Whitemouth, who did not press charges against their attackers, Barsky sought justice under the law. In *The Queen vs. Charles Wicks*, the assailant was charged before Chief Justice Edmund Burke Wood with "committing an assault with intent to do bodily harm on Keever [sic] Barsky, a Russian Jew, at Rosser Station on the C.P.R. on July 20," and sentenced to one month's imprisonment. For the Jewish community, something more had been gained here than merely the punishment of wrongdoing: though prejudice might still persist, there was hope for the future, with even-handed justice under the law.

By November of 1882, a number of the immigrants were able to leave the immigration sheds for the luxury of private accommodations in drafty wooden shanties. But with the resources of the local Jewish residents strained to the breaking point, some twenty immigrant families still had to endure a Winnipeg winter in the bleak government sheds, without sufficient fuel or food or warm clothing.

Sir Alexander Galt had made some Mansion House funds available for the relief of the refugees, but the money did not reach Winnipeg. In January 1883, a *Free Press* reporter assigned to look into the plight of these unfortunates offered his readers a graphic account of what he found, under the heading, "Hebrew Refugees Perishing from Hunger and Cold." The story captures indelibly the despair of the immigrant experience:

The George Frankfurter family, at home. Ca. 1905. Frankfurter was a dry goods merchant. Both husband and wife were actively involved in the community, Mrs. Frankfurter as a volunteer Sunday School teacher and in women's organizations.

Isaac and Bessie (Finkelstein) Ripstein, at the time of their marriage, September 1896. In 1889, at the age of fourteen, Bessie was the youngest speaker at the laying of the Shaarey Zedek synagogue cornerstone. She presented the trowel used in the ceremony to the Rev. Canon O'Meara, Grand Master of the Lodge of Freemasons, who conducted the service.

Twenty poverty stricken families are huddled together in various stages of misery in small rooms not large enough for one person to sleep in. A stove, a bench, and in some instances a small table, constituted the sole articles of furniture. The beds were made on the tops of boxes which at one time constituted the whole of their possessions. It being the Jewish Sabbath, several of the children were to be seen poring over part of the Scriptures, written in the Hebrew tongue, and the individual members of the families were all assembled together, each family in its own apartment. Fire was seen only in one or two of the stoves, the children being in bed, and the older folks huddled together for warmth, their scanty clothing offering slim protection from

THE INTENSE COLD.

In the first room visited there was a man suffering from asthma and bronchitis, and also a bad scald on his right hand and wrist. The man was old and weak, and totally unfit for work. The women had all along supported themselves and their old father and mother by scrubbing out stores, and what other work they could find to do. The coming of winter has put an end to that kind of work, and now the poor wretches are without any means of subsistence. Jews will never beg of Christians. They are forbidden doing so by the traditions and ordinances of their religion, and, in consequence, they may be reduced to the direst extremity without their Christian neighbors knowing anything of their sad condition. These Jews, true to the teachings of their religion, have made no complaints; and it was only the spectacle of many of the women on the street being poorly clad in calico garments that suggested the probability of there being suffering among them. In one cabin — for the apartments resemble the cabins of the Irish peasants more than anything else — a child lay dying of bronchitis brought on by exposure. The supply of fuel was about exhausted, and they had spent their last penny for bread some days before. All the families had been without bread or anything else to eat for two and a half days. A kind lady, who was made acquainted with the sad condition of these unfortunates, sent them

FORTY LOAVES OF BREAD

on Friday last. These loaves were equally distributed, and will keep them from starving for a few days longer. The supply of wood will also last for a few days, and then, with no resources, unless something is done for them, these poor people must starve. The marvel is that in the desperate strait to which they are reduced they have not been guilty of any unlawful act, such as stealing wood or any of the necessaries of life. The spectacle of foreigners perishing of hunger and cold in a Government building, though it be an emigrant [sic] shed, is not one calculated to inspire respect for the Government that would allow such a state of affairs. These Jews were brought here with the consent of the Government, and lodged in the emigrant sheds, and for the credit of the country, they should not be allowed to perish. It is a lamentable fact that much prejudice exists against the Jews, and on that account but few of them have been able to get lasting work. They all declare their willingness to work, and much prefer working to accepting the charity of their Christian neighbors.

The city council and many citizens responded to the article. At Holy Trinity Church, Reverend O. Fortin appealed from his pulpit during the Sunday evening sermon: "We shall not allow human beings to starve at our very doors." A public meeting attended by some prominent citizens was held at the Young Men's Christian Association, and a relief committee was organized. Philip Brown reported on behalf of the Winnipeg Jewish community that the local Jewish residents had raised $1200; and he offered his premises at 303½ Main Street as a depot for contributions of food and clothing. C. E. Hamilton, an executive of the Manitoba and North West Railway Company, took charge of the relief work, visiting the struggling families himself, along with Alderman McCrossan. Mark Samuel, chairman of the Anglo-Jewish Association in Toronto, sent $250, two Winnipeg skating rinks held benefit nights for the refugees, and local residents helped the newcomers survive that first winter by countless small generosities. An anonymous lady offered "two pies," another sent $1.65 — part of it given, she said, by a servant girl.

The coming of spring and the advent of Passover brought new hope that the newcomers would be settled on land west of Winnipeg, or that they would be able to start a productive life in the city. Some had begun to work as peddlers; others had even opened small shops. A hall was rented for Passover, in a building at the corner of Main Street and Logan Avenue West, above the store of "Brown and Coblentz, Clothiers," and people came from many miles away to celebrate this Jewish festival of freedom. By July 1883, the last of the previous summer's arrivals had left the immigration sheds near the mouth of the Assiniboine River, to settle in as best they could.

A Winnipeg Street Railway car on Main Street, 1890. One of the promoters of the company was Hyman Miller, a Jewish hardware merchant. The Weidman Brothers' store is on the extreme right.

The Community Takes Shape

The Manitoba that Jews came to in 1882 was changing rapidly from a fur-trading to an agricultural economy, as the expanding transcontinental railway linked the west with the east, and its travel lines spread out into the isolated farmlands. Mennonites and Icelanders had come to take up land in the 1870's, and in the 1890's increasing numbers of Ukrainians would bring their own traditions and farming skills to the province. In the encounter of different languages, religions, and cultures, tensions were inevitable, and the early settlers — particularly the English, Scottish, and French — resented the intruders. But just as the Icelanders some sixty miles north of Winnipeg had called their settlement "Gimli," meaning "Paradise," so all the immigrants had come in pursuit of a dream of happiness, and the prospering economy to which their labours contributed helped to achieve a more relaxed atmosphere in the community.

It was into this vast prairie landscape that the Jewish immigrant was thrown. Lacking the agricultural skills of the Icelanders, Mennonites, and Ukrainians, he was yet able to fit into the small town and the city of this great, sparsely populated land, as an artisan or merchant. Winnipeg itself was developing light industries and becoming the major distribution centre for the prairies, and here a large number of Jews settled.

The very early Jewish business neighbourhood was made up of small shops clustered around the C.P.R. depot along Main Street from Higgins Avenue to James Street. There were a number of shops that sold cigars, men's clothing, furs, dry goods, jewellery, baked goods, and groceries, and a growing number of tailor shops and second-hand clothes shops. While the Henderson Directory of 1880-1881 indicates that the original settlers were established, the directory of 1883 contains the names and occupations of quite a few of the more enterprising new arrivals who advertised their services: Miss Myers was a dressmaker at 194 Fort Street; B. Rosenthal was a tailor at 208 Main Street; D. Samuels was a butcher; F. Stirsky was a dealer in watches at 205 Main Street, and M. Drozdovitz a clothier at 723 Main Street; the Ripstein brothers sold groceries, liquor, and cigars at 690 Main Street; Harris Cohen was a carpenter, Sam Davis a painter, J. Goldstein a grocer, D. Israels a bricklayer, H. Levy a peddler, H. Rosenthal a merchant, T. Tapper a tailor. A kosher butcher shop was opened; meat sold first at fifty cents a pound and then dropped to twenty-five cents during the winter.

Within a remarkably short time, the Jewish newcomers were recognized as effective members of the larger community. In 1883 Louis Weinberg was appointed a Justice of the Peace, the first Jew in the Province of Manitoba to be raised to the magistracy. Hyman Miller formed a wholesale hardware company, held office in the Board of Trade in Winnipeg, and helped to promote the Winnipeg Street Railway Company.

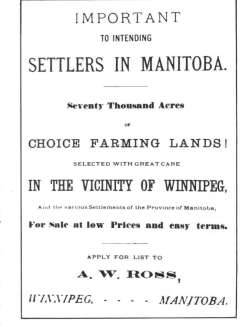

Immigration poster. Ca. 1880.

> ## Appeal for Aid to Erect a Synagogue.
>
> > " Father of all in every age,
> > " In every clime adored,
> > " By saint, by savage, and by sage,
> > " Jehovah, Jove or Lord."
>
> The Hebrews of Winnipeg have, by their united efforts purchased a lot on the corner of King and Common streets and are endeavoring to erect a Synagogue, wherein they can worship in a manner worthy of Him the God of their Fathers. Although somewhat numerous, our people are not overburdened with wealth, and we therefore appeal to a generous and charitable public for assistance to enable us to carry out our undertaking.
>
> Many of us have fled to this glorious and free country from climes where religious and political freedom are utterly unknown, bringing with us only our lives, the lives of some only of those dear to us and our traditions, leaving behind us the countries of our birth, our wealth, and the memories of innumerable and heartless persecutions.
>
> Here we wish to enjoy that freedom dear to every heart, *the right to worship God* according to our ancient laws.
>
> For His own wise purpose He has chosen to scatter His Jewish people over many lands, those whom fate and His kind hands have guided hither, seek to praise and worship Him as taught us by our traditions, handed down from Father to Son, since the time of Moses, and to raise here a Temple somewhat worthy of the great Creator; the God of Abraham, of Isaac and of Jacob.
>
> Contributions to the Building Fund can be sent to Philip Brown, chairman of the Building Committee, No. 606, Main street, Winnipeg, Manitoba. All contributions will be entered in the Golden Book of Life and thankfully acknowledged.
>
> | *Committee :* | *Committee :* | *Officers.* |
> |---|---|---|
> | D. Ripstein, | G. Frankfurter, | Philip Brown, Chairman. |
> | H. Weidman, | S. Ripstein, | T. Finkelstein, Treasurer. |
> | H. Gelgeran, | N. Zimmerman, | A. Benjamin, Secretary. |
> | H. Goldstaur, | J. J. Shragge, | Ch. Risky, Asst.-Secy. |
> | W. Goldbloom, | Jacob Heiman. | |
>
> Winnipeg, { Elul, 5649. / August, 1889.

A public appeal for contributions in 1889 preceded the building of the Shaarey Zedek Synagogue. This circular was discovered in the Manitoba Legislative Library among the papers of Thomas Greenway, then Premier of Manitoba.

The families of the merchants usually resided either behind the store or above it. The few who prospered moved to the adjacent residential areas on Martha Street, Lily Street, and the streets running to the river. Just north of the C.P.R. tracks were the homes of the Jewish labourers, carpenters, draymen, rag-and-scrap peddlers, painters, and milkmen, whose number gradually increased with every new flow of immigrants until the first World War. People called the area "Jerusalem" because of the predominantly Jewish population. In time, these artisans and tradesmen ventured still farther up Main Street, where the newer homes were located, and the city's colourful "North End" began to take shape. Meanwhile, as commerce and industry took over all the streets near the C.P.R. depot, many of the prosperous Jewish families who had lived there moved off across town to the grander new development of River Heights in south Winnipeg. Thus began the split in the Winnipeg Jewish community between the more affluent, more acculturated Jews of the "South End" and the self-consciously ethnic Jews of the "North End."

When the 1882 group of Russian Jews arrived, the handful of original Jewish pioneers had already begun the effort to satisfy their religious needs.

The look of well-being: the S. H. Narovlansky family, 1890. For some the west turned out to be the land of milk and honey.

A group had joined in prayer in a private home on Yom Kippur, 1879, the first congregation so constituted in Manitoba. By the following year there had been enough Jews in Winnipeg to hold services in the Orange Hall, and in 1881 the High Holidays were celebrated in the Oddfellows' Hall, with Abraham Benjamin, a scholar though not an ordained rabbi, coming up from the United States to act as cantor and reader and to teach the children. In the fall of 1882, after the arrival of the large group of Jews from eastern Europe, the greatly expanded congregation invited their gentile neighbours to attend the High Holiday services in Wesley Hall. Kieva Barsky and Jacob Shragge officiated, for there was still no regular rabbi, and the *Free Press* reported that the observers were interested and impressed.

There were other and sadder needs to be met. The night that the Russian group arrived, an infant died, and a few weeks later a boy was drowned in the Red River. A cemetery had to be provided, and in the winter of 1882-83 the community purchased an acre of land in Springfield for that purpose.

The newcomers did not mix easily with the resident Jews, and towards the end of 1882 formed, briefly, their own B'nai Israel Congregation. Nevertheless, with close to four hundred Jews now in Winnipeg, and the need for a synagogue most urgent, the entire group organized a building committee in 1883, and began a campaign for funds among Jews and non-Jews. In the meantime, that year's High Holiday services were held in the Albert Hall, with Rabbi J. Friedman from Montreal serving as religious leader. An executive was elected, consisting of both pioneer settlers and recent arrivals.

But the rift within the small community was becoming increasingly evident. The early settlers, English and German Jews, leaned towards a "modernized" reform Judaism on the American pattern, while the east European Jews clung to the traditional forms of their *shtetl* synagogue, complaining that the original Jewish residents had little interest in Jewish education, and not enough in religion. The coalition between "English" and "Russian" Jews, between reform and orthodox, proved unstable.

The reform group withdrew from the coalition in 1884 to form their own congregation, Beth El, and to found the Montefiore Hebrew Benevolent Society, "to promote some means to aid the erection of a Jewish

S. H. Narovlansky, livestock dealer and prominent Winnipeg citizen. Ca. 1890. By 1900, he was active in the Jewish Committee for the Canadian Patriotic Fund, to assist widows and orphans of soldiers who fell in the Boer War.

reformed temple, and to assist deserving objects of charity." The orthodox held services as the Sons of Israel Congregation, and fund-raising came to a halt. A truce was arranged in honour of the one-hundredth birthday of the Anglo-Jewish philanthropist, Sir Moses Montefiore, and in 1887 an official merger between the two congregations was achieved under the name Beth El of Israel. By 1889 enough money had been raised to proceed with building plans, and on September 3 the cornerstone was laid at the corner of King and Cameron Streets. Eight months later, on March 20, 1890, the new Shaarey Zedek Synagogue was dedicated.

The inherent differences within the new congregation once more proved divisive, however, and the orthodox withdrew to found their own congregation. Their first wooden structure, on Henry and Martha Streets, was destroyed by fire, but a new one was built directly across the street, and dedicated on August 24, 1893, as the Rosh Pina Congregation. The *Bikur Cholim* Society was formed, offering a sick benefit plan for a monthly premium of twenty-five cents. Each member was assured of nursing attention and part of the cost of doctor and medicine.

Meanwhile the exodus out of Russia continued, and a steady stream of Jews came to Winnipeg throughout the eighties and nineties, to stay or to proceed farther west.

A particularly colourful episode — colourful now, after its misery and hardship have faded — was the arrival in 1898 of a group of young "Foot-wanderers" from Romania. These were young men and women, incensed

"Foot-wanderers". Jewish emigrants from Romania pose for a group picture on the eve of their departure. Some of these young men reached Winnipeg in 1898.

by government persecution of their people, who had determined on a dramatic means of arousing the attention of Europe and the rest of the world. In bands of one hundred and two hundred, and carrying their possessions on their backs, they marched across Europe from one country to the next, towards their ports of embarkation for the New World. They were met and helped on their way by reception committees and eventually provided by the Jewish Colonization Association with steamship tickets to cross the Atlantic. The band that reached Montreal was welcomed with affection, and the J.C.A. undertook to place the young people in the promising lands of the great Canadian north-west. Their coming to Winnipeg was the first mass arrival since the Russian settlers of 1882-85.

The abortive Russian revolution of 1905 was followed by the largest flood of new immigrants ever to arrive in Winnipeg, and with this group the Jewish community began to assume its distinctive character. Not only was it necessary to provide for the physical wants of the poverty-stricken refugees, but their intellectual hunger had to be met as well. A free night-school for the teaching of English was established in Edwards Hall, where forty to fifty students, grey-bearded elders and clean-shaven youths alike, eagerly learned the A B C's of a different language and a different

Main Street, Winnipeg, 1910. Many of these small enterprises were operated by Jews.

life. The Jewish spirit too was enriched by the pressures of the newly-arrived majority, with their zest for a more vital communal life. Interest in traditional education increased and there was a revival of religious activity. The old, traditional *cheder* was transplanted to the Canadian west, and functioned side by side with the public school. Laughed at as *greeneh* (green ones), by their compatriots with a few more years on Canadian soil, these latest settlers were closer to the source of their heritage, and they were not prepared to lose themselves in a strange environment. For them, cultural survival was a conscious aim, a matter of principle.

This clamour for spiritual sustenance pointed the way to the eventual establishment of the splendid educational and cultural institutions that would form the backbone of the future western Jewish community. Paradoxically, the very strength of these urban Jewish institutions contributed to the undoing of a series of Jewish agricultural settlements, for the Jewish farm family was inevitably drawn back to the centres of culture.

Winnipeg's new Jewish residents established themselves so quickly in their growing city that by the first decade of the twentieth century, sons of some of the early pioneers were already achieving prominence; in the legal profession, as the first Jewish elected representatives to public office in Manitoba, as the founders of some important business establishments, and as the movers and shakers of the Jewish community itself. It was a time when men of boundless energy responded to the unlimited potential of a new situation. As Harry Steinberg put it in 1901, standing in front of his tiny "Montreal Great Bargain Store," in Manitou, Manitoba: "Small store, big name! Think big!"

Harry Steinberg, at the door of his Montreal Great Bargain Store, Manitou, Man., ca. 1901. Steinberg became an overall manufacturer in Winnipeg; in his later years he was known as the "Sholem Aleichem Yid," entertaining audiences with his readings from the Yiddish humourist.

3. THE LURE OF THE LAND

When Sir Alexander Galt sought to interest his Prime Minister in the "agricultural Jews" among the refugees from Russian persecution, he was perhaps unwittingly lending support to a dream cherished by the proposed settlers, rather than to a reality. Though many of the Jews had come from small towns and villages—and many, indeed, declared themselves to be farmers—very few actually had any experience in agriculture. What a great number of them did have, particularly among the more highly educated immigrants, was an extraordinary yearning for land that came from a sense of two thousand years of deprivation. In all the long years of exile, the annual round of Jewish festivals and holy days had recalled the cycle of seed-time and harvest, and generations of scholars had found an unfading validity in the social laws of the Talmud, with their basis in a rural economy. Now, as the secular young Jew earnestly strove to rid himself of the taint of the ghetto, it seemed clear to him that his people could only achieve a normal place in the world if they re-established their roots in the soil. Farming became more than an occupation—it was an ideology taught by serious philosophers and supported by a number of high-minded institutions. The dedicated new Jewish farmers were hardly prepared for the harsh realities of prairie sod-breaking.

Beginning in 1882, with the first Jewish farm settlement near Moosomin, Saskatchewan, a number of colonies were established. Most were in the western prairies, although there were Jewish farms at St. Sophie and

Amos Kinsey (holding reins) with his team and buggy; in the background, Kinsey's log house, which replaced his first sod shack. While not Jewish himself, Kinsey farmed at "New Jerusalem" from the colony's inception. Moosomin, ca. 1883.

JEWISH FARM COLONIES and SETTLEMENTS on the PRAIRIES

1	MOOSOMIN, Sask.	Founded	1882	8	ALSASK/MONTEFIORE, Sask.	Founded 1910
2	WAPELLA, Sask.	Founded	1888	9	NARCISSE/BENDER, Man.	Founded 1903
3	HIRSCH, Sask.	Founded	1892	10	CAMPER, Man.	Founded 1911
4	LIPTON, Sask.	Founded	1901	11	BIRDS HILL	
5	SONNENFELD, Sask.	Founded	1906	12	PINE RIDGE	Manitoba farm settlements founded during and after the first World War.
6	EDENBRIDGE, Sask.	Founded	1906	13	WEST KILDONAN	
7	RUMSEY/TROCHU, Alta.	Founded	1906	14	ROSENFELD	
				15	ROSSER	

✱ FARM COLONY   ● PRINCIPAL CITY

New Glasgow, near Montreal, and a few in British Columbia, Nova Scotia, and New Brunswick. These endeavours were assisted chiefly by funds from the world-wide philanthropies of the Baron and Baroness Maurice de Hirsch, and through such institutions as the Young Men's Hebrew Benevolent Society of Montreal and the Jewish Colonization Association. Nevertheless, despite all these efforts and the dedication of the colonists, the settlements seemed dogged from the start by insuperable difficulties.

Moosomin

Through the negotiations of Galt, twenty-six families from the 1882 group took up homesteads on the raw Canadian prairie a few miles southwest of Moosomin. Each had been granted 160 acres by the Canadian government and a loan of $400 by the Russo-Jewish Committee, and by the end of the first summer, the enthusiastic settlers produced a season's supply of potatoes and vegetables. Winter in their badly built houses proved a bitter hardship, and the wind-swept isolation unbearably lonely, but the group persisted—inexperienced, without technical advisors, on land that was not, after all, productive. Frost in August destroyed the crop in 1885, drought ruined it in 1886, a fire in the settlement wiped out the hay crop in 1889. Transportation was inadequate, and there were no schools, no one to teach the children. The colony, which had been nicknamed "New Jerusalem," either in hope or in derision, dwindled, as one by one the settlers drifted away, some of them—the Weidmans, Narovlanskys, Lechtziers—to achieve success in Winnipeg. The fact that Scottish and other homesteaders in the same district were equally unsuccessful a few years later, also for lack of proper advice and support, was small consolation for the failure of a new way of life.

Wapella

An equally determined band of settlers, under the leadership of Abraham Klenman and John Heppner, moved out in 1888 to land near Wapella, Saskatchewan; by 1892 the colony numbered twenty families. This group also had very little agricultural experience among its tailors, shoemakers, and unskilled labourers, but Wapella became the longest-surviving Jewish farm colony in the Canadian west, serving as a training ground for other would-be young farmers. Among the settlement's members in the early 1890's were the Ekiel Bronfman family, who later achieved power and prominence with the House of Seagram.

Wapella's initial support came from Herman Landau, a prominent Anglo-Jewish financier and the C.P.R.'s London representative. It received no assistance from government or public funds until several years after its inception, when some of the colonists obtained help from the Jewish Colonization Association. As the Russian persecution continued, a

Abandoned sod house at Moosomin, 1890.

BELOW
Mr. and Mrs. Simon Lechtzier, Moosomin pioneers. This photograph, with their son, Phillip, and his wife and children, was taken when the family was established in Winnipeg. Ca. 1900.

number of individuals working both privately and within the organized relief committees tried to arrange further settlement schemes. The chairman of the Russo-Jewish Committee of London, Alfred Wolff, exchanged letters on the subject in 1892 with Joseph Wolf and Hyman Miller of Winnipeg, and the Montreal Jewish community continued to play an active role. As late as 1897 Landau tried to negotiate with Sir Wilfrid Laurier for the establishment of a Jewish farm colony in Manitoba. But all their deliberations were too slow, as the need became more pressing with each new arrival of homeless immigrants.

Hirsch

One group of Russian-Jewish immigrants too impatient to wait for organizations and governments to settle their problems arrived in Winnipeg in the summer and fall of 1891. It was harvest time, and the friendly Mennonite farmers in the Gretna and Plum Coulee areas offered employment to the new arrivals. Needless to say, the work was eagerly undertaken by the Jews as a kind of apprenticeship for their life on the land.

Impatient with the protracted negotiations in Montreal on just where their farm colony should be located, Asher Pierce took his father, Jacob, and his brothers out to Oxbow, in south-eastern Saskatchewan, and they were joined in 1892 by forty-seven more Jewish families. The site they had selected was counter to the advice of the Jewish Colonization Association experts, who recommended the Canadian government offer of land in the vicinities of Red Deer, Prince Albert, and Regina. But the existing non-Jewish farmers near Regina protested vehemently that if Jews were imposed on the area they would keep out some interested and wealthy English settlers; and Pierce, for his part, insisted with equal vehemence that Oxbow was preferable because it lay within easier reach of the settled Jewish communities of Manitoba. It was, in some respects, a classic encounter, repeating the familiar pattern of prejudice and withdrawal: the gentiles objected, sight unseen, to the Jews, and the Jews pointedly chose to be near their own kind. Pierce's advice prevailed, and with the arrival at Oxbow of ninety-one men from Montreal and Winnipeg on May 2, 1892, the new colony was officially established a few miles away, east of Estevan, and named Hirsch, for the Baron and Baroness de Hirsch.

Though drought and hail and grasshopper plagues compounded the difficulties of the inexperienced farmers, the colony survived for about fifty years or more, as the children of the first settlers took their places on the land. A branch of the C.P.R. was extended to Hirsch, and the first two schools in the district were erected, providing both religious and secular education. A *shochet* was employed, and Saskatchewan's first synagogue was built, to be followed by another a few miles away. Here also a cemetery was located, now the oldest consecrated Jewish cemetery in Saskatchewan.

Jacob and Debora Pierce, shown with their grandson, spent the summer of 1892 at Hirsch in a tent.

OPPOSITE PAGE
TOP LEFT
The Wapella home of the Alexander Klenman family. Ca. 1900.

CENTRE LEFT
Ekiel Bronfman, Wapella pioneer and founder of the Bronfman clan. Ca. 1889.

BOTTOM LEFT
Fanny and Kalman Zelickson of Hirsch, Saskatchewan. Studio portrait. Ca. 1920.

TOP RIGHT
Solomon and Raina Barish at home on their Wapella farm, 1936. The poster on the wall shows Theodor Herzl, the founder of the Zionist movement.

CENTRE RIGHT
The Yackness and Fishtrom families, ca. 1900. The young boy is Isaac Fishtrom, who arrived with his parents, Mr. and Mrs. Moses Fishtrom, in 1892, when he was five years old.

BOTTOM RIGHT
The Pierce brothers and sisters, pioneers of Oxbow and the Hirsch colony. Ca. 1900.

TOP LEFT
Lipton homesteaders, ca. 1890. The house is whitewashed sod, with a thatched roof.

TOP RIGHT
Interior of Lipton farmhouse, ca. 1900. Creature comforts were no better than those in the *shtetl*, but the promise was greater.

BOTTOM LEFT
Tiferes Israel School, Lipton, Saskatchewan. Ca. 1910.

BOTTOM RIGHT
Open-air wedding at the Lipton Colony. Ca. 1915.

Lipton

Lipton colony, seventy miles north-east of Regina and originally named Qu'Appelle, was started in 1901 by forty-nine families from Romania, assisted by an advance of $200 to each family from the Jewish Colonization Association. Once again inexperienced in agriculture, the settlers were grateful to the local métis, who showed them how to construct log houses against the cold. But the Colonization Association's local supervisors were farmers and businessmen in the area who hardly took the Jews and their efforts seriously, and some administrative bungling by the supervisors left the colony without the means to become self-sustaining. Faced with the harsh realities of the land, many of the families left the settlement shortly after arriving. Eventually the colony attracted some Jewish immigrants from Russia, and it flourished for a time.

Sonnenfeld

Some fifty miles west of Estevan, in the south-eastern corner of Saskatchewan, Sonnenfeld was founded in 1906 by a group that included Israel Hoffer, Philip Berger, Meyer Feldman, and Max Feuer. These young men had received farm training in the agricultural school of the Jewish Colonization Association at Slobodka Lesna in Galicia, and had then worked as hired hands for the Hirsch settlement. The colony was named for Dr. Sigesmund Sonnenfeld, the Association's director.

Writing in a 1952 issue of *Saskatchewan History*, Israel Hoffer recalls that his first year's wages amounted to $125. With this amount he moved on to his homestead in June 1907, with his father and his brother Mayer, buying a team of broncos and harness, a cow and a calf, mostly on credit. Thus began what was to become one of the best-operated farms in southern Saskatchewan. Living conditions, as Hoffer describes them, were primitive for the first settlers: "Our staple foods were flour, corn meal, sugar, syrup, tea, coffee, and dried peas. We made butter and cheese and ate (wild) duck eggs secured from the numerous sloughs in the vicinity." Their water supply also came from a slough, and had to be boiled. They made a sod house which caved in, and then they lived in a shack with no roof. A more successful sod structure became their first permanent barn.

ABOVE
Teacher on horseback: Louis Rosenberg taught at Lipton and served as western manager of the Jewish Colonization Association. Later he became executive secretary for the Canadian Jewish Congress. Photo 1916.

TOP
Nucleus of a town: country elevator and store. Ca. 1915.

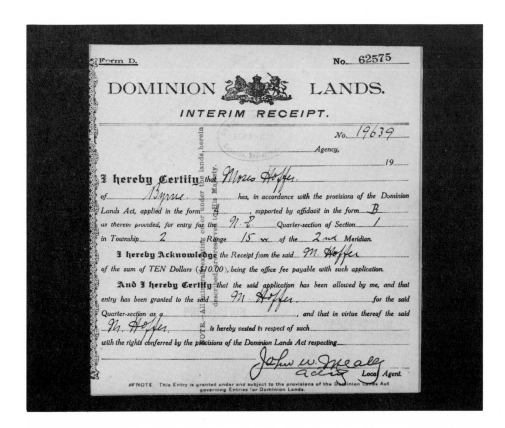

Receipt for land grant to Moses Hoffer, 1908.

LEFT
Hoffer colony patriarch: Moses Hoffer, father of Israel and Mayer. Ca. 1900.

RIGHT
Wedding of Rose and Mayer Hoffer, Rossburn, Manitoba, 1914.

Isaac Blatt and his sons, Henry and Jack, stooking wheat. Ca. 1930.

Edenbridge

Some seventy miles east of Prince Albert, the Vickar brothers, David and Sam, took up homesteads, and another new colony came into being. Part of a group of Lithuanian Jews who had settled near Capetown, South Africa, the Vickars had seen a Canadian Department of Immigration pamphlet offering 160 acres of virgin land in the north-west for ten dollars, to be owned outright. Accompanied by fifty-six families who had been living in the Transvaal during the Boer War, they left South Africa for Canada in 1906, and settled in the Carrot River area of Saskatchewan, where the rich and well-watered soil made good farm land. The Vickar brothers were soon joined by others, including one group of young Jews who had come to Canada's wide prairies from the clothing shops of London, England. One of them, Mike Usiskin, was the chronicler of the settlement, writing lyrically to the press about the life of the colonist.

The name of the colony was acquired a year after its inception, when the Canadian government informed the settlers that a post office was being

established and that a name was therefore required. The Jewish farmers suggested several "Jewish" names, like "Israel Villa" and "Jew Town," but these were turned down by the government as unsuitable. The name finally accepted, "Edenbridge," probably sounded pleasantly English and rather uplifting to official ears: "Paradise Bridge," it seemed to mean. What the post office did not know was that the compound concealed a private joke. "Eden" is a pun on *Yidden* (Jews), so that the town is called "Jews' Bridge"—an ethnic designation after all. The bridge, incidentally, is the steel span that connects the two sides of the Carrot River.

Narcisse or Bender Hamlet

In 1903, a Jewish colony was started in the Interlake district of Manitoba, fifty-two miles north of Winnipeg. Jacob Bender organized thirty Russian-Jewish families who had lived in Winnipeg for several years, to take up homesteads in the region. Originally named Bender Hamlet for its founder, it was renamed Narcisse in honour of Narcisse Leven, one-time president of the Jewish Colonization Association. It was modelled after the European plan of a village colony, but the land was ill-chosen, much of it rocky, swampy, and unsuitable for farming. At its height Narcisse had thirty-eight Jewish families, a synagogue, and a public school. Today only a cemetery remains as a monument.

TOP LEFT
"The Jewish Bridge" spanning the Carrot River at Edenbridge.

TOP RIGHT
Clearing the land: pulling tree stumps. Ca. 1920.

BOTTOM LEFT
Mike Usiskin at Edenbridge, ca. 1930, with Esther Levinton and Parella Miller.

BOTTOM RIGHT
Edenbridge synagogue, built 1912. The cairn was dedicated to the memory of the pioneers at a ceremony in 1968.

ABOVE LEFT
Immigrants arriving at Bender Hamlet, Manitoba. Ca. 1905.

ABOVE RIGHT
Bender Hamlet was modelled after the European plan of a village colony: twenty lots of eight acres each, with the homes grouped together to relieve the loneliness of farm life. Ca. 1920.

LEFT
City-bred Gertie Rodin taught school at Bender Hamlet and helped with the farm chores. Ca. 1916.

Rumsey and Trochu

Alberta's earliest Jewish farm settlements were the neighbouring colonies of Rumsey and Trochu, founded in 1906 about one hundred miles north-east of Calgary. With fertile land and enough moisture, the colonies were at one time among the most prosperous in the west. By the end of the first World War, however, a marked decline in population had set in, and today the farms have passed into other hands.

Alsask and Montefiore

Alsask and Montefiore came into being in 1910, in a drought-stricken, wind-blown area on the boundary between Alberta and Saskatchewan. The original Jewish settlers included a number who had previously farmed in Montana and North Dakota, but the district proved unproductive, as it did for many of the non-Jewish farmers who also attempted to locate there. Though the Jewish Colonization Association responded to an appeal for help, the settlements did not survive. A number of the pioneers are reported to have returned to the United States, to try their luck this time in the more bountiful acreage of California.

Camper and Other Colonies

In 1911 another group of Jewish farmers from the Ukraine homesteaded at Camper in the Interlake district of Manitoba. Their colony, named New Hirsch, was dissolved in 1924. Other farm settlements in Manitoba were established near Winnipeg, in Birds Hill, Pine Ridge, West Kildonan, Rosenfeld, Rosser, and elsewhere, but functioned only briefly.

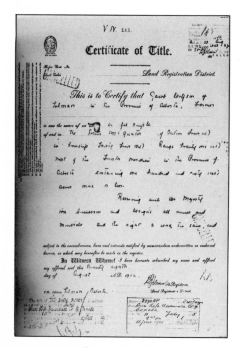

Certificate of Title issued to Jacob Wolfson, July 1915.

The Gurevitch family, Rumsey, Alberta. Ca. 1910.

LEFT
Leible Guttman on his homestead at Trochu, Alberta, 1913.

The Podersky family at their homestead at Lacombe, Alberta. Ca. 1910. Many Jewish families farmed individually, not as members of a colony.

Harvesting in Montefiore, Alberta, ca. 1910. Most of the settlers in this Jewish colony had farmed in North Dakota and Montana.

ABOVE
Hillel Sandock on the veranda of his house, Camper, Manitoba, 1920.

TOP
A musical picnic. The Levitt homestead at Camper, Manitoba, 1915.

One by one all these colonies, begun in hope and determination, dwindled into extinction. While Jewish farmers are still to be found across the prairie provinces, some of them on land that was homesteaded by their grandparents or great-grandparents, the pioneers' dream of a Jewish agricultural society has vanished. It was defeated ultimately not by physical hardship but by the impossibility of sustaining in a rural setting the kind of rich and complex community which Jews in every walk of life have always found indispensable. With synagogues, schools, lecture halls, theatres, and the bustle of organizations far away, and books and newspapers scarce, disenchantment set in all too quickly. Even in those colonies which apparently took root and prospered, opportunity for the young was lacking. In those early clusters of families, an elementary education was difficult to provide, and a Jewish education almost impossible. Inevitably, the sons and daughters of a colony's founders were drawn to the larger centres, with their institutions of higher learning, their Jewish cultural organizations, their avenues for professional advancement. With the younger generation gone, there was little to keep the aging pioneers on the land, and, like their counterparts, the Jewish storekeepers in the little prairie towns, they retired to the cities. Within fifty years at most, the organized Jewish back-to-the-land movement had come to an end.

The remaining farmers of Edenbridge were represented at a ceremony in 1968, when a monument to the pioneers was unveiled outside the rustic synagogue which they built in 1912. Its cemetery is still used by the Jews of Melfort and the surrounding community, but the cemetery at Hirsch has now become a historic site.

Cecil Gordon harvesting at Edenbridge, Saskatchewan. Ca. 1930.

"How Beautiful are the Fields"

In his book, *Canadian Mosaic*, John Murray Gibbon reprints a letter which was written to the Jewish Colonization Association, and which, he says, "reads almost like a Psalm of David." The writer of that letter, not identified by Gibbon, was Mike Usiskin, and his translator was Louis Rosenberg, one-time western manager of the Jewish Colonization Association of Canada:

I sit upon my plow and my eye is enchanted with the sight of the brown earth being turned upwards furrow by furrow. If the field is a long one and one starts with a straight furrow, it takes on the appearance of a Tallith, with broad blue stripes at the edges, and when the sun's rays strike the eye and the breeze blows the squadrons of little flies past, it seems as if the black strips of ploughed land twist and turn. It is a picture which I am not able to place upon paper. Later, when one has to run after the harrows, no matter how hard it is, the work draws like a magnet. The field behind takes on another appearance. From a piece of coarse, common cloth it becomes like linen, and another stroke of the harrow makes it into velvet, silk, or a piece of smoothly polished furniture. It serves as enchantment which prevents the feet from feeling tired.

How beautiful are the fields afterwards when they become green. This draws you and draws you and makes you willing to root out forests, turn over fields, even drink the sweat that pours from your forehead, and yet be satisfied.

And who can describe the rhythm of the binder, especially when you have enough feed for the horses and the horses feel their oats and the machine is in good repair. You sit upon the binder and you become one with the machine, and the joyfulness of the horses passes through the binder to you and you become a part of them. Should the field be good and the straw straight you cannot distinguish between the iron of the machine, the blood and bone of the horse, and the man. They form one happy piece of machinery.

If the joy of the land has faded for the children of the early dreamers, the lyricism of these words still expresses the zest of the Jewish pioneer in the unfolding horizons of his new country.

4. BRITISH COLUMBIA, 1860-1918

Just as the opening of the prairie provinces began with the fur trade, the first sizable settlement of Europeans in British Columbia developed around the Hudson's Bay Company's fort at Victoria, built in 1843, on Vancouver Island. Although a town was laid out at Victoria in 1852, it remained a trading post, and there were only a few scattered trading posts on the mainland as well, until the discovery of gold in the Fraser River in 1858 brought a rush of adventurers to the Pacific coast. The history of Victoria, incorporated as a city in 1864, is until 1887 virtually the history of the province. It was here that the traffic for the Cariboo gold rush originated, and with it the opening of Prince George on the northern mainland and of the British Columbia interior. As long as furs and gold held sway, Victoria was dominant. Vancouver came into its own as the century neared its end, after the C.P.R. had spun out its iron thread to the Pacific ocean.

Like the province itself, British Columbia's early Jewish community developed separately from the rest of Canada, until the completion of the railroad. Victoria's Jews were the first along the north Pacific to organize, beginning in the 1850's. Settlement in Vancouver came later, and both communities grew only slowly. It was not until the turn of the century that the effects of the mass influx of east European Jews after the 1882 pogroms reached the west coast.

The Jews who first made their way up the Pacific coast from the United States came singly, rather than in large, close-knit immigrant groups. Unlike the Russian Jews, they did not come under duress, fleeing persecution, but seeking adventure and opportunity in the rich west coast resources. Like the very earliest Jewish arrivals on the Atlantic seaboard, in central Canada, and even on the prairies, these colourful individualists were generally the sons and daughters of reasonably well-established families in England, Germany, or the eastern United States. Where the east European Jews were by long experience alienated from their host society, and intensely determined to transplant their own culture and religion to the Canadian environment, the Jews from the United States, England, and western Europe moved far more freely among their neighbours, and in British Columbia this difference was especially marked. East of the Rockies even the first Jewish immigrants came as a foreign element into a society whose character had already been established, but in the Pacific Northwest the first Jews were themselves among the pioneer architects of what was only later to become a province of Canada. The bond of a shared religion held them together, but they found a ready outlet for their energies in the developing economic, political, and social life of their communities, and organized Jewish activities developed slowly.

Adolph Friedman, a native of Latvia, is the first Jew known to have settled on British territory in the Pacific Northwest. As a very young man, he set out with thirty-five Scandinavian sailors from the port of Libau in 1840, via the Cape Horn route; and in 1845, after many stops and adventures, the group finally reached what is now the city of Tacoma, Washington. Friedman became a supplier to fishermen and homesteaders. Canadians can claim him only as a relative by marriage; though he came to Victoria to marry his cousin, Masha Stusser, the couple returned to live in the United States.

It is with the remarkable Oppenheimer family that settlers of Jewish origin began to leave their mark on British Columbia, and the fascinating story of these five brothers mirrors the pattern of the province's early growth. In 1848, Charles, David, Godfrey, Isaac, and Meyer left their native Bavaria for the United States, and they lived briefly in Ohio, in Texas, and in Louisiana. Two years after the 1849 discovery of gold in California, the Oppenheimers headed for San Francisco, in the wake of the thousands of people from the world over seeking instant wealth. It was as suppliers to these hordes of prospectors that the Oppenheimers perceived their own opportunity, and in 1858 they followed the Fraser River gold rush to Victoria. Charles was the first to arrive, and he set up a trading firm at Victoria. From this base the brothers moved out to the frontiers of mainland British Columbia and set up a two-way traffic, taking supplies in to the gold miners and bringing the gold out.

By 1859 there was one Oppenheimer store operating in Yale, on the Fraser, and another in Fort Hope; later, stores opened in Litton and Barkerville. There were Jews among the anonymous packers and pack-train operators who laboured through that inaccessible terrain, and other Jewish merchants among those who built their fortunes during the brief heyday of gold rush fever. Carl Strauss had stores in Barkerville and Williams Creek, and Felix Neufelder in Barkerville, Van Winkle, and elsewhere. With traffic extremely difficult, the Oppenheimers in particular badly needed to link together their multiple operation. It was thanks to their initiative that the famous Cariboo Wagon Road was begun in 1862, with a contract awarded to the Oppenheimer firm for the construction of the initial section. This was the first road into the B.C. interior, and the foundation of one of the first railway lines in the area.

The place names that date back to this time evoke the wild romance of the entire period—Hell's Gate Canyon, Jackass Mountain, Fort Hope, Soda Creek. Existence was as precarious for the frontier merchants as for the motley hordes of miners they served. Barkerville burned to the ground in 1868; in a lavish gesture as grandly dramatic as it was shrewd and practical, David Oppenheimer went off to San Francisco and returned with a fire engine. His brother Isaac was installed with all due ceremony as chief of the fire brigade, and Felix Neufelder served as a prominent member.

No less colourful among the early Jewish settlers was Frank Sylvester.

ABOVE
Among Victoria's first Jewish settlers, Francis Joseph (Frank) Sylvester, arrived on July 17, 1858.

TOP
David Oppenheimer (1832-1897), pioneer, entrepreneur, mayor of Vancouver.

FIGHTING FIRES FOR HONOUR
AND FUN

Victoria's first steam fire-engine,
purchased in 1868 by the Tiger
Engine Co. No. 2.

LEFT
Officers of the Tiger Engine Co. No.
2, 1864. Two Jewish members in the
group were H.E. Levy, second
assistant (back row, extreme left), and
Frank Sylvester, secretary (front row,
centre).

RIGHT
Isaac Oppenheimer, captain of the
Barkerville Fire Brigade, with his
trumpet, the badge of office. 1869.

Born in New York in 1837, he crossed the continent overland by
stagecoach at the age of twenty, arriving in Victoria on board the *S.S.
Pacific* from San Francisco on July 17, 1858. When his first enterprise, a
small store, failed, and he lost all his money, Sylvester joined the trek to
the high adventure of the first Cariboo gold rush. His diary records the
hazards all men faced when they set out to look for gold: "At one time I had
to cross a narrow saddle on a trail not less than a thousand feet above the
river, on a trail not over a foot wide, and the least misstep would have sent
one into the boiling river, faintly seen below." After three years in the gold
fields, Sylvester returned to Victoria, where he became an accountant with
J. P. Davies, an auctioneer. He married Davies' youngest daughter, Cecelia,
in January 1869, and set up independently as an accountant.

Victoria: Urban Beginnings

By this time Victoria was a thriving community, with a variety of
enterprises catering to a multiplicity of needs. Many of its pioneer businesses were located on Yates Street. Kady Gambitz established his first dry
goods and drapery store at 43 Yates Street, in December 1859, and then
opened a new store on Yates near the corner of Government Street. The

Yates Street, Victoria, in the 1860's. The establishments of the Sutro brothers and Joseph Boscowitz are in the foreground.

LEFT
The Franklin brothers of Victoria, B.C., Selim (left) and Lumley (right). Selim was a member of the Legislative Assembly of Vancouver Island and mayor of Victoria. Ca. 1860.

CENTRE
Henry Nathan Jr., a prominent Mason and an early British Columbia member of Parliament. 1871.

RIGHT
Marcus Wolfe, Grand Master of the British Columbia Masonic Grand Lodge, 1891-92.

Pither and Leiser wholesale operated on Yates Street, as did the wholesale tobacco business founded by the Sutro brothers, Emil and Gustave. It was on lower Yates Street that Joseph Boscowitz, the pioneer Jewish fur dealer and entrepreneur, set up shop, and as early as 1858 his fur store on Wharf and Bastion Streets was one of the first commercial establishments in Victoria. The enterprising Boscowitzes were the leaders in the sealing industry, operating their ships in the North Pacific, and they helped to develop the copper deposits along the eastern shore of Howe Sound.

The degree to which the Jewish pioneers of Victoria were integrated from the beginning into the life of the community can be seen by their prominence in civic affairs. Freemasonry played an important part in the young city's politics, and of the twenty-one names on the membership roll of the Victoria Lodge in its first year in 1860, six were Jewish: Lumley Franklin, a charter member and afterwards master; Gustave Sutro; Lewis Wolff; Moses Sporborg; Samuel Goldstone; and John Malowanski, who was the first candidate initiated into Freemasonry in Western Canada. In 1891-92 Marcus Wolfe was installed as Grand Master of the British Columbia Grand Lodge of the Masons, thus becoming the only Jew to reach the top of the Masonic order in Canada. Apparently the Hook and Ladder Company, the volunteer fire brigade, also had a prestigious role to play: it was in the 1860's, for positions in that august body, that Canada's first election by secret ballot rather than by open voting took place. On that occasion Nathan Koshland, who had come to Victoria in 1860, defeated J. S. Drummond for the post of assistant fire chief.

Jews were involved in politics on a larger scale as well. In 1860 Selim Franklin was elected to the second legislative assembly of Vancouver Island. He was, however, opposed to union between Vancouver Island and the mainland, and resigned his seat in the legislature when union was completed. He left the colony in 1866 and moved to San Francisco, where he became secretary of the Bank of California. That same year his brother Lumley was elected mayor of Victoria by a huge majority, and so became the first Jewish mayor of a city in British North America. Disagreeing with Selim, Lumley presided over the key meetings on union with the mainland, and after his retirement from public office, he was active in the movement toward Canadian Confederation.

Landing a cargo of valuable furs, Prince Rupert, B.C., ca. 1910. Top right, early trader Louis Ripstein.

Members of the Jewish community of Victoria on a sight-seeing tour, with J.B. Yaffe at the wheel. 1917.

Equally prominent on the federal as well as the provincial scene was Henry Nathan, who came to Victoria in 1862, and established the firm of Henry Nathan Jr., Wholesale Merchants. A staunch supporter of Sir John A. Macdonald, he was elected member for Victoria in the British Columbia legislature in November 1870, and remained until its dissolution in 1871. After the province joined Confederation, he was elected to the federal parliament by acclamation, as the first member for Victoria, and was re-elected during the 1872 general election. A prominent Mason, he also served as a director of what was to become the Canadian Pacific Railway.

A Cemetery and a Synagogue

At the same time as the first Jewish settlers of the Canadian west coast began to establish themselves economically and to take part in the on-going life of the settlement as a whole, they also felt their needs as Jews. Here as in many other places, one of the first moves towards a Jewish community came in response to a sorrowful—and practical—problem. Inevitably, death claimed some members of the small Jewish group, and a suitably sanctified burial ground had to be provided. A meeting held in Simpson's Store on Yates Street, on May 22, 1859, set the project in motion, and the cemetery was consecrated on February 5, 1860. Located at Cedar Hill Road, Victoria, this is the oldest Jewish cemetery in western Canada. Some eight months earlier the Victoria Hebrew Benevolent Society had been founded, with Abraham Blackman as president, and the development of the west coast Jewish community was on its way.

An organized congregation of worship and a temple came next. Although there were only about one hundred Jews in Victoria, the decision to begin a building campaign was made at a meeting held one warm Sunday afternoon at the end of August 1859, in Gambitz's Ladies' Wear Store on Yates Street.

Yates Street, Victoria: Gambitz's first dry goods and drapery store was located here. From an 1862 drawing.

ANNO VICESIMO SEPTIMO ET VICESIMO OCTAVO

VICTORIÆ REGINÆ.

※※

No. XIX.

An Act to incorporate the Israelite Congregation named "The Emanuel of Victoria, Vancouver Island."

WHEREAS a Congregation of Israelites of the City of Victoria being desirous of fulfilling the Ordinances of their Religion, have formed themselves into a Congregation under the Style of "The Emanuel of Victoria, Vancouver Island," and have established certain Rules and Articles embodied in Articles of Constitution for their Government : Be it therefore enacted by the Governor, on Her Majesty's Behalf, by and with the Consent and Advice of the Legislative Council and Assembly of Vancouver Island and its Dependencies, as follows :

I. That the existing Members of the said Congregation, and all such Persons as from Time to Time hereafter may become the Members of the same according to the Articles of Constitution aforesaid, or any Articles of Constitution for the Time being in Force under the said Constitution, shall be a Body politic and corporate in Deed and in Law, by the Name of "The Emanuel of Victoria, Vancouver Island," for carrying into Effect the Fulfillment of the Ordinances of the Israelitish Persuasion according to the orthodox Order, and shall for all legal Purposes be known by such Appellation, and shall have a corporate Seal, with the Name of the said Corporation imprinted thereon, in the Words following : " The Emanuel of Victoria, Vancouver Island," and shall be governed by such Articles of Constitution as may be for the Time subsisting by virtue of the said Constitution. *Incorporation of the Congregation Emanuel.*

II. That a Copy of the Articles of Constitution aforesaid, shall be deposited with the Colonial Secretary, verified by the President and Secretary of the said Congregation, within fourteen days from the passage of this Act, and that a copy of *Articles of Constitution, &c., to be deposited.*

any

Received my Assent this 7th day of July, 1864.

A. E. KENNEDY,

GOVERNOR.

VICTORIA, VANCOUVER ISLAND :

PRINTED BY AUTHORITY OF THE GOVERNMENT BY HARRIES AND COMPANY.

1864.

Temple Emanu-El, Victoria, as it looked in 1863, before its alteration by a "modern" facade. It remains the oldest synagogue in continuous service in Canada.

The cornerstone of the temple was laid with great pomp and ceremony on June 3, 1863. Since some of the participants wanted a Masonic ceremony, it was decided that two cornerstones would be laid, one by members of the congregation and one by the Masonic fraternity. A procession was formed at the rooms where the community had formerly worshipped, and it marched to the site of the new building, headed by the band of *H.M.S. Topaz*, which was then in port at the Esquimalt docks. In order came the Germania Singing Varein, the Hebrew Benevolent Society, the St. Andrew's Society, the French Benevolent Society, and the German Benevolent Society, and they were joined on the site by the Grand Lodge of Free and Accepted Masons, all in full regalia. Not least in the procession were the Chief Justice of the city and the Mayor. According to reports of the event, Mr. Meyer Malowanski offered the opening prayer, the congregation being without a minister, and Mr. Samuel Hoffman delivered the address. Clearly the temple dedication was a grand civic occasion, and the Jews in Victoria at that time were simply one more element in the variegated tapestry of west coast pioneer life. The consecration of their house of worship as Congregation Emanu-El, on September 13, 1863, confirmed that they, too, had arrived.

Vancouver: the Frontier and the City

While Jewish settlement started in Victoria, the city remained the centre of Jewish activity for a relatively short time only. Cariboo gold ran dry, and without the gold rush trade, supplying the sealing industry alone became unprofitable. While most of the pioneer families remained in Victoria, with its favourable climate and beautiful scenery, it was Vancouver that held the promise of the future, as a shipping and lumbering centre, and eventually as the western terminus of the C.P.R. The Oppenheimers were in the vanguard of the change.

When David and Isaac Oppenheimer transferred their operations from Victoria and were joined by brothers Meyer and Charles, Vancouver was

Vancouver, ca. 1895.

still only a town. Imaginative and venturesome in business, the brothers turned their attention to transportation and to shipping. David Oppenheimer's tramway company linked Westminster and Vancouver, and he headed the B.C. Dyking and Dredging Company. Promoting trade between Canada and Australia, he established the steamship communications that ensured Vancouver's future as a terminus for the C.P.R., and he deeded to the railway one-third of his land holdings.

Prominent also in civic affairs, the Oppenheimers took a leading part in the incorporation of the city in 1886, and in the extension of the C.P.R. from Port Moody. David and Isaac both served as aldermen in the second city council, having been elected by acclamation for Ward Five. In 1888 David Oppenheimer was elected Mayor, serving without remuneration for four years. He entertained visiting dignitaries at his own expense, and for a time used his own office as city hall. During his term as mayor he developed the first water supply service, laid sidewalks, and built bridges. A man with a unique sense of public service, he was generous to both Jewish and non-denominational causes. He turned over some of his land holdings for municipal parks and schools. It was David Oppenheimer who had the foresight to set aside the land for Vancouver's Stanley Park, and on December 14, 1911, a statue was erected there in his honour.

Another of Vancouver's pioneers was Samuel Gintzburger, who arrived in British Columbia in 1887. Born in Switzerland, he tried his hand at fur trading, seal hunting, and mining for both silver and gold, before achieving prominence in Vancouver as elected official, founder of Temple Emanu-El and the Hebrew Free Loan Association, and consul for Switzerland. Rosina Gintzburger, his wife, also played a significant role in the community, being particularly concerned with the immigrants coming to the port of Vancouver.

Jacob Izen, who arrived in 1898, was one of several Jews in the early theatre and motion picture business in Vancouver. Something of a mystery is Louis Brier, a native of Romania, who worked in the gold fields of the Yukon from about 1897. Quite unknown in Vancouver, he nevertheless left part of his large fortune to the Vancouver Jewish community; the Louis Brier Home for the Aged of B.C. was opened in his name. Besides all these residents of the province's two major centres, there were Jews in Burnaby,

Pither and Leiser Ltd., wholesale, was established on Water Street, Vancouver, in 1900. The firm started in Victoria in 1858.

Jacob Parker, front left, with family and friends, at a favourite tourist attraction, Vancouver's hollow tree. Stanley Park, 1910.

New Westminster and Chilliwack; in Trail and Nelson in the interior; in Prince Rupert and Prince George and even farther north, in New Hazelton. Some of them have become part of the folklore of the country. "Johnny the Jew" was a legendary trapper who worked the bush near Prince George for forty years; "Silver King Mike" was a Jewish packman in the Kootenays before the coming of the railway, and later a storekeeper in Nelson.

Towards a Future Community

Vancouver's oldest congregation, Temple Emanu-El, was functioning in 1887, one year after the city's incorporation. Initially the temple's services were strictly Orthodox, and conducted by the members themselves, but in 1890 it adopted the semi-Reform services with its first rabbi, R. Rosenstein. When this change took place, the Orthodox community established the B'nai Yehudah, or Sons of Israel, in 1907.

By this time there had been a large influx of Jews to Vancouver, and some one hundred families were settled there. Part of the same immigration wave that brought Jews to the prairies from eastern Europe, these

Vancouver's first synagogue, B'nai Yehudah, established 1907. Ca. 1911.

newcomers came in the main from the same *shtetl* background as their brothers east of the Rockies. They too brought with them their Orthodox faith, their customs and traditions, so that while the Reform group at the coast had reached its plateau, the Orthodox community was on the ascendancy. By 1911-12 the Sons of Israel had their small synagogue at Pender Street and Heatley Avenue. About the time that the community reached 250 families, in 1917, the Orthodox congregation was renamed Schara Tzedeck. In 1910, with the community still quite small, the Hebrew Aid and Immigrant Society was formed to assist the various immigrants who were beginning to arrive from Europe via Japan and China. The Vancouver Hebrew Free Loan Association, founded in 1915, provided financial help to the newcomers. Jewish education achieved a major advance in 1918 when a school was combined with the new synagogue erected by the Congregation Schara Tzedeck. Nathan M. Pastinsky was then engaged as cantor, *mohel*, and *shochet*, and afterward as rabbi. Because the Jewish population was scattered over a wide area of the city, a second branch of the school was maintained in the west end.

During all this period the Pacific coast Jewish communities seemed to have no more than nominal contact with their counterparts in the rest of Canada. It was, in part, to counteract the isolation of the Jewish communities scattered across the prairies and British Columbia that the Canadian Jewish Congress was organized in 1919, but the cohesive force of the Congress did not become effective until the 1930's. Vancouver came fully into its own as a major Jewish centre, with a vital, developed community life, only after World War II.

The Vancouver Junk Co., 841 Powell Street, was founded in 1902 by Abraham Goldberg, who came to the city from Seattle. Ca. 1912.

ABOVE
Mary Livingstone, wife of comedian
Jack Benny, was the stage name of
Vancouver-born Sadie Marks, seen
here, left, with her sister and a friend.
Ca. 1920.

ABOVE LEFT
An outing on the Capilano River,
North Vancouver. Ca. 1917.

Vancouver's first Schara Tzedeck
synagogue, at 700 East Pender Street
West, completed in 1921. The arched
windows and doors and the tile roof
are characteristic of Mediterranean
style synagogue architecture.

Dr. Samuel Blumberger, pioneer
Jewish physician in B.C. Ca. 1863.

Enterprise With a Flair

A number of memorable "firsts" claim their due place in the early history of Jews in British Columbia.

The first Jewish physician in the west coast province was Dr. M. H. Boscowitz. He arrived in Victoria in February 1863, and offered his medical services as a "German Physician, Surgeon and Obstetrician, fully conversant in four languages." Vancouver's first Jewish doctors were Samuel Blumberger and Samuel Petersky. Blumberger came from Riga, Latvia, graduated from McGill in 1906, and travelled to the Orient as a ship's doctor before setting up his shore practice in 1909. Petersky, also a McGill graduate, was the first native-born Jewish practitioner.

Mr. Justice Samuel D. Schultz, the first Jew to be appointed to the bench in Canada, was the son of another noteworthy figure; his mother, the former Elizabeth Davies, was the first Jewish woman to be married in B.C. Samuel was born in Victoria in 1865, graduated from Osgoode Hall Law School in Toronto, and practised in Nelson, Victoria, and Vancouver. He was appointed Judge of the County Court at Vancouver in 1914. Briefly active in politics, he served as an alderman for North Vancouver in 1909-10, and he was also a delegate to the Zionist convention held in Winnipeg in July 1917.

It was at the residence and hardware store of Zebulon Franks, at 42 Water Street, that the earliest Jewish religious services in Vancouver are said to have taken place — perhaps even as early as 1887, when Franks arrived from Russia. Highly educated, he was a leader of the Orthodox group in Vancouver, and the founding president of its B'nai Yehuda congregation.

In the lives of these pioneers, however, personal adventure was inseparable from professional, economic, and social achievement. The west coast attracted some unusual people, and there was a flair for the dramatic even among seemingly ordinary citizens.

David Belasco, the famous U.S. theatrical genius, was the son of an English Jew and a gypsy mother, Humphrey and Reina Belasco, who moved to Victoria from San Francisco in 1858, when David was five. Humphrey tried his hand at acting, and briefly went off in search of Cariboo gold. David was an avid reader, and his father thought his young son might become a rabbi, but the child was stage-struck from an early age. Having done some walk-on parts at the Victoria theatre, he ran off when he was eleven to join a travelling circus, and a show business career was launched. A highly successful producer, adapter of plays, and starmaker, Belasco also wrote the libretti for Puccini's *Madame Butterfly* and *Girl of the Golden West*.

A graduate engineer, Frederick Augustus Heinze made his fortune in Butte, Montana, before coming to Trail Creek Landing in 1895 at the age of twenty-six. There he built a two-furnace copper smelter just above the

CENTRE
Mr. Justice Samuel Schultz,
(1865-1917), the first Jewish member
of the judiciary of Canada.

BOTTOM
Hardware and household goods: the
Franks store, 42 Water Street. Ca.
1902.

Columbia River. He also constructed a narrow-gauge railroad from the boat landing at Trail, and organized the Columbia and Western Railway Co. His holdings, sold in 1898 to the C.P.R., became the basis for the Cominco smelting and fertilizer enterprise in Trail.

Simon Leiser, who started as a grocer on Victoria's Johnson Street, joined the importing firm that became Pither and Leiser Ltd. in 1893. He was prominent in the sealing industry as well, and personally operated his ship, the *Wanderer*, in the northern waters. He became a director of the Royal Jubilee Hospital, was associated with the Victoria Opera House Company, and took a leading part in the building of the Royal Victoria Theatre.

The Prince Rupert clothing store opened in 1908 by Isidor Director and Maurice Cohen was the first Jewish business establishment in northern British Columbia. The town was not yet incorporated at the time, and the partners began as squatters. Director once walked the 450 miles between Prince Rupert and Prince George, "just to see the country."

George H. Salmon and his father-in-law, Adolph Robinson, made a five-hundred-mile automobile trip to Fraser Lake, in the interior of northern British Columbia, in 1911. The route they followed was the famous Yukon Trail.

TOP LEFT
Reina and Humphrey Belasco, with future impressario David. Ca. 1853.

TOP RIGHT
Frederick A. Heinze, front centre, developer of smelting operations at Trail, B.C. Ca. 1897.

BOTTOM LEFT
Businessman and patron of the arts, Simon Leiser. Ca. 1890.

BOTTOM RIGHT
The Simon Leiser establishment, 14-16 Yates Street, Victoria, in the 1880's.

First Jewish business in northern British Columbia, on Third Avenue, Prince Rupert, operated by Isidor Director and Maurice B. Cohen. 1910.

By car to the B.C. interior, 1911: George H. Salmon and his father-in-law, Adolph Robinson (with beard).

Buckskin Romantic

Morris Moss was the epitome of the romantic Englishman who found a niche in the story-book history of the Canadian frontier. The son of a well-to-do family of English Jews, he was university-educated, a marksman, a horseman, and a sailor, and he came to Victoria in 1862 to take up a position as agent with a firm of fur traders. Over six feet tall, bearded and handsome, he became the darling of Victoria society. But his heart was in the dark forests of his childhood reading, and after a few months he abandoned the amenities of Victoria for life among the Indians at a trading post at Bella Coola. When a trip for supplies later that year ended in shipwreck, Moss lived off the land for three months on a small island, until he was rescued by Indians. By that time, however, his trading post had been plundered, and he came back to Victoria penniless.

Morris Moss, socialite and adventurer.

Some government service followed, when Moss was persuaded to act as "Indian expert" for the Legislative Council, handling everything from murder charges to customs. But distant adventure was an irresistible lure, and in 1867 he went off to build a house and store on the site of an old Hudson's Bay Company post at Bella Coola. He found and named the "Hebrew Mine" — and squandered a fortune trying fruitlessly to develop it. He ran a trading post in the Queen Charlotte Islands, travelled up the Skeena by canoe, and joined a party searching for claims near the Alaska boundary.

Sealing attracted his restless energy next. Moss was in his element at the helm of his own ship, and he had soon built a most successful business in furs. When United States officials confiscated his two schooners in the Bering Sea, claiming that he was violating the American monopoly on sealing in the area, the case achieved international prominence, and Moss was finally awarded damages by an arbitration court in Paris.

Once again the buckskin-clad adventurer returned to Victoria, to the proper respectability of a fine home and the presidency of the synagogue, the B'nai B'rith lodge, and the Victoria Club. At the age of forty-two he married the twenty-two-year-old Hattie Bornstein, and a year later their son was born. A period of apparently placid domesticity followed. Then, on a June morning in 1896, Moss went off on a brief trip to look into some mines in Washington State — and vanished out of sight. His death was reported in Denver, Colorado, four years later.

Moss Street in Victoria, and Moss Bank and Moss Passage in Millbank Sound are all named after Morris Moss.

5. THE PRAIRIES, TO 1920

From 1901 to 1919 the number of Jews in the three prairie provinces rose from under fourteen thousand to twenty-five thousand. Although most of the immigrants flocked to the larger urban centres, a significant number of the early settlers went out to smaller towns and villages. There, from the turn of the century to the thirties, the Jewish country storekeeper played an important role.

Jews located wherever there was a line elevator, a railway station, a Main Street. They came from towns in Europe with strange sounding names: Proposk, Bratzlav, Szchvisloshch, Pogrebishtch, Priluka, Pavolich; and they made their new Canadian homes in western towns with names that were surely just as strange: Snowflake, Plum Coulee, Bannock, Porcupine Plain, Whiskey Gap, Michichi, Skookumchuck, Woodpecker. Dotted along the newly extended railway lines, eight or ten miles apart, each town might consist of a two-room railway station, a blacksmith shop, a post office, one or two grain elevators, one or two churches, a school, a restaurant (usually run by Chinese), and a general store (usually run by Jews).

The people who started to clear and cultivate the land on the prairies were mostly peasants from eastern and central Europe. Few could speak English, and many could not even understand the language of their neighbours of different ethnic backgrounds. The Jewish merchant, himself newly arrived from czarist Russia, Poland, or Romania, spoke the language

Dave Brownstone's store, at Rush Lake, Saskatchewan. Ca. 1914.

and understood the ways of the new settlers, but as a rule he had also acquired some knowledge of English, and if necessary he picked up an Indian dialect as well.

Freighting in his supplies by wagon train from the railhead, the storekeeper sold groceries, shoes, clothing, yard goods, outerwear, underwear, harness, hardware, household remedies, kerosene. In return he bought eggs, butter, cheese, raw furs and hides from the neighbouring farmers, whom he carried on his books from seed-time to harvest. He was the district's advisor as well as the provisioner, and his store was the social centre and the meeting place, the light on the dark prairie at night. When the thirties brought drought and depression to the west, merchant and farmers suffered alike. Some of them survived, others fell by the wayside.

Of those storekeepers who remained, some eventually prospered as the towns grew in population and importance. Usually there was only one Jewish family in the district, so that these rural Jews led lonely lives. Once the first mutual strangeness had worn off, the small-town Jew generally participated energetically in the social activities of his gentile neighbours; but like his counterparts in the enthusiastically conceived Jewish farm colonies, he lacked a community, a synagogue to worship in, an extended family of co-religionists with whom to celebrate his holidays. Moreover, he increased his isolation by insisting that his children have more education than the country schools could provide. The children, once educated, found urban career opportunities, and rarely came back home to settle. Sooner or later their parents retired and followed them back to the

BOTTOM LEFT
J. Ratner and family, Vanguard, Saskatchewan. Ca. 1917.

BOTTOM RIGHT
Queen's Hotel, owned by J.D. Diamond, Plum Coulee, Manitoba. Ca. 1918.

BELOW
Sophie and Harry Freedman's "Famous Store," Pontiex, Saskatchewan. Ca. 1920.

S. Cohen (with white beard) in front of his general store at Oak Bank, Manitoba, ca. 1920. A barter deal appears to have been arranged: the exchange of produce for the plough which the farmer proudly displays.

sociability of the city. If today the rural population on the prairies as a whole has diminished, the movement from country to city was accelerated among the isolated Jewish merchants. Within a few decades the Jewish storekeeper, once a familiar figure in the small town, had all but vanished.

Anatomy of a Community: Manitoba

In the larger, urban centres, as soon as the new Canadians could divert some of their energy from keeping food on the table and a roof overhead, Jewish community life began to acquire its characteristic patterns. Because it had the third largest Jewish community in Canada, after Montreal and Toronto, Winnipeg produced the most highly developed cultural, religious and educational institutions in the west, and its Jewish schools, both religious and secular, were an extraordinary achievement. On a lesser scale, more diversified cultural institutions also came into being in Regina and Saskatoon, in Edmonton and Calgary, and in Vancouver, thereby providing a Jewish focus for the smaller towns.

From Mondays to Fridays, Jews, like all members of the community, worked at many tasks. Evenings and Sundays they donned their finery, visited relatives and friends, or ventured a little further into new affiliations. Still attached to their old country roots, they gravitated towards acquaintances from the same European towns or district—for there were regional differences between Russian Jews, Polish Jews, Romanian Jews, Lithuanian Jews, and Galician Jews—and they formed *landsmanshaften*, associations of fellow countrymen. Winnipeg's proliferation of *landsmanshaften* reflected their founders' need for familiar faces and voices: the Austrian-Polish Farband, the Bessarabier Society, and the Romanier Society were named after the country of their members' origin, and the Kiever Society after the large city in the Ukraine, while the Bobrover Hilfsfarein, the Propoisker Society, the Nikoliever Farein and the Pavolicher Society identify an attachment to very small towns indeed. In many ways, these organizations served as the backbone of family and community life. From the "Society," one borrowed money to help pay hospital or fuel debts, to

Hard times for immigrants: unemployment in World War I. Winnipeg, 1916.

meet university fees for sons and daughters, or to buy furniture. Above all, it was a place to meet *landsleit*, people from one's own home town, in comfortable sociability.

The loan function of the *landsmanshaften* was part of a larger self-help movement in the immigrant Jewish community. Behind the growth of these "free loan" associations lay the spirit of the old-country *Gemilut Chasadim* societies. The name *Gemilut Chasadim* literally means "doing of loving kindnesses." With a wisdom harking back to Talmudic teaching, the operative principle held that a loan was not to be considered charity, and therefore damaging to the recipient's self-respect, but simply a temporary support, perhaps even an obligation upon the group as a whole. Transplanted to the new world, the loan associations provided people in every walk of life with funds to weather an emergency or to start a business.

The history of the Winnipeg free loan societies dates back to 1909, when thousands of Jewish immigrants were arriving from Europe in need of assistance. At that time the United Hebrew Charities were established, controlled by the well-to-do Jews of the South End, and then matched by the North End Relief Society on the other side of the C.P.R. tracks. On January 22, 1913, the first Winnipeg Free Loan Society was organized, and the concept was so appealing to the Jewish community that in 1914 alone

LEFT
~The Shragge sisters, Minnie and
Annie. Winnipeg, ca. 1905.

RIGHT
Dr. Oscar Margolese at his office
door. Ca. 1908.

Abe and Tanya Klimoff on an outing.
Winnipeg, 1910.

David Morosnick's Farmers' Market, in Winnipeg's North End. Ca. 1911.

The staff of Cameron's Tailoring Shop, Winnipeg, ca. 1912. Mr. Cameron (wearing a vest, centre) is surrounded by his employees, most of them Jewish. Second row right, Solomon Swartzman.

Edel Brotman in his Winnipeg liquor store. Ca. 1915.

Aaron Grosney in his confectionery store at 470 Selkirk Ave., Winnipeg, 1918.

RIGHT
Riva Lercher (Mrs. Sam Kanee),
right, and her sister, Mrs. Sarah
Bokhaut. A New Year's card,
ca. 1900.

ABOVE
Sonia Shanas, upper left, and friends.
Ca. 1915.

TOP
Only four years after their arrival in
Winnipeg, a studio portrait for the
folks back home. Rose and Meyer
Gutkin. Ca. 1910.

no fewer than fourteen loan organizations were formed and chartered. By 1926 there were thirty-two separate Hebrew loan societies, with a combined membership of one thousand, and a combined capital of over $200,000. Apart from the loan groups specifically identified with *landsmanshaften* — the Propoisker, the Nikoliever, the Bessarabier — there were the Zion Loan Association, the Winnipeg Jewish Aid Society, the Achdus Free Loan Association, the Hebrew Sick Benefit Association, the Hebrew Friends Society, the Hebrew Fraternal Lodge, the Hebrew Free Loan Society, and many others. Like the *landsmanshaften*, all these self-help groups also served as social clubs for their members.

The same sense of group responsibility manifested itself in other ways. When World War I broke out, the Western Fund for the Relief of War Sufferers was founded, and funds were collected in every western Canadian city, town, and hamlet where Jews lived. The war relief movement, in turn, helped to set an organized immigrant aid program in motion.

The prominent Jewish service order, B'nai B'rith, came to Canada in 1875, with the establishment of lodges in Toronto and Montreal. Founded in New York in 1843, the order's constitution declares its dedication to the causes of "supporting science and art; alleviating the wants of the poor and needy; visiting and attending the sick; coming to the rescue of victims of persecution; providing for, protecting, and assisting the widow and orphan on the broadest principles of humanity." The third Canadian lodge was Victoria Lodge No. 365, established on September 7, 1886, while Vancouver's B'nai B'rith came into being much later, in 1910. Winnipeg's first lodge was inaugurated in 1911; Calgary, Edmonton, and Saskatoon followed, and by the early 1920's there was a sizable membership in Yorkton, Leader, and Estevan.

It was in pursuit of the principle enunciated in the order's original

charter of "promoting the highest interests of the Jewish people" that the Winnipeg lodge took a stand in 1920 against the low-key public relations policy of the Constitution Grand Lodge. In the uneasy aftermath of the first World War, Henry Ford, the automobile magnate, had allowed his prejudice against Jews to flare out openly. His Detroit daily, the *Dearborn Independent*, had launched a virulently antisemitic campaign, centred on *The Protocols of the Elders of Zion*, a re-issue of the slander first circulated in czarist Russia, the fiction that Jews were plotting a take-over of world business. At the same time, on the other side of the Atlantic, London's *Morning Post* was making some circulation-boosting capital by tying Jews to the opposite political camp, calling them "Bolsheviks" and promoters of "world revolution." The customary response of the B'nai B'rith and other Jewish community groups to such unpleasantness was quiet, low-profile influence and pressure, but the maverick B'nai B'rith lodge in the spirited toughness of Winnipeg was not content with self-effacing politeness. In November 1920, the Canadian Anti-Defamation Committee was organized in Winnipeg, with Max Steinkopf as chairman, S. L. Goldstine as treasurer, and Rabbi Herbert J. Samuel, of the Shaarey Zedek Synagogue, as secretary, and it conducted an active publishing campaign against the pervasive hate literature. The skirmish was a rehearsal for the battle against the antisemitism that accompanied the growth of fascism in the 1930's.

TOP LEFT
Winnipeg street scene, ca. 1889. L. Abremovich owned the Evil Eye store. The name is a piece of wry humour, intended to ward off bad luck.

TOP RIGHT
Leopold Meltzer, a formal portrait. Ca. 1900.

BOTTOM LEFT
George Frankfurter's store was located at the corner of Logan and Main, Winnipeg. Ca. 1890.

BOTTOM RIGHT
Leopold Meltzer (centre), in front of his furniture store, Selkirk Ave., Winnipeg. Ca. 1902.

The noted writer, Sholem Asch (arrow), arriving at the C.P.R. Station, Winnipeg, in May 1913, to raise money for European relief.

A montage of some of the Jewish organizations and institutions active in western Canada in the first half of this century. Many continue to function today.

TOP HATS

The *tsilinder* or top hat was worn on special occasions — weddings, High Holidays, public functions. Not always a sign of affluence, it was quite often supplied as a studio prop, along with the gold watch fob, to stress the subject's dignity and importance.

ABOVE LEFT
Jacob J. Shragge. Ca. 1890.

ABOVE RIGHT
Sholem Aleichem's Winnipeg uncle, *Fetter* Nissel Zimmerman. Ca. 1890.

LEFT
Edel and Leah Brotman, ca. 1910. The Brotmans were members of the Wapella farm colony, and later moved to Winnipeg.

BELOW
Board of Directors: the laying of the cornerstone of the Winnipeg Hebrew Free School, July 28, 1912.

The Western Communities: Alberta and Saskatchewan

Although Jews had begun to settle in Alberta in 1889, it was not until 1901 that the Jewish population became large enough to record statistically; that year's census lists 242 Jews in the foothills province, out of the 16,717 in Canada. In 1906 Jewish communities officially came into being in Calgary and Edmonton, with the establishment of congregations in those two cities. Small Jewish groups were also living in Lethbridge and Medicine Hat, and in rural areas throughout the province. To these should

William Diamond, of Calgary and Edmonton. Ca. 1906.

TOP RIGHT
Mr. and Mrs. Jacob Diamond, Calgary. Ca. 1892.

BOTTOM RIGHT
Gutnick's grocery and confectionery store in Lethbridge, Alberta. Ca. 1900.

be added, of course, the Alberta Jewish farm settlements of Rumsey and Trochu Valley, about one hundred miles north-east of Calgary, also established in 1906.

In Calgary the first religious services took place in 1894 on Rosh Hashanah and Yom Kippur in the old Masonic Hall, with Jacob Diamond as reader. This first *minyan* (the ten men required for a congregation) was made up of two residents from Edmonton, two from Calgary, five commercial travellers just passing through, and one farmer from Lacombe who came to Calgary to be with his own people during the High Holidays.

Diamond was the first Jew to settle in Calgary, arriving from Ontario as a peddler in 1888, when the town's entire population was about fifteen hundred. In 1904 there were just four Jewish families living there, and it was still difficult to find a *minyan*. Land for a cemetery was obtained in that year, and a burial society was organized about two years later. By 1906 it was possible to organize a congregation, with a membership of about twenty-five. Services were held in a public hall, and Diamond was president and cantor, until H. Sissinsky was engaged as *shochet* and cantor.

The Ladies' Aid Society, the first Jewish charitable organization in the city, was organized in 1906 to cope with the influx of Jewish immigrants. In 1911, when there were about seventy-five families and, according to the census, 604 Jews, land was purchased for a synagogue; completed a year later, it was named Beth Jacob. A council to manage the Jewish community's various institutions was elected in 1912, and in the same year the Hebrew Free School or Talmud Torah was organized. One of the first teachers was Judah Shumiatcher, and M. Rubin was the principal. The school had financial difficulty until about 1919, when members of the Zionist Society together with members of the Beth Jacob Congregation established a viable basis of support. A branch of the Jewish fraternal society known as the *Arbeiter Ring*, the Workman's Circle, appeared in

ABOVE
Mr. and Mrs. John David Dower and a friend pose against a photographer's set. Calgary, 1911.

TOP
Jewish employees in a Calgary laundry, 1909.

ABOVE LEFT
Abe Aron, trading with the Indians
in northern Alberta. Ca. 1910.

ABOVE RIGHT
Abraham Gutnick bagging flour,
MacLeod, Alberta. Ca. 1912.

The Guttman, Waterman, and
Pepper families with their friends,
gathered for a party in Calgary.
Ca.1910.

Abraham and Bella Singer and family, Calgary. Ca. 1919.

Morris Ghitter's mens' wear store, 9th Ave. S.E., Calgary. Ca. 1914.

1912, and it maintained a variety of cultural and social activities, establishing a short-lived school in 1920. Nine years later a successful I. L. Peretz Institute was founded. The year 1917 saw the formation of the B'nai B'rith Lodge; during World War I Calgary's Jews joined in the effort to raise funds for Jewish war victims, while at the same time they participated in the town's Patriotic and Red Cross Societies. These varied achievements appear all the more remarkable when one considers that it was not until 1926 that Calgary's Jewish population exceeded one thousand.

Abraham Cristall and H. Segal were the first Jews to settle in Edmonton, arriving in the 1890's, and they were instrumental in giving the fledgling community of the following years some Jewish character. William Diamond came to Edmonton in 1905 from Calgary, where he had joined his brother, Jacob, in 1892. He was one of the founders of the Edmonton Hebrew Association, which was established in 1906 to assist the various community organizations needing financial support. Until 1906 there was no place of worship, no provision for giving the few children a Jewish education, no *shochet* to supervise *kashrut*, and no Jewish burial ground. Land for a cemetery was purchased in 1907. The community was further prodded into action by the arrival that year of a very energetic young man, A. H. Goldenberg, who began to advocate the erection of a house of worship when most people argued that the community was still too small. Long before the funds were raised, a contract was let, and in August 1911, the cornerstone for the House of Israel was laid, in the presence of the lieutenant-governor and other dignitaries. H. Goldstick became the religious leader, until he was succeeded in 1912 by the Rev. A. Pinsky.

A very early Jewish arrival in what is now Saskatchewan was Max Goldstine, who settled in Qu'Appelle in 1877, when the district was still called Assiniboia; but Saskatchewan's Jewish communities, like those of Alberta, developed most effectively in the larger cities.

RIGHT
A well-stocked general store: the Moses Lyons store, Edmonton. Ca. 1913.

BELOW
Abraham Cristall (1868-1944) was one of the first Jews to settle in Edmonton, in 1893. He was also one of the founders of the Beth Israel Synagogue and other institutions.

Regina received its first Jewish settlers in 1904: Mr. Prosterman from Russia, D. Cohen from Austria, and Mr. Blumenfeld from Romania. By the time Saskatchewan became a province in 1906, with Regina as its capital, it was possible to gather a *minyan* in the city. In 1912 there were about twenty Jewish families there, and in September 1913, the population was large enough to inaugurate its first synagogue, the House of Jacob, in a debt-free new building. The first rabbi was M. Kaliff, and a Mr. Wasserman, who farmed in the immediate vicinity, acted as *mohel* and *shochet*. A Talmud Torah was organized in 1913 with forty children and two teachers, and for a number of years occupied a series of rented buildings. The Regina Jewish community celebrated the opening of its new Talmud Torah building in 1924, at an official ceremony on September 7, attended by government officials and by guests from Winnipeg: Rabbi I. I. Kahanovitch, M. J. Finkelstein, and H. E. Wilder. The school at that time had 165 pupils; its president was Z. Natanson.

A Hebrew Sick Benefit Society was formed, and by 1929 Regina had a Jewish Cultural Centre with facilities for lectures and dramatic presentations, and a library of Yiddish, Hebrew, and English books. All of these

Harry Woolfe at the Royal North West Mounted Police riding school, Regina, 1916.

Joe Schwartzfeld and his family, Regina, 1921.

TOP LEFT
Chaim Freiden, scrap-metal dealer. Moose Jaw, early 1920's.

TOP RIGHT
The dry cleaning room, Arthur Rose Dry Cleaners, Saskatoon. Ca. 1913.

BOTTOM
The finishing room, Arthur Rose Dry Cleaners, Saskatoon. Arthur Rose is standing at the door; Elsie Rose is seated at the sewing machine. Ca. 1913.

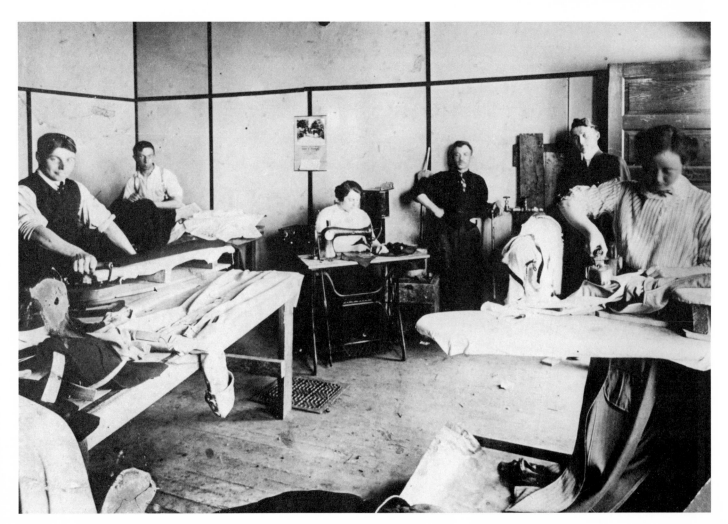

institutions were co-ordinated from 1912 on by the Regina Hebrew Federated Community.

The first Jews to settle in Saskatoon were H. Sklar and W. Landa, who arrived in 1908 and were joined in the same year by M. Volansky, J. Mallin, R. Rose, S. Henerofsky, and S. Goodman. They were all present at the first *minyan* for the High Holidays, held that year at the home of Mr. Sklar, along with some travellers stopping over and some settlers who had come in from neighbouring towns for Rosh Hashanah and Yom Kippur. A year later Mr. Birnbaum, a new arrival from Europe, officiated at the holiday services, once more in Mr. Sklar's home. As more families arrived, a small hall was rented for religious services, and in 1910 the first *shochet*, Rev. M. Selchenko, was engaged. Services were held the following year in the Cahill Block, and Saskatoon acquired a *Chevre Kedisheh* (burial society). The Hebrew Ladies' Aid Society arrived on the scene in 1912. Even from these early stages the community directed its efforts towards the erection of a synagogue; the official opening took place finally in September 1919, once again with Rabbi I. I. Kahanovitch officiating.

East of the large Jewish community of Winnipeg, a smaller number of settlers found a focus in the twin cities of Fort William and Port Arthur, now combined as Thunder Bay. There were twelve Jewish families in 1907, and in the succeeding years the city organized its own branches of the familiar institutions: a synagogue, a B'nai B'rith Lodge, a Zionist organization, a Ladies' Aid Society, and a Young Judea group. One of the two teachers at the Talmud Torah, which came into being in the 1930's, was Bora Laskin, later to become Chief Justice of Canada.

Mr. and Mrs. Herman Yacht. Moose Jaw, ca. 1918.

The Eureka Brick Works, Estevan, Saskatchewan. A number of Jews including Solomon Feuer, J. A. Steinberg, Sam Altman and Joseph Berger worked here in 1909.

The Extension of Community Services

Characteristic of Jewish communities of any size in Canada, and particularly of those dominated by east-European immigrants and their descendants, is the concern for the provision of services such as health care for those unable to pay for it privately, shelter for orphaned children, and homes for the elderly. This concern stems, of course, from Jewish self-administration in the circumscribed *shtetl* society, and from the ancient Talmudic injunction to *tzedakah* (charity or righteousness).

In the mushroom growth of the Jewish population in Winnipeg during the first quarter of the century, medical care for poor Jews was an early necessity but an enormous undertaking. Nothing came of various schemes until 1926, when a free clinic was started on a modest scale in a house on Pritchard Avenue. A building was constructed in 1929, marking the beginning of the Mount Carmel Clinic, on Selkirk Avenue East. Jewish doctors and pharmacists volunteered their services, and although the clinic never reached the dimensions of a hospital, medical care and some prescriptions for needy Jews and non-Jews alike were offered free of charge.

Today Selkirk Avenue is no longer a Jewish district, and the crush of needy Jewish immigrants in unmanageable numbers has ceased. The Mount Carmel Clinic continues to provide medical and social services to the working poor, the métis, Indians, Spanish-speaking Chileans, and others who now live in the area, and it operates a day nursery for deprived children. Its financial support has been taken over by Winnipeg's general charitable fund, the United Way, and by the provincial government and some private agencies.

As early as 1912, Winnipeg Jews had organized the Hebrew Ladies' Orphans' Home Association, and by 1913 two rival institutions existed, the Esther Robinson Orphans' Home on Robinson Street and the Canadian Jewish Orphans' Home on Selkirk Avenue, the latter founded jointly by the Hebrew Ladies' Association and the B'nai B'rith. Pogroms in Russia and World War I left many children homeless, and a number of them were rescued and brought to western Canada. In 1916, to take care of these and local children, the two Jewish orphan homes amalgamated as the Jewish Orphanage and Children's Aid of Western Canada, and moved to a rented home at 1280 Main Street. The founding committee, incidentally, rejected the offer of R. S. Robinson to donate $5,000 to the new home on condition that it too be named in honour of his mother, Esther; a public trust, the committee argued, must not be a vehicle for *koved* (personal honour). In 1920, a permanent home was built on Matheson Avenue with funds raised in Jewish communities across western Canada. It operated until other forms of child care took over in 1948.

At the other end of the life-span, the Jewish Old Folks' Home, also established in 1912, undertook to care for the now aging pioneers of the

Board of directors of the Mount Carmel Clinic, Winnipeg, 1929.

Queen Esther contest at Purim, in aid of the Mount Carmel Clinic; Winnipeg, 1940.

DEPARTMENT OF PROVINCIAL SECRETARY.

M A N I T O B A

      I hereby certify that "THE ESTHER ROBINSON JEWISH ORPHANAGE AND CHILDREN'S AID SOCIETY OF WINNIPEG," has been incorporated under the provisions of "The Children's Act," being Chapter 30, of the Revised Statutes of Manitoba, 1913, on, from and after the 4th day of April, A.D., 1914.

      DATED at the office of the Provincial Secretary, in the City of Winnipeg, this sixth day of April, A.D., 1914.

B.L. Baldwinson.

Deputy Provincial Secretary.

Certificate of incorporation, the Esther Robinson Orphanage. Winnipeg, 1914.

western Jewish communities, and almost immediately opened its doors, in a rented home at 143 Euclid Avenue, to five elderly men and women. Larger quarters were obtained in 1919 at 424 Manitoba Avenue, and when these too became inadequate, a vigorous building-fund campaign was conducted throughout western Canada. The initial stage of the present modern building, on Magnus Avenue East, was erected in 1940. Now known as the Sharon Home, the structure has been expanded to meet growing and changing needs. In later years, similar institutions were founded in some of the other prairie centres.

In Vancouver, the Jewish Home for the Aged of British Columbia was incorporated in 1946, under the auspices of the Jewish Men's Cultural Club and the Ladies' Auxiliary. A sixteen-room home formerly occupied by the I. L. Peretz School was purchased, partly with money from the Louis Brier estate, although additional funds were required.

Rehearsal at the Queen's Theatre, Winnipeg, 1918, for an Orphanage benefit.

Jewish war orphans from Europe after World War I. Ca. 1920.

Men at prayer in the synagogue of the Old Folks Home, Winnipeg. Benjamin Sarner, director, is standing at right. Ca. 1922.

Crossing Swords with the Czar of Russia

Max J. Finkelstein graduated in Law from the University of Manitoba in 1904. Six years later he defended Savaa Federenko against the government of the czar of Russia.

For the sons and daughters of immigrants, the transition from uncertain newcomers to accredited Canadians could be rapid, and education was the key. Max J. Finkelstein arrived as a child with his parents in the late 1880's, completed public school, and in 1897 passed the entrance examinations to the Collegiate Institute with the highest marks in Manitoba. He matriculated to the University of Manitoba in 1900, winning several scholarships, graduated in Law in 1904, and was called to the bar. In 1910, M. J. Finkelstein achieved international prominence when he acted for the defence in the celebrated Federenko case.

Savaa Federenko was a Russian radical who had shot a village watchman, Samson Osadchuk, on January 5, 1908, in the hamlet of Levkovka, Russia. Federenko had been hiding in the home of a friend, and had assumed, perhaps correctly, that the watchman, approaching with a policeman, was about to make an arrest. He fled to Winnipeg. A murder charge was laid, and an order obtained for his extradition from Canada. At this point, Federenko gained support among recent immigrants from Russia who were themselves intensely opposed to the czarist regime, and it was the Jewish community who first organized his aid. But as evidence of czarist brutality mounted, with reports of the case in the international press, many establishment figures such as the mayors of Winnipeg, Toronto, and Montreal, and the novelist Ralph Connor (C. W. Gordon) joined the group for the defence. Federenko's legal team, Finkelstein and N. F. Hagel, K.C., succeeded in having the extradition order quashed on the ground that the charge was political.

The case had a further twist. Under pressure from the Russian government, the Privy Council restored the extradition order, but Federenko had disappeared, and was never apprehended.

Finkelstein's dramatic appearance on the legal scene was the prelude to an extended career of public service in B'nai B'rith, the Zionist Organization, the Canadian Jewish Congress, immigrant aid, and many other community concerns. A politician who never sought public office, he nevertheless achieved widespread recognition.

6. RELIGION WITHOUT FEAR

Jews identify themselves both by their religion and as a community group, for Judaism as a faith is itself strongly community-oriented. The practice of the Jewish faith requires the presence of a group of worshippers, in the conduct of everyday life as much as in the celebration of holidays, and this need has been a shaping influence on the development of Jewish settlement in Canada.

Judaism is founded on the Mosaic Ten Commandments and the Pentateuch, or the first five books of the Old Testament, and on the commentaries of the Talmud and later scholars. The essence of the Jewish faith is its intense monotheism — its worship of one undivided God — and its emphasis on ethical practices rather than formal dogma. There is no priesthood as such in Jewish worship; "rabbi" means simply "master," in the sense of "teacher." In present-day practice a rabbinical candidate is formally ordained when he has completed a specific program of studies, but in ancient custom ordination simply meant that an older scholar certified a younger man as truly learned and therefore capable of pronouncing judgment. Traditionally, a rabbi was a man who had become known for his learning, wisdom, and piety, and in this capacity was entrusted with the administration of community affairs. It is still as teacher and guide that the rabbi exercises authority, but the synagogue is actually governed by its lay members. Further, the service is entirely congregational: ten adult male Jews gathered together constitute a *minyan*, a viable congregation entitled to hold a full service of worship.

In a synagogue today, the rabbi conducts the services, assisted by a *chazzan* or cantor who leads the congregation in prayer, chants the sung portions, and conducts the choir, if one is used. There are certain other religious functionaries who are not rabbis, but whose services are essential to orthodox Jews: the *mohel*, who has been specially trained to perform the ritual circumcision; and the *shochet*, who supervises the ritual slaughter of such animals as Jews may eat, in accordance with the strict requirements of the code of *kashrut*. Originating in Biblical times, the dietary code specifically forbids the use of dairy foods together with meat.

Generally speaking, religious Jews today belong to one of three groups, Orthodox, Conservative, and Reform, which are distinguished by matters of practice rather than by basic beliefs. A further distinction dates back to the third or fourth century and, again, marks a historical and cultural divergence rather than a difference in faith between the *Ashkenazim*, or Jews from Germany and eastern Europe, and the *Sephardim* (from the Hebrew word for Spain), Jews from southern Europe, North Africa, and parts of the Middle East. With the increasingly frequent movement of people from one part of the globe to another in today's world, Jews are often surprised to encounter someone whose life style is very different from their

Rabbinical garb generally retains some traditional elements, but adapts to current clothing fashions.

ABOVE
Ashkenazi rabbi, Holland, ca. 1700. Shown is the broad-brimmed hat and full-length rabbinical coat. Engraving by Jehiel Michael.

ABOVE CENTRE
Sephardic rabbi, Holland, ca. 1824. Clean-shaven, he wears a three-cornered hat and wig of the period, and is distinguished by his white clerical bands. Engraving by David Leon.

ABOVE RIGHT
Reform rabbi, Germany, ca. 1840. Clean-shaven, he wears a skull cap, white clerical bands, and *tallit* or prayer shawl, draped over his long black gown. Lithograph by Naphtali Frankfurter.

The *shochtim* (ritual slaughterers) of Winnipeg pose for a studio portrait in 1906.

own, but who shares with them an ancient heritage of faith.

Orthodox Jews generally adhere strictly to the forms of worship laid down by rabbinical authorities hundreds of years ago. They observe the Sabbath scrupulously, follow the full round of worship and prayer, and seat men and women separately in the synagogue. A Conservative congregation will permit some modification of ritual, allowing, for example, the seating of men and women together. For Reform Jews, an adjustment of ancient practices to contemporary conditions is held necessary in order to maintain the essential faith. For example, many Reform Jews find the dietary laws no longer valid.

Strict adherence to orthodoxy requires that men and women cover their heads at all times, although the injunction is now honoured chiefly at the synagogue or during prayer. (Conservative congregations generally require head covering in the sanctuary; Reform synagogues do not.) Traditionally, a *yarmulke* (skullcap) serves this function for the male worshipper, and he drapes over his shoulders a *tallit* (prayer shawl), usually made of wool and in a specified design. A very orthodox Jew wears a *tallit katan* (small *tallit*) under his outer garments during his entire waking day, and uses *tefillin* (phylacteries) during morning prayer. These are two small black leather boxes containing passages from the Pentateuch, which are bound to the arm and the head.

Rabbi Shumuel Abba Twersky, the *Mekarever Rebbe.* The descendant of a dynasty of Chassidic rabbis, the *guter yid* (holy man) had a "court" of disciples in Winnipeg's north end. Ca. 1930.

Sofer or scribe: Manus Switzer repairing worn passages in a *Sefer Torah.* The Scrolls of the Law must be letter-perfect, and the scribe ranks high in the religious hierarchy. 1961.

Publisher-to-be Mel Hurtig conducting junior services. Edmonton, ca. 1940.

Celebration

The Jewish Sabbath is observed from just before sundown on Friday to just after sundown on Saturday as a day of complete rest and abstention from work, as the Lord commanded Moses in Exodus 31. One outstanding exception to the prohibition of work is allowed: when human life is in danger, everything possible must be done to save it. Since the Sabbath is a gift of God, "an everlasting sign between Me and the children of Israel," it is celebrated as a joyous liberation from the cares of the workaday week. Tradition requires that every household, however poor, prepare to receive the Sabbath as an honoured guest, according to its means: with clean clothing, with the best food it can afford, and a table laid with special care.

Blowing the *shofar*: a call to repentance at *Yom Kippur*. Ca. 1910.

Yom Kippur, the Day of Atonement, in the synagogue. Poland, 1878. Painting by Moritz Oppenheim (1856-79).

It is the privilege of the mistress of the household to usher in the Sabbath by lighting and blessing the Sabbath candles, and the meal is preceded by the *kiddush*, the benediction over wine. Worship and study occupy the following day, and the *havdalah* (the farewell prayer at the end of the Sabbath) ushers in the week in a mood of sadness and regret.

Most solemn of all times in the round of Jewish observances, the ten penitential days or High Holidays from *Rosh Hashanah* (the New Year) to *Yom Kippur* (the Day of Atonement) are a period of soul-searching and personal accounting, when the fate of each man for the coming year is inscribed in the heavenly Book of Life. Special prayers of entreaty are said, and the services are marked by the blowing of the *shofar* (ram's horn). Customarily, people exchange greetings and wishes for "a good year." *Yom*

Children lighting the Chanukah candles at the Rosh Pina Synagogue, Winnipeg. Ca. 1960.

The Purim Ball at the Academy of Music, New York, 1865. This charity ball was a highlight of the New York Jewish social season. The guest in the box-like costume and pointed hat (right) is dressed as a Chanukah *dreidl* (top).

Purim players. The custom of presenting plays at Purim originated in Europe in the Middle Ages. Woodcut, 1720.

Elaborately illustrated page from the Book of Esther, read in the synagogue on the eve and the morning of Purim.

Kippur is a fast day, when all adults are required to abstain from food from sundown to sundown. Orthodox Jews often wear a *kittel*, a white robe, to indicate their awareness of a purity of purpose at this time.

Coming in the late autumn, just five days after *Yom Kippur, Sukkot* (the Feast of Tabernacles) is a joyous celebration that still retains the characteristics of its origin as a harvest festival. The festive meals are eaten in a *sukkah*, a temporary outdoor shelter such as the harvesters once used; and the services include the use of a *lulav*, a palm branch bound with willow branches, and an *etrog*, a citron grown in Israel. The last day of this eight-day festival is *Simchat Torah*, which marks the end of one year's reading of the Torah and the beginning of the next.

Chanukah, the festival of lights, celebrates a comparatively recent event, the victory of the Jews over the Syrian tyrant Antiochus, probably in the second century B.C. Central to the observance is the miracle of the cruse of oil: when the invaders were driven out, a quantity of oil only sufficient for one day burned in the newly rededicated Temple of Jerusalem for a full eight days. The festival is marked by the lighting of the *Chanukiah*; the *Chanukah* lamp; in its most familiar form the *chanukiah* is a nine-branched candelabra, a variant of the seven-branched *menorah* traditional in Jewish worship. Children are given gifts, customarily of coins, and a holiday *dreidl*, a spinning top, spells out the words, "a great miracle happened there." Significantly, Israeli children today spin a *dreidl* with the altered inscription, "a great miracle happened *here*."

Reaching much farther back into ancient history, *Purim* commemorates the deliverance of the Jews by the beautiful Jewish Queen Esther from the annihilation plotted by the wicked Haman, advisor to the Persian king Ahasuerus. Falling in late winter or early spring, *Purim* has become a season of particular merrymaking. Friends exchange gifts of sweet foods, *shalach monot*; many Canadian Jews continue a tradition of making small triangular cakes, called *homentashen*, supposedly in the shape of Haman's hat. During the service, children delight in creating an uproar with their *graggers* (noisemakers) every time Haman's name is mentioned, and a spirit of carnival prevails. This is the season for masquerade balls and amateur theatricals: performances by *Purim shpiller* (*Purim* players) go back to the Middle Ages in Europe.

In the spring of the year, the Passover holiday, *Pesach*, centres on the exodus of the Jews from Egypt under the leadership of Moses. Because the Israelites, in their hasty flight, took no bread with them, only *matzo* (unleavened bread) may be used, and the very dishes in which food is ordinarily prepared and served must be replaced by utensils reserved for Passover, in observance of the festival's particular *kashrut* laws. At the *seder*, the festive Passover meal, the youngest child present has a special role to play, asking the traditional Four Questions that initiate the retelling of the ancient story of slavery and liberation.

Shavuot, celebrated seven weeks after Passover, is another harvest festival associated in Biblical times with the offering of first fruits to God. Tradition emphasizes that this holiday commemorates the giving of the Tablets of the Law on Mount Sinai.

TOP
Pre-Passover ritual, Amsterdam, 1725: ridding the house of leavened bread.
From a painting by Bernard Picart (1663-1733).

BOTTOM
Passover *seder* in Amsterdam, 1725. The head of the household formally hands
his wife a piece of *matzo*, as the family members pause in the reading of the
service, and the servant, seated at table with his masters, reaches to replenish
the wine. From a painting by Bernard Picart (1663-1733).

Passover *seder* in Galicia, Central
Europe, 1915, with two members of
the Austrian Imperial Army as guests.

The Pearl family at the Passover *seder*,
Winnipeg, 1929.

Milestones

While the customs of the various ethnic groups in a multi-ethnic society generally borrow from each other, and the outward style in which Canadian Jews mark important occasions has changed greatly from the folkways of eastern Europe, two events firmly retain their cultural significance and their ties to tradition. The *Bar Mitzvah* ceremony, which marks a boy's coming of age at thirteen, has been given added emphasis in North America, and the wedding continues to affirm deeply ingrained Jewish values.

The first definite reference to the ritual of *Bar Mitzvah* occurs in the thirteenth century, but rabbinic literature contains indications that the custom goes back to even earlier times.

Bar Mitzvah is Hebrew for "son of duty," one who is obliged to fulfill the commandment. According to Jewish tradition, the youngster who is *Bar Mitzvah* is now fully responsible for his own actions and for carrying out all the religious duties of an adult Jew, and he may be counted in a *minyan*, a religious quorum.

The focal point of the ceremony is the calling of the young man to the reading of the Torah, generally during the services on the Sabbath before his birthday. The father participates by reciting a blessing, and the grandfather or other relatives may also take part in the service. In recent years, some Conservative synagogues and most Reform temples have introduced the *Bat Mitzvah* for Jewish girls, the equivalent of the *Bar Mitzvah* for boys.

In the same way that at coming of age the young person is admitted to full membership in the congregation, the guests at a wedding renew their sense of family and welcome the new family unit with an age-old greeting: *"Chosen Kalleh, Mazel Tov!"* ("Good luck to the bride and groom!")

The marriage service requires the presence of a *minyan*, and may take place in the synagogue, in the home, or, according to the traditional custom, out of doors. The bride and groom stand under a *chuppah* (canopy), said to be symbolic of the bridal chamber. In some communities, the bride walks around the groom seven times at the ceremony's beginning. The rabbi recites the blessings over a cup of wine from which both bride and groom drink, and the groom places a plain gold band on the bride's finger, saying, "You are betrothed to me with this ring, in accordance with the religion of Moses and Israel." Then follows the reading of the *ketubah*, the marriage contract, which is given to the bride to keep, and the recital of the "Seven Benedictions." At the end of the ceremony the groom breaks a glass underfoot, a sign that in the midst of joy one should remember the destruction of the Temple by the Romans.

Often beautifully inscribed in ancient Aramaic, or sometimes handwritten in Hebrew, the *ketubah* of former times was a decorative, artistic document, reflecting the art forms of the country of its origin. Today, while

The Bar Mitzvah speech, highlight of the boy's coming-of-age ceremony. Germany, early 19th century. Painting by Moritz Oppenheim.

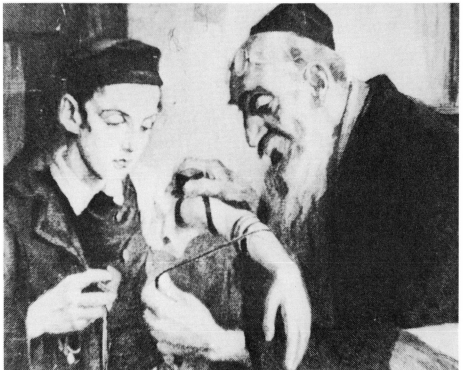

Instruction in wearing *tefillin*. Poland, early 20th century painting by Bender.

the document is generally a printed form filled in by the rabbi, the *ketubah* still sets out the woman's rights and privileges in the marriage. For hundreds of years, Jewish women have enjoyed rights which, until a century ago, other women did not have. A Jewish woman could not be married without her consent, even in the arranged marriages of days gone by. Her *ketubah* was a legally binding contract, which guaranteed that her husband was responsible for her support; and if divorced or widowed, she was entitled to a financial settlement. Thus, if the fostering of *sholom beyit*, harmony in the home, is the special charge of the Jewish wife, the strength of her position is established under the marriage canopy itself.

TOP
Jewish wedding in Venice, Italy, 1601: bride and groom with the rabbi under the traditional canopy,
flanked by their parents — men on the left, women on the right. Woodcut.

BOTTOM LEFT
Outdoor Jewish wedding at Frankfurt, Germany, early 19th century. A prayer shawl draped over the
heads of the bride and groom takes the place of the canopy. Painting by Moritz Oppenheim.

BOTTOM RIGHT
Jewish wedding in Poland, ca. 1920. The young couple are under the wedding canopy, surrounded by
their families. Some of the men wear the traditional fur-edged hat, or *shtreimel*. Painting by Mané Katz.

TOP LEFT
Alex Cohen and Rifka (Rose) Diamond. Both came from Russia about 1905, and were married in
Winnipeg in 1910. Alex's parents, Frank and Fanny, pose with the bridal couple.

TOP RIGHT
Wedding of Flossie Finkelstein and Frank Huffman. The party poses in front of the bride's home. Winnipeg, 1906.

CENTRE RIGHT
Honeymoon express to Minneapolis and St. Paul: wedding of Sybil Meyers and Edward Kopstein.
The bridesmaids pose with their shepherdess's crooks, the latest in wedding elegance. Ca. 1914.

BOTTOM
Wedding of Rhoda Lechtzier and Maurice Halter, Winnipeg, 1904.

Bride and groom, fifty years later: Nachum and Ziporah Ratner, at their golden wedding anniversary. Plum Coulee, Manitoba, 1916.

The six Ratner ladies at the fiftieth wedding anniversary of Nachum and Ziporah Ratner. Plum Coulee, Manitoba, 1916.

TOP LEFT

Ketubah or marriage contract, Yemen, 1795. The ornate design shows a middle-eastern influence.

ABOVE

Ketubah: marriage certificate of Harry Singer and Fanny Dudelsack, Son-nenfeld Colony, 1923. Printed form,

ABOVE

Ketubah in Hebrew and English: marriage certificate of Ralph Louis Halter and Anne Weidman, Winnipeg, 1918. The rabbi was

TOP RIGHT

Ketubah or marriage contract, Jerusalem, 1844. The circled symbols across the centre represent the twelve tribes of Israel.

ABOVE

Ketubah, completely in Hebrew: marriage certificate of Max Steiman and Rose Sereth, Winnipeg, 1905.

The Synagogues

From the very earliest times in the Canadian west, in small towns and tiny settlements, the synagogue was the centre of most community life. It served its members for traditional Friday evening and Saturday morning services, at religious holidays, for weddings, *Bar Mitzvahs*, and funerals, and it was sometimes used by the community as a lecture hall, a Sunday school, a library, and a place for meetings and social functions. Led by the rabbi, the synagogue ministered to all the religious needs of the community.

Free to practise their faith in their new homeland, the Jews quickly established religious roots. Throughout the Canadian west, wherever there were ten Jews for a *minyan*, a congregation was assembled, with one of its members serving as a *Baal Tefillah* or prayer leader. In 1901, for example, soon after their arrival in Lipton, Saskatchewan, from Romania, Jewish homesteaders gathered for a special thanksgiving service. In small towns and larger cities, the acquisition of a permanent house of worship

Interior of a synagogue at Nancy, France, showing the reader's stand (centre) and the ark, or receptacle for the Scrolls of the Law (left). Ca. 1810.

TOP LEFT
Interior of the old Shaarey Zedek
Synagogue at the corner of Henry and
King, Winnipeg, dedicated in 1890.

CENTRE
Exterior of the first Rosh Pina
Synagogue, Winnipeg, dedicated in
1893. Although a modest structure,
the Rosh Pina shows design features
similar to the elegant Temple
Emanu-El in Victoria.

BOTTOM LEFT
The last service in the old Rosh Pina
Synagogue, Winnipeg. 1952.

Interior of the old Rosh Pina
Synagogue, Winnipeg. 1950.

RIGHT

The House of Israel, Calgary. The box-like contemporary style still retains the traditional circular central window and two small side windows. Ca. 1949.

BELOW

The synagogue in Fort William (Thunder Bay), Ontario. The Mediterranean influence, the curved roof, occurs frequently in synagogue architecture. Instead of the usual side windows, two semi-circles flank the door. Ca. 1910

came next, as soon as the Jewish population was sufficient. Synagogues were built very early in the development of Melfort, Oxbow, and Wapella, Saskatchewan, and Medicine Hat and Vegreville, Alberta. In Winnipeg, the start of the 1882 immigration boom was quickly followed by the city's first two synagogues, the Shaarey Zedek in 1890 and the Rosh Pina in 1893, and in the greatly enlarged community divergent groups formed their own congregations.

The Holy Blossom Congregation began in September of 1904, with High Holiday services at which Rabbi D. A. Bonheim, a Reform rabbi from Las Vegas, officiated. Then, modifying its Reform orientation slightly, the congregation was reconstituted in November 1905 as the Shaarey Shomayim, with Rabbi Elias Friedlander of Montreal in the pulpit, and it began the construction of a synagogue on Dagmar Street, just opposite the old William Avenue library. Increasingly attractive to younger, English-speaking Jews, the Shaarey Shomayim achieved a meeting of minds in 1913 with the generally Conservative Shaarey Zedek, and the two congregations merged, under the latter name, in the building on Dagmar Street, and with Rabbi Herbert J. Sondheim of Glasgow, Scotland, as minister. An ardent patriot, Sondheim dropped his Germanic surname at the outbreak of World War I, and became Herbert J. Samuel. He was followed by Rabbi Solomon Frank, who came to Winnipeg in 1926 and served the Shaarey Zedek Synagogue for twenty-one years.

In 1904, while some of the English-speaking families in Winnipeg were turning towards Reform Judaism, the Orthodox Jews organized the building of a synagogue on Schultz Street in North Winnipeg. The Beth Jacob,

as it was named, cost $7000, an enormous amount of money for a congregation of generally modest means, and it could seat seven hundred worshippers. The leaders of the new congregation set themselves the task of finding a universally respected Orthodox rabbi, who could deal authoritatively with questions of Jewish religious law, and who would serve Winnipeg and the scattered communities across the west. In 1907 they brought to the city Rabbi Israel I. Kahanovitch, a noted scholar, who was to become a definitive force among the Jews of western Canada. By the late 1930's, Rabbi Kahanovitch had been instrumental in organizing a rabbinic council in Winnipeg, which provided a central administration for the community's religious affairs.

While the Shaarey Zedek continued as the single spiritual centre for the South End Jews, no fewer than fourteen synagogues were established in the North End of Winnipeg in the century's first three decades, from the B'nai Abraham in 1906 to the Ashkenazi in 1930, all of them following Orthodox observance. On the prairies, perhaps because of the preponderance of settlers from eastern Europe, with their traditional background, the Reform movement never took firm hold. Nor was there, as in eastern Canada, a pronounced division between Orthodox and Conservative groups. Rather, the lines of opposition were drawn up between the divergent philosophies of the religious Jews and the secular-minded, in a continuing family squabble. That the battle has now subsided may be a mark of greater sophistication — or of less passionately held convictions.

Portrait: the Rabbi

He was a matchmaker, a peacemaker in family troubles, a job-finder, a home-seeker for the homeless, a teacher. He was a builder of institutions, an ardent Zionist, a platform speaker of stature, a champion of people and causes. A patriarchal figure, with his flowing beard and his long black *kappoteh* (surcoat), Rabbi Kahanovitch brought an old-world dignity to the office of Chief Rabbi of Western Canada, and a boundless humane warmth to all his relationships with people.

Born in Volpa Grodno, Poland, on October 8, 1872, Israel Isaac Kahanovitch received his Hebrew training at the famous theological seminaries at Grodno and Slabodka, Lithuania, and was ordained as a rabbi at the age of twenty. He was married in 1896 to Rachel Clayman, and continued his studies until 1905. In 1906, after the Kishinev pogrom, he came to America to take up a post in Scranton, Pennsylvania. A year later, he was invited to Winnipeg by the Beth Jacob Congregation, the largest in Winnipeg's North End.

The Jewish community in Winnipeg at this time numbered five thousand. Here, north of the C.P.R. tracks, several small Orthodox synagogues were functioning without a spiritual leader. The rabbi came to fill this void,

ABOVE
Chief Rabbi I. I. Kahanovitch and
kashrut officials. Winnipeg, ca. 1907.

BELOW
The rabbi's wife, Rachel, as an infant,
with her parents, Mr. and Mrs.
Koppel Clayman, and her brothers.
Rachel was born in Leeds, England.

and to extend his spiritual authority, within a few years, from Fort William to Victoria.

He was concerned with every aspect of Jewish life, from the most mundane to the most visionary. Immediately on his arrival he took on the task of organizing *kashrut*, observance of the dietary laws. A supervisory body was established, providing for jurisdiction over Jewish butcher shops, and assuring salaries for religious functionaries. The rabbi helped organize the Talmud Torah, the Hebrew Free School; he encouraged the founding of the farm colonies at Camper, Manitoba, and Sonnenfeld, Saskatchewan; and he participated in Zionist work, and in the founding of the Canadian Jewish Congress. Indeed, Rabbi Kahanovitch's story parallels the development of the western Jewish community, and his boundless energy epitomizes the dedication of its members. At a time when the city's institutions were financed by the nickels and dimes donated by small wage-earners, the Rabbi himself could be seen on Sunday mornings going from house to house, with his *shammes* or sexton in tow, knocking on doors to collect for a variety of worthy causes.

As part of his regular responsibilities, he performed countless wedding ceremonies, and he presided over divorce proceedings, making sure that both parties were justly treated. He settled disputes between people who trusted him implicitly. He supervised loans, he administered charity, and he drew up business contracts as binding as they were straightforward. One such contract, translated here from the Yiddish of the rabbi's records, reflects something of the daily doings in early Winnipeg. It spells out the terms of employment of Hershel Rosenstock (who was also a teacher) by Moshe Goldenberg, the owner of a candy store:

1. That Mr. Rosenstock must deliver to the customers not less than two loads a day, with the exception of Saturday. 2. On the days when there are no deliveries Mr. Rosenstock is to work inside from 8 in the morning until 6 in the evening. 3. Also Mr. Rosenstock is to look after the horses. 4. For this Mr. Goldenberg must pay Mr. Rosenstock $70.00 a month. 5. Wages every two weeks. 6. In addition Mr. Rosenstock is to receive a half percent commission from his deliveries, which he is to be paid every week.

This account and many other such agreements are preserved in one of several dog-eared business ledgers, its entries in several hands, and its pages decorated with the scrawls of the lively Kahanovitch children.

The rabbi's reputation for integrity was such that a Dr. Herbert M. Rosenberg advertised, in the fall of 1912, that he was willing to treat the poor free of charge, if the patient presented a written request from Rabbi Kahanovitch. Many impoverished Jews took advantage of the offer.

A pillar of old-fashioned orthodoxy, the rabbi was never doctrinaire, but saw Judaism in a larger context. A revealing incident took place in Calgary, when a group of young Jewish parents came into conflict with the city's established religious community. When these secular-minded people attempted to open their own school, to educate their children in Yiddish and in Jewish history and literature rather than in religious practice, they were blocked by the supporters of the Talmud Torah, who called them unbelievers and threatened excommunication. Rabbi Kahanovitch was invited to give judgment. As was his wont, on those frequent occasions when the business of his far-flung community summoned, he boarded the day coach of the C.P.R., carrying his phylacteries, a change of linen, and a

Pages from the Rabbi's marriage records, 1907 to 1945.

little packet of kosher food, to make the two-day journey across the prairie. In Calgary, a crowded meeting seethed with tension, as the orthodox made their demands. The rabbi's response was characteristic. Stroking his beard and adjusting his *yarmulke* he admonished the orthodox: "You have objections to the curriculum taught in the Peretz School? You are in error. In the Winnipeg Peretz School the children are educated in the Jewish spirit. Any group of parents seeking to enrich the lives of their children in their mother tongue is doing the Lord's work." With scripture and with good humour he asked for an end to the dissension in Calgary; and it was by the same breadth of vision that he helped weld together all the separate clusters of Jews in western Canada.

In a lighter vein is the story of the rabbi's devoted follower who found himself one Sabbath with a forbidden but irresistible cigarette in his hand as his revered master approached. Desperate, he shoved his hands into his pockets and turned nonchalantly to greet the rabbi. A few moments of grave conversation ensued, and then the rabbi moved away with a piece of urgent advice: "Charlie, take your hands out of your pockets! You'll burn your pants!"

The rabbi's own finances were never secure. Weddings brought in some funds, when the groom remembered, and could pay, but the main income came from the contributions of a small circle of supporters. In their house

Chief Rabbi Israel Isaac Kahanovitch
in 1945.

on Flora Avenue, the rabbi and his wife, the *rebbetzin*, brought up five daughters and three sons, and there petitioners of all sorts came and went. The rabbi insisted on goat's milk, and the white goat tethered in the yard sometimes escaped to play havoc with the wash on the line, or to intrude into a solemn council in the living room. From the basement might come the sounds and smells — and the occasional explosion — of a young scientist's curiosity, and the rabbi himself took a benign interest in all the stray animals his children brought home. Presiding over all this, the *rebbetzin* patiently endured, a resplendent figure in black satin on the Sabbath and other state occasions.

The death of Rabbi Kahanovitch, in June 1945, marked the end of an era in the history of the Jewish community of western Canada. A tribute paid to him by H. E. Wilder, co-publisher of the *Israelite Press*, Winnipeg's Jewish newspaper, serves to sum up the man and his achievements:

> A fluent speaker, an engaging personality, possessing a rich store of Judaic knowledge, tinged with a veneer of secularism; he was orthodox, without fanaticism, liberal, without transgression; he was easily at home with all the factions except the hard-headed extremists whom he deliberately, yet tactfully, ignored. This many-sidedness enabled him to become Chief Rabbi, with spiritual authority over practically all the congregations in the city and western Canada.

7. THE HERITAGE IN LITERATURE

Moses Mendelssohn, 1729-1786.

Ahad Ha-Am (Asher Ginzburg), 1856-1927.

Chaim Nachman Bialik, 1873-1935.

By the early 1900's, the cultural and spiritual tides that were sweeping through the Jewish communities of eastern Europe had brought about a subtle change in the character of the Jewish immigrant arriving in western Canada. More and more young people had been exposed to urban life and new ideas before departing for America. Many no longer adhered to the orthodox ways of their fathers, but were caught up in the "modern," secularized progressivism. Much to the horror of their elders, they no longer defined their Judaism in terms of an all-embracing religious commitment, but rather in terms of an inherited culture and of the social values which that culture had taught. As the twentieth century dawned, a significant number of Jewish immigrants to Canada consciously sought a new focus and a new meaning for their lives in the heritage of language, literature, and history.

The departure was itself rooted in tradition. Proud of a literary legacy that goes back thousands of years, Jews have long thought of themselves as *am hasefer*, the people of the book. Moreover, because of the vicissitudes of their long history, today's Jews are heirs to two languages whose intertwined development reflects the nature of the Jewish experience.

Hebrew was the language of the ancient Israelite tribes, whose nomadic existence has been recorded in the first books of the Old Testament. A semitic tongue, like Moabite and Phoenician, Hebrew evolved throughout the centuries, coming under strong Aramaic influence after the dispersal of the Hebrews by the Babylonians about the sixth century B.C. It was in Hebrew that the *tannayim* (teachers) of the second and first centuries B.C. composed the prayers that still form the basis of Jewish worship, and in the late Middle Ages, when the centre of Jewish population had shifted to Europe, Hebrew was enormously enriched by the great Jewish liturgical poets of Italy, France, and Spain. But paradoxically, while it survived and flourished as a written language for sacred and artistic purposes, it was replaced in daily speech by a variety of local dialects of eastern Europe.

The beginning of modern Hebrew is associated with the eighteenth century *Haskalah* (Enlightenment) movement, the conscious attempt at modernizing Jewish society initiated in the circle of the German-Jewish philosopher, Moses Mendelssohn. Convinced that Jewish emancipation required social and intellectual unity with the non-Jewish world, the savants of the *Haskalah* were the founders of a modern secular literature in Hebrew, which came into full flower by the end of the nineteenth century, in the work of such later *Haskalah* poets as Abraham Lebensohn and Judah Leib Gordon. From the 1880's on, inspired by the dream of a national homeland and the then new Zionist philosophy, writers like Ahad Ha-Am

Jacob Gordin, 1853-1909.

(Asher Ginzburg), Chaim Nachman Bialik, Zalman Schneour, and David Shimoni achieved a high level of literary excellence.

For the east European ancestors of most of Canada's Jews, the language of daily life from the Middle Ages on was Yiddish. A correlate of medieval German, Yiddish is distinguishable as a separate tongue by the thirteenth century or earlier. Its syntax and vocabulary are basically Germanic, but it uses the Hebrew alphabet in its written form. The vocabulary has retained a large amount of Hebrew, and has also absorbed a substantial number of Slavic and English words. With its homely origins in the market place and at the fireside, Yiddish was long considered an inferior tongue, fit only for women and the ignorant, and some of the most delightful works in early Yiddish are romances and folktales expressly designed for such lesser readers. One such work is the *Bovo-Buch* or *Bovo-Maase*, composed in Italy at the beginning of the sixteenth century by Elija Levita. This verse epic about the knightly adventures of Prince Bovo of Antona achieved an almost legendary popularity. For the pious Jewish housewife of the nineteenth-century Russian *shtetl*, the font of knowledge and a constant comfort was the *Tzenah v'Renah*, a combination of moral instruction, practical advice, and Biblical tales. Remarkably, Yiddish became a lingua franca, the common tongue in which all the Jews of Europe could communicate, across the national and linguistic boundaries of their host countries.

Mendele Mocher Sforim, 1836-1917.

The Enlightenment philosophers had little regard for this "jargon" of the vulgar, but found they had to resort to it in order to reach their intended audience. Thus they paved the way for the classical masters of the Yiddish language: Mendele Mocher Sforim, Isaac Leib Peretz, and Sholem Aleichem. These three, with their contemporaries, cemented the bond among Yiddish-speaking Jews throughout the world, and the books which the Jewish immigrants brought with them to the vast and fertile prairies of western Canada did much to fill the gaps that were inevitable in the existence of a people far removed from their own kind.

For a generation of dramatists, novelists, and poets, newly transplanted to the American soil, Yiddish continued to flourish, a shining vehicle for the joy and the grief of theatrical spellbinders like Jacob Gordin, David Pinski, and Peretz Hirschbein, and lyric poets like Jehoash (Solomon Bloomgarden), Abraham Reisin, and H. Leivick. Morris Rosenfeld and Morris Winchevsky were the voices of sweat-shop despair, and hundreds of thousands of readers devoured the robust novels of Sholem Asch, even before their translation into English. The Nobel Prize awarded in 1978 to Isaac Bashevis Singer honours not only the writer himself but also the long tradition of Yiddish literature in which he stands.

Peretz Hirschbein, 1880-1948.

Sholem Aleichem,
1859-1916.

Sholem Aleichem surveys New York's
East Side. Cartoon by Lola, 1914.

LEFT
Isaac Bashevis Singer, 1904-.

RIGHT
Sholem Asch, 1880-1957.

"Prince of the Ghetto"

Isaac Leib Peretz (1852-1915), perhaps the foremost Yiddish man of letters, elevated the parochial Yiddish language and literature to national stature. In the words of his biographer, Maurice Samuel, he became essentially the "prince of the ghetto," conscious always that he was "entrusted with the timeless treasure of his people, the accumulated inheritance of many generations." As Sholem Aleichem's wry tales have come to represent the humour and breadth of the Jewish spirit, and as Mendele Mocher Sforim is regarded as the "grandfather" of modern Yiddish literature and its foremost satirist, so Peretz mirrors the austere moral grandeur that sustains his people in their harsh existence.

A graduate in Russian jurisprudence, a practising lawyer, and then an employee of the Jewish Communal Bureau in Warsaw, Peretz had begun to

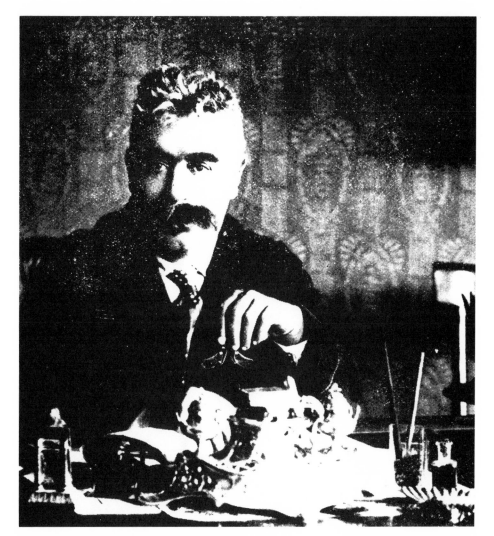

I. L. Peretz at his desk. Warsaw, 1890.

write at the age of fourteen. After experimenting with Polish and Hebrew, he finally chose Yiddish as his most effective medium. His first major poem, *Monish*, appeared in 1888, and his first collection of Yiddish tales was published in 1890. His literary reputation was further enhanced by *Chassidic Tales*, begun in 1894, and by the plays to which he turned his attention in the early 1900's.

Peretz was as concerned with the social function of his work as with its literary form, and he gave expression to the ferment that swept Jewish life from the mid-nineteenth century to World War I. A letter to Sholem Aleichem conveys his earnest purposes:

> As we shall express new ideas, we must give them new forms, new expressions, since the old garment doesn't fit the new one; the expressions will at first appear strange, but in the end they will penetrate the reader's mind and enrich his intellect. For that reason I have made no effort to limit my thoughts and to curb them to the common speech. On the contrary, I have resorted not to his speech but to the language that best expresses the riches most strongly, so that the uneducated reader might educate himself.

Both the pain and the endurance of the common man are the subject of Peretz's work. The most famous of his tales, "*Bontche Shveig*" ("Bontche the Silent"), captures and cries out against the soul-numbing hardship of the ordinary man's lot; his "Or Even Beyond" raises to mystical heights the supreme Jewish virtue of charity. His heroes and heroines, never wavering in their faith, stir the reader to love, to pity, and to fierce indignation.

Peretz was the bell-ringer, the town-crier, who tried to awaken his

RIGHT
Five Yiddish writers, ca. 1908. Left to right: Abraham Reisin, I. L. Peretz, Sholem Asch, Dr. Chaim Zhitlovsky, H. D. Nomberg.

BELOW
Ohel Peretz: shrine of Peretz in Warsaw, erected in 1925. The remains of Peretz and two of his comtemporaries, Jacob Dinesohn and S. An-Ski, are housed here.

people to a desire for a better life. Even as he set down the sights and sounds of the ghetto and the names of its legendary heroes, he spelled out an emphatic lesson for the future. In "Between Two Mountains," an encounter between the famous Talmudist, the rabbi of Brisk, and the equally famous *chassid*, Reb Noah of Biale, becomes a confrontation between old-style formalism and the new religion of joy. The rabbi of Brisk concedes finally that loving service to humanity is the highest worship of God.

Woodcut of I. L. Peretz against a *shtetl* background. 1915.

IMAGES OF THE SHTETL:
EXCERPTS FROM THE
WRITINGS OF I.L. PERETZ

From "My People"; illustration by N. Kozlowski: "I am the son of the chosen, eternal wandering people .... We have been chosen for shame and mockery, woe and anguish, blows and pain; we are the weakest and the least ... but that is precisely why my people is spurred on to the farthest reaches of human justice, to the most distant post on the road to human freedom; to the final victory over physical might, over physical coercion."

From *Der Kuntzenmacher* ("The Magician"); illustration by Marc Chagall: "He motioned with his hand, hocus-pocus, and two silver candlesticks appeared in mid-air in the room .... A snow-white table-cloth fell from the ceiling and covered the table ... [and] the silver candlesticks came down and stood on the table .... At the magician's behest a platter of ceremonial Passover foods appeared, wine-glasses and bottles of wine, and *matzos* and all the other things necessary for a kosher and happy *seder* .... Then they knew that the magician had been the prophet Elijah."

BELOW
From "Or Even Beyond"; illustration by Dewdney. [The unbelieving Litvak has watched secretly as the Rabbi of Nemerov, on one of the Penitential Days, puts on peasant clothes, cuts a large faggot of wood in the forest and, still in the guise of a peasant, brings the wood to a poor, sick woman, enjoining her to trust in her mighty God in heaven. The story concludes:] "In after years, if [the Litvak] heard anyone say that on the morning of the awesome Penitential Days the Rabbi of Nemerov ascended to the heavens, he never laughed, but only added quietly, 'Or even beyond.'"

BOTTOM
From "The Bass Viol"; illustration by S. H. Dewdney: "The bass viol kept up its plaintive notes while the guests listened in rapt silence, as though under a spell. Then the sky divided, and high in the depth beyond depth a light trembled, and out of the light came music. The celestial hosts were saying their midnight prayers. A choir of angels sang, bands of angels played, and the melody of Abraham's bass mingled with the heavenly tune and became one with the song that trembled in the midst of the light on high."

New Directions

Peretz and his generation helped bring about a radical transformation in Jewish life and thought that released a tremendous amount of creative energy among ordinary people as well as among intellectuals. The Jews who left eastern Europe after the defeat of Russia by Japan, and after the failure of the Russian Revolution of 1905, were fairly well-educated, skilled workers and artisans who saw in America the hope for a more fulfilling life. Some brought with them their radical zeal for political progress, and others the Zionist dream of a national homeland; all shared a deep-rooted devotion to the Jewish people.

This was the spirit that shaped the North End of Winnipeg. It was a time of new beginnings: new schools, new organizations, new ventures of all kinds. Winnipeg began to be known on the North American continent as a great Jewish cultural centre, to which poets and writers and actors and lecturers were pleased to come, sure of their welcome by an eager audience. Although the newcomers were in the main forced to become workers in the shops and factories, the night schools were filled with avid students anxious to learn English and to make new friends. Tirelessly seizing new opportunities, and often urged on by working wives, they became the lawyers, doctors, dentists, and teachers of their generation, and sometimes the factory owners and shopkeepers. Simultaneously, and often at odds

The Scotland Woolen Mills on strike, 1906. The striking employees, a number of Jewish workers among them, enjoy an unusual outing at St. John's Park, Winnipeg's North End.

A serious-minded group at City Park, Winnipeg, 1906.

Winnipeg's Socialist-Territorialists were self-conscious intellectuals, and dedicated to the ideals of comradeship. Some studied poses vary the formality of a group portrait. Ca. 1907.

Newcomers, part of the 1905 group. Seated centre, Rose Alcin; to her right, Fanya Golden Cherniack; leaning on chair, J. Alter Cherniack. Winnipeg, ca. 1906.

with each other, they hewed out the foundation of a strong new community, translating inherited values into new forms.

At times the oppositions that divided secular from orthodox Jews flared into intense hostility. Disagreeing about the place of religion in a modern Jew's existence, they split again over the importance of a national home for Jews, breaking apart into a broad spectrum of political parties, each championing its cause with fervent dedication. They became partisans of either Yiddish or Hebrew, and built rival schools to educate children in their own passionately held ideals.

For a short time, as the newly arrived immigrants flocked together seeking security in each other, Winnipeg's North End reproduced something of the closeness of the old *shtetl*, and something of the energy the *shtetl* had generated. Today, the invisible geographic barriers are down, and the children and grandchildren of the immigrant generation find new outlets for the inherited values.

A group of young "radicals". Top row, centre, J. A. Cherniack; directly below, his wife, Fanya; top right, Joseph Guravich; centre row left, Berl Miller. Winnipeg, ca. 1910.

Portrait: "A Silken Young Man"

Boris Joseph Ginsburg was one of that dominant group of Jewish immigrants who arrived in Canada after 1905. His story is interesting not so much because of any outstanding public achievements but because it reflects the lives of many of his contemporaries.

Born in 1889, in Bobroisk, Russia, he mastered the general high school program by studying at home, sat for his matriculation examinations in Warsaw, and was admitted to the Kiev Commercial Institute. His courses there ranged from Hygiene and Mathematics to Government and Philosophy, and included five languages: Russian, Polish, German, French, and Latin. Having graduated at the age of nineteen, he enlisted for two years in the Russian army and then became a reporter for the *Bobroiske Gazette*, pursuing an early flair for writing. A dissatisfied restlessness drove him to join the stream of young people emigrating from Russia; he arrived in

B. J. Ginsburg, as shown on his report card from the Kiev Commercial Institute, 1908.

B. J. Ginsburg, seated right, with the staff of the *Broboiske Gazette*, 1910.

Canada on the ship *Megantic* from Liverpool in September 1912, at the age of twenty-three.

Bernard, as he was called in his new country, worked for a time in Fort William, Ontario, and then moved to Winnipeg in the fall of 1913 to enroll at the University of Manitoba. He tried engineering first, and then switched to medicine. To support himself he became a sales agent for the Book of Knowledge. An ardent social democrat, he gravitated towards the progressive young people whose cultural and social clubs were proliferating on the Winnipeg scene. When the Jewish Radical School, later renamed the I. L. Peretz School, was founded in 1914, its first teachers were I. Hestrin and the young Bernard Ginsburg. He taught evenings, attending college during the day and selling books door-to-door in his spare time. Graduating in 1917, he served for two years in the Canadian Army Medical Corps, commissioned, according to his documents, as "Lieutenant and Captain." Then he turned again to employment of a socially useful, rather altruistic nature, and worked for a time as secretary to the Jewish War Relief Agency in Winnipeg. The salary was nominal, and Ginsburg found himself in financial difficulties. In a letter to his president, B. Sheps, he made a very modest and diffident request: "I would appreciate receiving a raise of eight dollars a month, so that I can meet the increase in my room rent. Please let me know if under the circumstances the organization finds itself in, whether it will be possible." The organization compromised: he was given a four-dollar raise.

In the early twenties he succeeded in bringing his parents from Russia to Winnipeg, and settled at last into the quiet routine of his profession. For the greater part of his life he practised medicine in the McIntyre Block, in a shabby, neglected office furnished with kitchen tables and battered chairs,

Dr. B. J. Ginsburg in the army barracks, Winnipeg, 1917.

B. J. Ginsburg in lieutenant's uniform, with the staff of the Jewish Radical School, 1918. Seated right, Dr. B. A. Victor.

and lit by light bulbs dangling on long cords from the ceiling. These surroundings were a startling contrast to Ginsburg himself, with his aristocratic bearing and immaculate clothes, and his elegant home on Scotia Street. A competent physician, he yearned nevertheless for a different fulfillment, like so many of his generation whose dreams went beyond the exigencies of daily existence. One ambitious scheme dear to his heart was probably a little ahead of its time: in 1947 he conceived of a splendid festival of Jewish music, literature, and art, but the detailed plans never materialized.

Writing was his avocation. While he had a completely literate command of the English language, he chose to write in a fine and precise Yiddish, filling a miscellaneous collection of notebooks with fragments of description and character sketches for future use. Some of his short stories, novellas, and literary essays, marked by a fastidious decorum, were published in a number of American Yiddish magazines, and he carried on a voluminous correspondence with the best-known Yiddish writers of the day. The major work of his life was a full-length novel, *Generation Passeth, Generation Cometh*, also written in Yiddish; translated by his niece, it was published when he was sixty-eight years old, in 1957. In his last years, aloof finally from the mundane doings of the community, he found a kind of companionship in the fictional people he created. He died at the age of seventy-three, on March 21, 1962.

There is a phrase in Yiddish for the young man of refined tastes and exquisite sensibility who is somehow set apart from the common herd. "A *zeidener yunger man*," Jews say affectionately, "a silken young man." Dr. Ginsburg was not an ordinary man, but in the rarity of his aspirations he had much in common with the extraordinary immigrant generation to which he belonged.

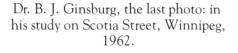
Dr. B. J. Ginsburg, the last photo: in his study on Scotia Street, Winnipeg, 1962.

8. IN THE COMMUNITY

Winnipeg by 1920 was a teeming, polyglot city, echoing with the voices of immigrants from many parts of the world. As Jews vacated their homes on Jarvis, Dufferin, and Stella, and moved northward into better residential areas, their places were taken by immigrant Ukrainians, Poles, and Germans. By and large, the Jews tended to cluster east of McGregor Street, with its streetcar tracks running along the weedy centre strip. Boyd and College Avenues had some solid homes by that time. St. John's was comfortable; Machray and Cathedral had some pretensions to affluence, or what the average citizen considered affluence. Eastward from Main to the Red River, the well-to-do Jews lived in style, gradually encroaching on the "English," who occupied the leafy, elegant Scotia Street running along the river to Kildonan Park. Still farther north, in the open fields of West Kildonan and Old Kildonan, were the vegetable and dairy farms, some of them Jewish, that supplied the city. Many people who grew up in the North End have fond memories of the milkman who arrived every day by horse and wagon, to ladle out milk from his big cans into the housewife's containers.

Within these bounds were most of the Jewish schools and societies, the butcher shops and grocery stores and all the other community services — the North End, home to a generation. For the child who grew up here, amid the variety and security that the large group offered, the experience of being Jewish was vastly different from the sense of being an outsider that marked the isolated child of the small-town Jewish storekeeper, or even the children in the smaller Jewish communities outside Winnipeg. Life in the North End was not without its tensions, however. The full viciousness of anti-Jewish violence did not really cross the Atlantic, but the Jewish children — the boys, mostly — were fair game for toughs and bullies. Many a youngster resorted to going several blocks out of his way, to and from school, to avoid trouble. For all that, it was a comfortable, familiar world.

By the end of the 1920's, some Jews had become part of the growing middle class: shopkeepers, small manufacturers, wholesalers; or self-employed craftsmen: tailors, shoemakers, plumbers, electricians, carpenters, tinsmiths. They were also part of the new group of workers, who became closely connected with the trade union movement. The number of Jewish workers in the early periods of immigration had been small, but it increased with the stream of people from eastern Europe. By the end of the nineteenth century, the ranks of Jewish labour had become sizable. By 1907 Winnipeg had Jewish workers in the candy factories, the overall and knitting plants, the meat-packing industry, and the railway shops.

Jews took part in the growing needle trades industry of the 1930's, both as workers and union organizers and as developers and employers. The

OPPOSITE PAGE, TOP
Boys as well as men were employed at the Kemp Manufacturing and Metal Co.
plant on McDermot Avenue in Winnipeg, and many of the workers were Jewish.
Ca. 1904.

OPPOSITE PAGE, BOTTOM
The staff of the Galpern Candy factory, Dufferin Ave., Winnipeg. Ca. 1917.

BELOW
A watchmaker and jeweller: Max Steiman at the door of his "Busy Bee" store on
Main Street in Winnipeg, ca. 1905. The store was established in 1890.

largest number of workers who produced ladies' wear belonged to the International Ladies' Garment Workers' Union; those who produced men's wear, to the Amalgamated Clothing Workers of America. Many were also to be found in the cap and hat and the fur industries, and in the building trades — here, too, on both sides of the economic fence. In the Winnipeg General Strike of May 1919, when the city was brought virtually to a standstill by the concerted stand of many unions against the conditions imposed on them by their employers, and the seething tensions came to a head in violence and bloodshed, there were Jews on both the strike committee and the employers' Committee of One Thousand. In the 1930's, Jewish workers and union organizers were to be involved in strikes in the fur industry, the cloak trade, and the baking industry, often against Jewish employers.

Civic unrest was part of the growing pains of the west during this period, and the Jews of the immigrant generation, experiencing a parallel expansion of their own horizons, were intensely involved. A delight in the thrust and counterthrust of ideas has always been a Jewish characteristic, rooted perhaps as far back in the past as the disputations of the Talmudists, and the learned man of the *shtetl* commanded respect even from the man of means. In the new world, when all Jews were only a memory away from the same *shtetl* and the same steerage arrival, a man might very well change his work clothes for a suit and tie in the evening and be listened to attentively on a political platform or a school committee.

The devotion of the ordinary working man to politics can be gauged by the story one Winnipeg old-timer tells about his own youthful career. Back in the twenties he was an ardent socialist earning a living as a driver for City Dairy, delivering milk along a regular route of factories and shops. The factories were a golden opportunity to promote unions, and he spent more time organizing the workers, he recalls, than selling them milk. On one occasion, when his efforts to persuade the factory hands had grown even more heated than usual, he came out into the street to find his horse and wagon gone from the curb where he had left them. Momentary panic gave way to a thought. He telephoned the office — and sure enough, the horse was just plodding its way into the yard, faithfully trundling the load behind.

Practical considerations did often take second place to the earnest idealism of those days, but social change came into being out of just such firebrand unworldliness. It was due in large measure to the efforts of both the Jewish workers and their union organizers that the Dominion government and various provincial legislatures began to investigate the appalling working conditions prevalent at the time, and that better labour laws were eventually enacted.

Within the Jewish community, two labour-related organizations provided their membership with an interesting mix of social insurance,

All dressed up: Nate and Carl Safran of Calgary, in 1920.

OPPOSITE PAGE TOP
The Shumiatchers of Calgary in 1919, with Peretz Hirschbein, Yiddish poet and playwright. While on a speaking tour of western Canada in 1918, Hirschbein met and married Esther Shumiatcher, also a writer (third row back, first and second figures on the right).

OPPOSITE PAGE BOTTOM
Ladies' ready-to-wear and tailoring: Louis Gutkin (left) and employees, Selkirk Avenue, Winnipeg, 1920.

political involvement, and cultural activity. The Workmen's Circle, or *Arbeiter Ring*, was a fraternal insurance and self-help society with branches in the United States and Canada. Founded in New York by immigrants in 1900, it helped form unions in industries where Jewish workers predominated. As a central interest, however, the Workmen's Circle operated schools and summer camps, which fostered the Yiddish language and culture. Its close counterpart and to an extent its rival was the Jewish National Workers' Alliance, or *Farband*, a Zionist-oriented educational and mutual benefit organization founded in North America in 1913. The *Farband*, in turn, helped to establish Jewish folk schools which reflected its own complex of ideals.

A socially significant paradox in both these institutions is that their membership included, side by side, employers and employees of the same factories and shops, momentarily forgetting their economic differences in the fellowship of common principles. Within such close ties, anomalies could and did occur. The president of North Winnipeg's largest Jewish bakery, Sam Rachootin, had started as a bread-truck driver himself, and he continued to contribute generously to left-wing groups, still identifying himself instinctively with the workers from whose ranks he had so recently come. He was understandably flabbergasted when his own employees walked out on strike. "I don't understand it," he protested to anyone who would listen. "I give them money for all their causes, and they're trying to do me in!"

B'nai B'rith picnic at Howe Sound, B.C., June, 1923.

One of the last of the old-style milkmen: Louis Chochinov, Winnipeg, ca. 1925.

BELOW
Podersky and Co., auctioneers: their first store in Edmonton, ca. 1925.

A Dream of Homeland

On the international scene, the Zionist movement came into prominence at this time, bringing into full focus the endless Jewish vision of a return to the ancient soil. The dream of return is as old as the Babylonian Exile, and enshrined in the very language of prayer: "Next year in Jerusalem," the Passover service concludes. Two thousand years of longing crystallized finally in late-nineteenth-century Europe into the political Zionist movement, with Theodor Herzl as its messianic force, and the first Zionist Congress was held in Basle, Switzerland, in 1897. The movement's premises were that Jews are a people or a nation, that many of them cannot or will not assimilate with other people because they wish to retain their own identity as a national community. The Zionist goal was the establishment for the Jewish people of a national home in Palestine, guaranteed by law. At the end of World War I the British Government, which held the Mandate for Palestine, was persuaded by the British Zionist and chemist, Chaim Weizmann, to issue the Balfour Declaration, endorsing a Jewish national home in Palestine. When the Mandate terminated in 1948, the State of Israel was proclaimed by the United Nations, with Weizmann as its first president.

Nurtured in the impoverished deprivation of the European experience, and deeply rooted in the religious and cultural heritage of the Jewish immigrant, the Zionist cause was expressed even more enthusiastically in the freedom of the new world. The Basle Congress inspired a great mass

A meeting of the Zionist and Social Society in Vancouver, ca. 1914.

Balfour Day in Winnipeg, ca. 1918. A Zionist parade celebrates the declaration by British Foreign Secretary Balfour in support of "the establishment in Palestine of a national home for the Jewish people."

The Talmud Torah, Flora and Charles Streets, Winnipeg, July 1917. Clarence I. De Sola, president of the Zionist Organization of Canada, arrives to open the national convention.

"Hail to the redemption of Israel:" Balfour Day parade in Regina, 1918.

Galut parade on Portage Avenue, Winnipeg, 1918. *Galut* (exile) denotes the dispersal of the Jews from their Biblical homeland. The parade honours Britain for the Balfour Declaration.

Arrival of Chaim Weizmann (centre, with beard), world Zionist leader, in Regina, 1921.

Pageant to mark the Weizmann visit to Regina, 1921. Centre figures represent freedom and justice; left, Zion as ancient monarch; right, Britannia.

"Mandate" picnic on the anniversary of the Balfour Declaration by Britain, the mandate power. Prince Albert, Saskatchewan, 1922.

meeting in Montreal on January 23, 1898, for the purpose of forming a
Zionist society, and in the same year an overflow meeting convened at a
synagogue in Winnipeg brought the organized Zionist movement to western Canada. Within a very short time the essential Zionist desire to
"return" took on the colouration of the diverse ideological certainties
among Jews. Labour Zionists or *Poale Zion* separated from the more conservative General Zionists, and within Labour Zionist ranks a slightly more
doctrinaire fragment identified itself as "Left *Poale Zion*." Orthodox religious Jews saw the Zionist program as the fulfillment of their ancient faith,
and formed their own Mizrachi Organization, the third of the major
divisions in the Zionist movement.

Across western Canada, from the early years of the century, the ideals
of Zionism became part of the vigour and excitement of the growing Jewish
communities. In 1913 the Vancouver Zionist and Social Society raised
funds for its cause, and in the same year Dr. Nahum Sokolov, a prominent
member of the World Zionist Organization, was honoured at a banquet in
Winnipeg. The fifteenth National Conference of Zionist Federations of
Canada was held in Winnipeg in July 1917, the year of the Balfour
Declaration, and also the year when Hadassah, the women's Zionist
organization, was officially incorporated. Vancouver's Jewish women
established their Hadassah chapter in 1920. Balfour Day was marked for
several years in Winnipeg, Regina, Saskatoon, and other centres by a grand
public parade. Prince Albert held a Mandate picnic in 1922 and Regina
welcomed a visiting Chaim Weizmann with a public reception and still
another parade. All in all, Zionist activities, both serious and light-
hearted, were woven into the fabric of Jewish life, and another dimension
was added to the complex relationship between the Canadian Jew and the
country of his adoption or birth.

Tema Churchill, of Winnipeg, poses
with Golda Meir in Palestine, 1931.

Religious Education

Among all the forms into which the vitality of the developing Jewish community was channelled in the years after World War I, the most characteristic was, perhaps, its substantial and effective school system, as an increasingly confident immigrant generation expressed its values in the education of its children.

Throughout the west, in the cities as well as the farm colonies, the first steps in Jewish education were under synagogue auspices. The earliest school in Winnipeg was opened in 1883 by the English-speaking members of the reform synagogue incorporated the next year as the Beth-El Congregation. Some of the first Jewish residents of the city served as volunteer teachers: Philip Brown, Mrs. George Frankfurter, Louis Vineberg, and Miss Millie Brown. Held on Sundays, these supplementary classes taught the Hebrew language and religion, and they were reorganized and renamed the Shaarey Zedek Hebrew School, with thirty-nine pupils, when the two congregations merged in 1891. In 1902 the Shaarey Zedek School had one hundred students, so that the congregation was encouraged to erect a new

The students and some of the teachers of the Winnipeg Talmud Torah (Hebrew Free School), ca. 1910.

ABOVE
A 1922 class in the old Talmud Torah, Charles and Flora Streets, Winnipeg, with Mr. Kowalson as teacher.

A class in the private Hebrew school of Meyer Averbach (front row, centre). Winnipeg, ca. 1925.

Confirmation class, the Shaarey Zedek Synagogue, Winnipeg, 1926. Left to right: Bernice Shragge Berkowitz, Estelle Frankfurter, Claris Udow Freedman, Gertrude Morganstern Orenstein, Ruth Udow Pollock, Florence Barish Kanee.

school building on the lot adjacent to the synagogue, on King and Common. But with the immigrant population shifting northwards across the busy C.P.R. tracks, the school closed its doors in a few years.

It was with the advent of the eastern European Jews, beginning in 1882, that a more elaborate educational instrument began to develop. For these immigrants the preservation of orthodox worship and traditional life-style was almost instinctive, and the provision of a teacher for their children as immediate a need as bread and butter. The old country *melamed* re-appeared almost at once, as private teachers began giving religious instruction to boys after their regular public school classes, sometimes in the boys' homes, and sometimes in a new-world version of the *shtetl* school, the *cheder*. In Winnipeg, the first recorded *cheder* was opened by the Rev. J. Friedman in 1884, and others followed.

By the early 1900's several synagogues were holding classes after regular school hours for a growing number of children, but their facilities were badly overtaxed, and many parents wanted a more extensive Jewish education. In response to the increasing demand, the Zionist Society opened a school in 1905, at Dufferin and Charles in North Winnipeg, to teach in Hebrew and in accordance with modern educational principles. Finally, in 1907, the B'nai Zion Congregation proposed that Hebrew education be made the responsibility of the entire Jewish community. Chief Rabbi Israel Kahanovitch called for support of the proposal, and largely through his efforts the Winnipeg Hebrew School, or Talmud Torah, was formed. A board of directors was elected and a building purchased at the corner of

The laying of the cornerstone for the Edmonton Talmud Torah, 1927.

Talmud Torah kindergarten, Regina, 1929.

Dufferin Avenue and Aikins Street to house the new school, with its 150 students and the four teachers of the original B'nai Zion Hebrew school. In 1912 the cornerstone was laid for a greatly expanded Talmud Torah on Flora Avenue and Charles Street, just two blocks further north, and construction was completed a year later. With its capacious auditorium, the building became the community centre for North End Jews: a synagogue for the Sabbath and holidays, a meeting hall, a ballroom, and the site of many a wedding reception, lecture, and bazaar. The pioneer Moses Finkelstein was even then aware of its vigorous multiplicity:

> A peculiar feature of the meetings held in the Talmud Torah, worthy of mention, is that often a visitor will be gratified to find at the same time under the same roof a sombre charity board meeting down below, a fiery nationalistic gathering in an upstairs classroom, a caustic socialist assembly in an adjoining room, and a delightful ball in the concert hall above.

The school continued to grow and branch out, following the shifting population further into the North End of Winnipeg.

Educational facilities developed in a similar pattern in other cities across the west. In Edmonton, Mr. H. Goldstick was hired in 1906 to act as the spiritual leader of the Jewish congregation, and also to teach the children of two of its members; in 1912 the Talmud Torah was incorporated as a separate body. Saskatoon held classes in rented rooms even before it had a synagogue, and the purchase and maintenance of the first Talmud Torah building, in 1915, was the work of the entire community. In Regina and Calgary, it was with the support of Zionist groups in particular that Talmud Torahs came into being. Vancouver's efforts to provide facilities for Jewish education date back to 1913, when two sisters conducted Hebrew classes in a house on Heatley Street, and problems of space continued even after the formal incorporation of a Talmud Torah in 1918. For many years the school shared facilities with the Congregation Schara Tzedeck, in a building completed in 1920; the Talmud Torah did not attain a building of its own until 1943.

While Jewish parents insisted on a proper education for their children, often at considerable cost, they sometimes made a revealing distinction in their choice of curricula. In cities like Winnipeg, Vancouver, and Calgary, where schools with a secular orientation eventually offered an alternate form of Jewish teaching, it was not at all uncommon for the girls in a family to attend a secular school, with its primary focus on Yiddish rather than Hebrew, while the boys were enrolled in a Talmud Torah. Obviously the male child had to have a thorough grounding in Hebrew and religion in preparation for his *Bar Mitzvah*, but a secular education in the less prestigious Yiddish was sufficient for the female. Often, of course, parents simply sent their children, male or female, to whatever school happened to be nearest, without much concern for ideology.

Banners and Ideals

The secular Jewish schools which made their appearance in many of the larger centres of North America during the early decades of this century reflected the character and ideals of one outstanding group of immigrants. These men and women who had come from czarist Russia after the abortive revolution of 1905 called themselves "radicals." Having witnessed the failure of the Russian movement for reform, they were convinced now that the old world was dying, and that the new world offered the bright promise of social betterment for all mankind. In search of that elusive goal, they became "socialists" or "social democrats," and the more unconventional thinkers declared themselves "anarchists," opposed on principle to the tyranny of any form of government. Some anarchists showed their defiance of society's mores by refusing to go through the formality of marriage, though the households they set up were as solidly middle class as their peers'. As Jews, moreover, all these "radicals" were particularly concerned to couple the resolution of Jewish problems with their dream of emancipation for all people. Their encounter with the blight of antisemitism in the ranks of the Russian labour movement had not shaken their certainty that a world free of oppression and hunger would be a world free of hatred. Like the earnest philosophers of the *Haskalah* movement, some of them believed that in that glorious future the intractable Jewish separateness would simply disappear; preaching "assimilation," they served to stimulate further attempts to define Judaism by other self-conscious Jewish intellectuals. The "socialist territorialists" sought answers in the opposite direction, insisting that Jews needed to re-establish a society in a sovereign state of their own, and there was a flurry of interest in South America as a possible location. The Zionists looked to Palestine for a solution to the woes of stateless Jews, and the Labour Zionists, specifically linking the Jewish hunger for land to the hopes of progressives the world over, dreamed

Members of the *Poale Zion* (Labour Zionist) party record the 1930 visit to Winnipeg of party leader Zerubavel (centre, bearded).

The *Arbeiter Ring* or Workmen's Circle School Committee, Winnipeg, early 1920's.

BELOW LEFT
Left-wing comrades in Winnipeg pose for a studio portrait under the photos of Lenin and Marx and the banner of the hammer and sickle. Ca. 1926.

BELOW
The group seems to have acquired one more member as they dramatize their earnest intellectual pursuits. Ca. 1926.

A visiting philosopher makes a point:
Winnipeg Yiddishists with Dr. Chaim
Zhitlovsky, at the home of Dr. and
Mrs. B.A. Victor, Winnipeg, 1942.

of a future when a socialist Jewish state would proudly take its place among the emancipated democracies of the world.

For all the alarmingly militant sound of party labels, there was a strongly theoretical and utopian element in the political fervour among the Jewish immigrants of the 1905 group. In many respects, it was simply the expression of the inherited Jewish commitment to humane values, and much of its energy was poured into the building of educational institutions. Like the Talmud Torah and the schools for religious instruction initiated by the various synagogues, the special classes organized by the secularists were conceived of as supplementing the general education provided by the public schools, as adding that necessary Jewish component for the rounded development of the Jewish child. But the progressive-minded activists of the new school movement, turning their backs on all religion as stultifying and oppressive, sought rather to familiarize their children with Jewish beliefs and customs as part of their background, and to teach Jewish literature and history according to approved modern methods. Generally speaking, the Zionist groups fostered the teaching of Hebrew, the modern and revitalized Hebrew that would become the language of a new Jewish state. For those who did not entirely equate the future of their people with a particular homeland, but sought to shape a Jewish identity that was integrated with and yet distinct from the larger community wherever they lived, Yiddish was generally the language of instruction, as the vehicle most expressive of the course of recent Jewish history. The dispute that brought Rabbi Kahanovitch to Calgary was typical of the antagonism between the orthodox and the secular at that time, and the rivalry between different kinds of secular schools was almost equally intense.

Secular Education

In May 1914, a Yiddish-speaking young people's cultural organization and a group of social democrats in Winnipeg founded the Jewish Radical School. A single room in the Aberdeen School, on Salter and Flora, was rented for after-four classes several times a week, with the Yiddish language central to its secular curriculum. A year later, the school was renamed the I. L. Peretz School, in honour of the Jewish writer, who had just died. In the following years several new institutions appeared, and at their height of success these secular schools achieved a combined enrollment of several hundred pupils annually. The Workmen's Circle School, founded in 1920, developed out of the socialist sector of the community, and was located in the Liberty Temple, a labour centre. Here Jewish history and the Yiddish language and literature were taught, with the social democratic philosophy as the under-lying principle. In 1940 the extreme left wing forced the Workmen's Circle out and started its own Sholem Aleichem School, with the same curriculum, but slanted towards theoretical communism. The Labour Zionists supported the Peretz School, but in 1930 they formed a short-lived Folk School to foster Zionist ideals and to teach in Hebrew rather than Yiddish.

West of Winnipeg, Jewish secular schools developed along similar lines. A branch of the *Arbeiter Ring* was active in Vancouver in the early years, and in 1924 a Sholem Aleichem Folk Institute, the forerunner of the Peretz School in Vancouver, was formed as an alternative to the Talmud Torah's religious curriculum. The Peretz School opened in the mid-1940's. Calgary had an I. L. Peretz School in 1929, which has played an important role in the Jewish cultural and educational life of the city.

The establishment and maintenance of these schools, with their classes held in the evenings and on Sunday, required an enormous effort on the part of people who were still in the process of achieving their own economic security. All the more remarkable, therefore, was the introduction by the Winnipeg Peretz School in 1920 of an all-day school in which younger children could receive their entire education. On the urging of the school's women's auxiliary, the *Muter Farein*, a kindergarten had been established in 1918, and when these children reached school age the dedicated supporters of the school undertook to provide for the teaching of both the regular public school curriculum and a full program of Jewish studies, half a day devoted to each. As the program continued, grade by grade, the crowded schedule left little room for amenities such as physical education, and music and art were often squeezed in as extras after four, but most of these children grew up comfortably bilingual and more than competent in the regular school studies.

The first class of the Jewish Radical School, Winnipeg, at the Aberdeen School on Salter and Flora Streets, where classes were held; I. Hestrin (left), and B. J. Ginsburg (right), teachers. 1914.

Winnipeg's Peretz School was among the first institutions of its kind on the North American continent to offer a day school program. The *Arbeiter Ring* and Sholem Aleichem Schools both had kindergartens during their life spans, and the Talmud Torah instituted its own day program in 1944. The Ramah School day program dates from 1959, with classes to the sixth grade, and the older institutions have also expanded, so that today the Peretz School takes the child to the seventh grade, and the Joseph Wolinsky Collegiate, an offshoot of the Talmud Torah, offers its students a complete high school education. Though similar undertakings

The first group of students of the I. L. Peretz School, Calgary. Ca. 1929.

The Winnipeg I. L. Peretz School rhythm band, winners of their class in the Manitoba Music Festival, 1933.

I. L. Peretz School, Winnipeg, souvenir book cover, 1927, marking the school's thirteenth anniversary. Book title (boxed, centre) is "Seedlings."

in other cities in Canada and the United States have had limited success, Winnipeg's achievement is unparalleled.

The gap in curriculum between the secular schools and the Talmud Torahs narrowed with the years, as the young radicals mellowed, acclimatizing both economically and culturally. Agnostics who, in their youth, refused to enter a synagogue, modified their views and developed a benign tolerance of the past and its religious trappings. In the course of time, a "radical" grandfather might even wear a *yarmulke* and a prayer shawl to celebrate a grandson's *Bar Mitzvah*, or stand under the *chuppah* at a granddaughter's marriage.

A healthy mind in a healthy body: Workmen's Circle School gymnasts, Winnipeg, ca. 1924.

Graduation class, 1925, of the Workmen's Circle School, Winnipeg, with teachers and school executive.

Picnics, Parties, and Purposes

To be a student in one of these schools did not mean simply sitting at a desk. It meant being part of a community, an extended family, where your classmates were the children of your parents' friends, and the school itself was a social centre.

As regularly as the children attended classes, parents attended school meetings or lectures by visiting writers and philosophers, or came for a "reading circle," a sociable evening of tea and talk. If some parents needed to be persuaded that a Jewish education was important, the school committee argued with them to have a child enrolled; or if the family had no money for tuition, children were accepted free, and the deficit assumed as part of the school's operating costs.

Running a school could occupy all of a committee member's attention, and especially so at bazaar time, the year's biggest fund-raising event. Qualified teachers were always in short supply, but capable men from among the school supporters were pressed into service, and many a doctor, dentist, or lawyer put himself through university by teaching in a Hebrew or Yiddish school. Dedicated to the common ideal, teachers spent countless hours on school activities. Their salaries were low, and they sometimes accepted partial payment when the treasury was empty.

This was a time when parents saw each child as a Jascha Heifetz, a Mischa Elman, or an Artur Rubenstein, and every home aspired to a piano in the living room or violin lessons for its budding musicians. It was a busy life. Since daytime classes served only a small proportion of the students enrolled in any of the Jewish schools, most youngsters habitually rushed home at four for a glass of milk, out again for an hour or two at their Jewish studies, and back for supper and homework and piano or violin practice. Somehow the children still managed to join in the noisy games of the street.

This was a time when families gathered and partied over simple fare, when a spread of herring and potatoes was in itself a banquet. Entertainment meant a Purim costume ball, organized by the Society or the Club or the School, with the ladies vying for Queen Esther's crown and the men enjoying the swagger of fancy dress. A summer outing was a picnic on Sunday afternoon in the park, with the whole family, including aunts and uncles and cousins; in the winter there was sleighing or "tramping" or tobogganing. The holiday festivals marked the round of the year, drawing families even closer together.

The Lighter Side of Life

LEFT
Jacob and Bertha Plotkin in a romantic pose: Purim Ball in Winnipeg, 1908.

RIGHT
Abe Klimoff and Harry Krivoshea, two Jewish members of Bill Moore's Orchestra. Winnipeg, ca. 1919.

For ladies only: a picnic at Elm Park, Winnipeg. Ca. 1905.

When Flossie Finkelstein Huffman threw a "stag" party for her future sister-in-law, Sara Ripstein, in 1911, the ladies dressed as men — but allowed two or three males into their midst.

Pajama party in Winnipeg, February 1929.

"Stag" party for a bride: hi-jinks in Regina, ca. 1914.

CARS AND MORE CARS

"Modern" machines were the pride of their owners, and an unfailing attraction for bystanders.

TOP
Dr. Oscar Margolese made house calls in style. Winnipeg, 1906.

CENTRE
Ben Grossman chauffeured Edward, Prince of Wales, during a royal visit to
Victoria in 1919. Grossman bought this Oldsmobile in 1907.

BOTTOM
The scion of an 1877 Manitoba settler sports a brand-new automobile in 1907:
Roy Frankfurter and friends enjoy an outing, as pedestrians watch.

TOP
The young people of the Lipton, Saskatchewan farm colony admire a model "T"
Ford. Ca. 1920.

CENTRE
Six men, and passenger space for only two: Lipton, ca. 1918.

BOTTOM
A car's running-board made a convenient seat for picture-taking: the Masarsky
family of Winnipeg in 1923.

Purim carnival in Fort William, 1912.

BELOW
Members of the Workmen's Circle in Vancouver take time out from serious matters to climb Grouse Mountain. 1910.

Jack Spindel as a seventeeth century dandy, for a Regina Purim Ball in 1913.

Eva Finkelstein, first Jewish woman awarded a B.A. at the University of Manitoba. 1896.

May Bere Mereminsky (Merem) was the first child psychologist in the Winnipeg schools. A 1915 graduate from the University of Manitoba, she later moved to Palestine.

A Passion for Learning

As the sons and daughters of the Jewish immigrant generation grew up, they entered universities in ever-increasing numbers, urged on by their parents. In the eyes of all these people, struggling to put deprivation and want behind them, the privilege of higher education was not only for the rich. By skimping and saving, or by borrowing from friends and relatives or from the loan societies, parents of very modest means gave their children a few more years of specialized study, that they might achieve a greater fulfillment and independence.

Social conditions at the time had a direct bearing on the professions which these young people tended to choose. For all the boundless opportunities of the new world, the Jew who sought to enter an occupation, trade, or profession had to take into account the unspoken social barriers that denied him acceptance. There were, for example, very few Jews employed as clerks or managers in the large department stores, where the public would encounter them, although a number worked discreetly behind the scenes as tailors or dressmakers or other craftsmen. There were almost no Jews in the civil service, although many by this time had been elected to public office. Teacher training was open, but the Normal School graduate was at the mercy of school boards. The Jewish young man or young woman who went out to apply for employment with credentials in hand knew that to be identified as a Jew was a hindrance, and often an absolute barrier.

Law, medicine, and dentistry were chosen by a large number of aspiring Jewish students, for in these professions the qualified person was self-employed, not dependent on an employer for a position, and therefore not subject to age-old social prejudice. In these earlier years there were not many Jewish architects, engineers, accountants, actuaries, or university professors, but a very marked concentration in the three favoured professions. In Winnipeg in 1932 there were forty-four Jewish lawyers, twenty-eight doctors, and eighteen dentists, a higher than average percentage of professionals relative to the total Jewish population. Even so, training in these professions was frequently hard to get.

In medicine, effective hindrances to advancement were all but codified. To achieve a career as a doctor, a student must first be accepted in an accredited medical school, and enrollment in all medical schools was — and is — regulated by the medical profession itself. The Manitoba Medical College in the thirties operated, tacitly, under a quota system, regulating admission according to lists of "preferred" and "non-preferred" applicants, the "non-preferred" being, of course, the foreign-born and other such visibly "different" persons. In particular, there was a ceiling on the number of Jews admitted in any one year, however outstanding their qualifications.

These facts were brought to light in 1942 and 1943 by a small group of

Dr. Sophie Granovsky Parlin was born in Elizavetgrad, Russia, arrived in Winnipeg in 1908, and graduated in Medicine from the University of Manitoba in 1919. Ca. 1920.

BELOW RIGHT
Menorah Society executive, 1919-20.

BELOW
Program cover, Menorah Society, University of Manitoba. Early 1930's.

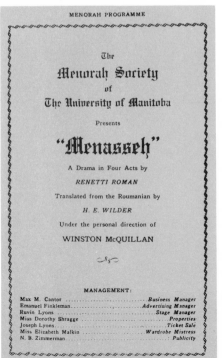

students, mostly graduates, working as the Avukah Society Fact-Finding Committee. Avukah ("torch" in Hebrew), founded at the University of Manitoba in 1936, was a chapter of a North American Zionist students' federation. The Avukah committee confronted the University with a carefully prepared analysis of statistics on admission to Medicine for the previous ten years, and, by taking their case to the Manitoba Legislature, forced the Board of Governors to take cognizance of the covert discrimination. In December 1944, the University finally agreed that the selection of students for the Medical College "shall be made without regard to the racial origin or religion of the applicants."

The push of young Jews for a university education is graphically illustrated by statistics. In the academic year 1930-31, across Canada, one out of every 316 Canadians of all origins was registered in an institution of higher learning, but in the same year one out of every ninety-six Canadian Jews was attending university, seeking the extra qualification of academic training. Gradually all the professions opened, as social attitudes changed slowly and unevenly, and racial barriers faded. Sam Freedman, who graduated in law in 1933, went on to the chancellorship of the University of Manitoba in June 1959, and became Chief Justice of Manitoba in March 1971. By that time the sons and daughters of all immigrants had free access to all Canadian institutions of higher learning, and found a much more ready acceptance in all walks of life.

The Lively Arts

In Winnipeg from 1904 to the early 1940's the Yiddish theatre was a favourite form of entertainment. Travelling Jewish theatrical companies had been performing in the city since the 1890's, and in 1904 a Yiddish theatre was organized, composed of local talent, under the name of the Jewish Operatic Company. The production of *Meshiach's Tzeiten (When the Messiah Comes)*, by the Yiddish playwright Abraham Goldfaden heralded a long and varied series of stage presentations. Tragedies, musical comedies, variety shows—all played to large and appreciative audiences. The home of Jewish drama in Winnipeg was the Queen's Theatre on Selkirk Avenue. Originally St. Giles Church, it was bought in 1907 by the Hebrew Sick Benevolent Society, later the Hebrew Sick Benefit Association, together with a group interested in the Yiddish stage. Until the 1930's, when the depression brought the era to an end, the Queen's reflected the diverse and changing tastes of its folk audience.

There Jews were in their element. Wives brought sandwiches for their husbands, who had come straight from work, and the performers on stage competed with the pop of soda-water bottle-caps and the crunch of apples. Peanut shells and Purity Ice Cream Honey Boy wrappers littered the floor. After a performance, the empty theatre looked like a battlefield when the conquerors have departed. The Queen's was the empire of Winnipeg's home-grown impresarios: Morris W. Triller, Morris Gussin, Morris Waisman, the Swerdlows; and here the Jewish Operatic Company presented its extravaganzas: *The Jewish Hamlet, The Jewish King Lear, Bar Kochba, The Sacrifice of Isaac, The Greenhorn, The Prince of Palestine*. Season after season the eager audience flocked in, lured by the promise of "A Gripping Tragedy, in Five Acts, with Singing and Dancing."

A slightly higher calibre of theatre was offered by the Yiddish Dramatic Club, organized by some of the serious intellectuals of the 1905 immigrant group: Ben Sheps, Hymie Roller, Bertha Prasow, Fanya and Alter Cherniack, and Berl Miller, among others. With Yiddish drama and literature then at its creative best, the club's amateur casts—housewives, shopkeepers, and tailors by day, and thespians by night—presented *Mirele Efros* by Jacob Gordin, *Tevyeh der Milchiker* by Sholem Aleichem, *The Dybbuk* by S. An-Ski, and other plays by David Pinski, Leon Korbin and Jacob Gordin.

A further addition to local theatre was made in the twenties and thirties by the Menorah Society, the association of Jewish university students, who offered a number of ambitious productions in English. Among the directors, stage managers, and performers listed in the society's old playbills are the names of many young people who went on to distinguish themselves in law, medicine, business, and politics.

The Jewish immigrants' insatiable appetite for the Yiddish stage drew a procession of illustrious visitors to western Canada. Sponsored by the

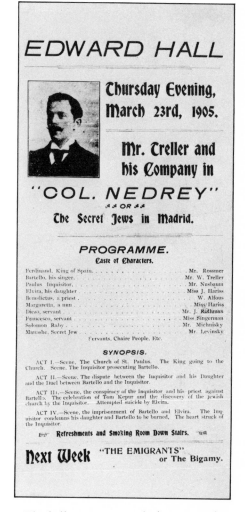

Playbill: gripping melodrama, with music. The Edward Hall was an annex of the Shaarey Zedek Synagogue, Winnipeg.

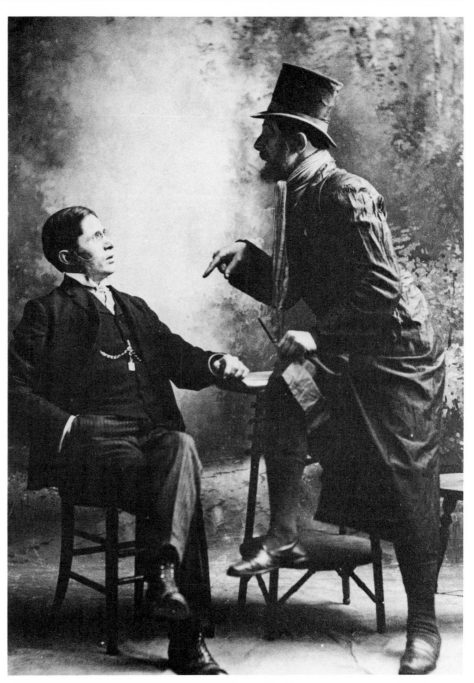

A scene from *Meshiach's Tzeiten* (When the Messiah Comes), by Abraham Goldfaden, with Morris W. Triller as director and star. Winnipeg, 1905.

Founding members of the Yiddish Dramatic Club, Winnipeg, 1906.

The Yiddish Dramatic Club, Winnipeg, had doubled its membership by 1908.

Farband and the *Arbeiter Ring*, guest stars "direct from New York," like Maurice Schwartz, Jacob Ben Ami, Jacob Adler, Madame Kenny Liptzen, and Rudolph Schildkraut performed in Winnipeg and then toured the west, where they were received with equal enjoyment.

Enthusiastic singers formed the Winnipeg Folk Choir in 1910, and achieved an expanded repertoire as the Jewish Community Choir, under Moses Jacob. In addition to its regular concerts the choir occasionally accompanied some of the famous cantors that visited Winnipeg. Jacob was succeeded by Benjamin Brownstone, who also conducted children's choirs at the Jewish schools. The Jewish Community Orchestra and the Jewish Women's Musical Club both contributed to Winnipeg's musical variety.

From Winnipeg to Prince Rupert, Jews participated actively in the performing arts of the general community. They played in symphony orchestras, supported local drama groups in small towns and large cities, and were voracious concert and theatre goers. As is frequently the case with minority groups, the arts became one avenue by which Jews reached out into the dominant society.

Winnipeg, 1910: the concert of three great cantors with the Winnipeg Jewish Folk Choir, under Cantor Moses Jacob, was a memorable occasion.

Joint Recital

of the
Three World
Leading Cantors

**Hershman, Roytman
and Kwartin**

WEDNESDAY JANUARY 9th
Board of Trade

Wedding in Kasrilivkeh (Sholem Aleichem's archetypal little town) was presented by a large amateur cast in Winnipeg in the early 1920's.

The Jewish Press

Shortly after the arrival of the east European Jews in Canada, Yiddish newspapers and periodicals began publication, to satisfy a deep-felt hunger. The Yiddish-speaking newcomers of the 1882 immigration were highly literate in their mother tongue, and they desperately needed a source of world and local news, a place where one could enjoy a novel in continuing instalments, or ponder an article of topical interest, or exchange views with the writers of other letters to the editor, or even ask for advice on personal problems. For the small-town dweller, news from the big city was especially important, to break through the walls of isolation.

In Winnipeg, several attempts were made to found a Jewish newspaper. In 1900 the Yiddish-language *Wiederklang* (the *Echo*) began publication, but it lasted only a few months. The *Winnipeg Courier*, also in Yiddish, appeared briefly in 1910, *Dos Volk* (*The Jewish People*) in 1912, and *Kanader Yiddishe Shtimme* (*Canadian Jewish Voice*) in 1921. None of these survived.

The only Yiddish newspaper still in existence in western Canada first rolled off the press in Winnipeg on September 23, 1910, as *Der Kanader Yid* (*The Canadian Israelite*). It changed its name to *Der Yid* (*The Israelite*) in May 1912, and then to its present name, *Dos Yiddishe Vort* (*The Israelite Press*) in August 1915. The fortunes of the paper rose and then declined with the changing character of the Jewish community. Issued first as a weekly, it flourished under two gifted editors, H. E. Wilder and Mark Selchen, and actually became a daily for a short time beginning in 1928. But with the decline in the number of subscribers for whom Yiddish was essential, the paper retrenched as a semi-weekly, and ultimately reverted to weekly publication, kept alive largely through the tenacity of one of its founders, Frank Simkin.

The *Israelite Press* is not alone in its problem of dwindling circulation. In New York, where a population of over 2,500,000 Jews at one time supported a thriving output of Yiddish newspapers and periodicals, only one daily survives, the *Forward*, and it appeals regularly for financial assistance from its readers. It used to be said that when an old Jew died, the *Forward* printed one paper less; and the same observation could be made of the *Israelite Press*. Western Canada's only Yiddish newspaper has suffered near-extinction and revival more than once, but it retains a tenuous hold on life.

An early Anglo-Jewish journal published briefly in Calgary. 1914.

The Anglo-Jewish Press

As the newcomers learned to speak English, and began to feel more at home with their environment, the Anglo-Jewish press made its appearance. The *Guardian*, first published in 1920 by the *Israelite Press*, lasted only half a year, but the *Jewish Post*, founded by Ben M. Cohen in 1925, and

אידישע וואָרט

THE ISRAELITE PRESS

Vol. 11, No. 4. Winnipeg. Fri. Jan. 12, 1923.   Published every Tuesday and Friday.

די אירגינעל אדישער צייטונג אין מערב קענערא

דר. וויצמאן וויל רעזיגנירען?

זאל האבען פארלאנגט מער מאכט

שלאנג פאר אלפרעד מאנד אלם פרעזידענט

אלוועלטליכע ציוניסטישע עקזעקוטיוו וועט נים אננעמען רעזיגנאציע

לאנדאן, יאנ. 11. (א.ק.ב.)

פראנצויזישע סאלדאטען שוין אריין אין עססען

ווינער באריכטע

וואלדימיר מעדעם'ם לויה זונטאג

רעוו. סעמועל און א. אסאוויסקי אין סאסקאטאן, זונטאג, 21-מען יאנואר

געזעלשאפטליכע נאמיצען

דער באזאר פון יענע באזארען

עפענט זיך דיזען זונטאג

מערב-קענעדער שטעם וועלען זיך באטיילינען אין קרן-היסוד קאמפיין

גרויסער עולם ביי הדסה פארזאמלונג

באנקעט לכבוד הרב זלאטניק

מערב-קענעדער שטעם וועלען זיך באטיילינען אין קרן-היסוד קאמפיין

צום ביאליק יובילעי

מעלודיע קאמבינאצי פאדר און הערט צו שטוצען פאר פריעדגעסער

אנגעקומענע אימיגראנטען

פראגענם נארמען צוריקנעוון וון אין רומענישע שולען

OPPOSITE PAGE

The front page of the *Israelite Press* for January 12, 1923, reflects reader concerns: Dr. Chaim Weizmann threatens to resign as president of the World Zionist Organization; French soldiers enter Essen; a large crowd attends a Hadassah meeting; a violinist will play a program honouring the noted writer, Bialik; and appearing inside is the first instalment of a new novel, *Love and Revenge*.

Beginning in 1925, a number of Vancouver publications finally evolved into the present *Jewish Western Bulletin*.

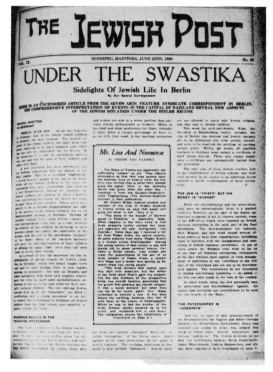

the *Western Jewish News*, started by S. A. Berg in 1926, continue publication to this day.

A publication initiated by the Vancouver Jewish community in the 1920's is still in circulation as the weekly *Jewish Western Bulletin*, but a Calgary attempt made in 1914 to publish the *Canadian Western Jewish Times*, for all the western communities, did not succeed.

On the front pages of all these Jewish publications, sombre world events have succeeded each other with grim inevitability, but the lively doings of the community itself provide a fascinating counterpoint, telling of weddings and Bar Mitzvahs, of school activities, visiting theatre groups, and lectures. Ben Cohen once told a young editor with rather inflated notions of his paper's function that the one indispensable part of the *Jewish Post* was the society page. Shrewd businessman that he was, Cohen had his finger on the pulse of his readers. It is the birth announcements, the club notices, the tea invitations that reflect the realities of daily life and the concerns of ordinary people.

TOP
Nazism comes to the fore in Germany: front page of the *Jewish Post*, 1933.

BOTTOM
The *Western Jewish News* reports on the Middle East, 1958.

Sports

Athletic activity was not part of the tradition that came with the Jewish immigrants from eastern Europe. True, the *Rambam* himself, the great Maimonides, who was a physician as well as a revered commentator on Talmudic law, had advocated "body movement" to maintain health, but the pale young scholar of the *cheder* and *yeshiveh* was more likely to study Maimonides than to follow his precepts on physical exercise. On the other hand, the Maccabi movement, the world union of Jewish athletic associations, was founded in 1895 in Berlin, Budapest, St. Petersburg, and Constantinople, and by 1910 had over fifty branches—evidence that

LIKE FATHER, LIKE SON

N. Cohen (right) won the Manitoba 440-yard dash in 1897.

urbanized, acculturated Jews did indeed participate in sport. But the old-country grandmother, transplanted to the Canadian prairies, generally frowned on her grandson's boisterous outdoor games. Playing chess or checkers she could understand, but she was sure that a boy who kicked a ball around the street would grow up a bum, a loafer. The young persisted, of course, and part of the driving ambition of the immigrant group was channelled into competitive sports. In these very early years, playground games were often a contest between the children of different ethnic groups. Winning was a distinct boost to one's ethnic pride, and a loss only a temporary setback, to be overcome tomorrow.

Laurie Cohen, son of N. Cohen, was Canadian 100-yard champion in 1924.

TOP
Hockey champions of Winnipeg's east side: the Zionist Athletic Club, 1903.

BOTTOM
A Jewish team won the soccer championship of the University of Manitoba in 1915. Bearded, centre back, the Rev. Herbert J. Samuel, of the Shaarey Zedek Synagogue.

TOP
The YMHA baseball team, Calgary, ca. 1924.

BOTTOM
The YMHA hockey team at the St. John's College rink, Winnipeg, 1924.

Leible Hershfield holds his audience entranced by a daring leap over eleven men, in a gymnastic display at the Winnipeg YMHA in 1937.

By the turn of the century, the Jewish community in Winnipeg had matured sufficiently to produce its first sports champion and to establish for its young people an organization that included sports among its activities: in 1895 the Young Hebrew Social Assembly was founded, as a cultural, social and athletic club, and two years later Nathan Cohen won the Manitoba 440-yard dash. (Cohen's feat, incidentally, has a sequel: his son Laurie became the Canadian 100-yard champion in 1924.) The Social Assembly became the Young Men's Hebrew Association (YMHA) in 1899, and received its first charter in 1919.

The Y's involvement in sports expanded greatly over the years, with lacrosse, basketball, soccer, and softball teams competing in city leagues in the years between the two wars. After their participation in amateur sports in the 1920's and 1930's, a number of Jewish athletes went on to become professional players, making sports their careers; several were particularly prominent in the Canadian Football League.

Today YMHA centres, open to men and women of all creeds, operate in Winnipeg and in other major centres in western Canada. No longer primarily involved in fielding competitive teams, they work in the area of physical fitness and recreation, with an extensive youth program and a wide range of lectures, study and drama groups, and similar activities.

There are not many Jewish players in professional sports today. As a general rule, the amateur baseball stars and football heroes of a generation or two ago enjoyed the satisfactions of team sports during their formative years, but went on to establish themselves in other careers.

Politics

Jews are inveterate committee people. Long accustomed to having a voice in the running of their own communal affairs, they gravitate naturally towards the processes of representative government. It is at the legislative level that they tend to seek redress for the inequities they have encountered, even in a democratic society. Once they have put down roots and recognized that where they live is home, many Jews seek election to the various levels of public office.

The right to hold public office in Canada had to be specifically acquired by Jews. It dates from the Quebec Bill of Rights sanctioned by King William IV and proclaimed in 1832, declaring "persons professing the Jewish Religion intitled [sic] to all the rights and privileges of the other subjects of His Majesty in this Province." Since then, though ethnic origin continued for a long time to affect the nomination of candidates and the decision of voters, it has been a mark of the essentially open nature of the Canadian democratic structure that public office is accessible to any properly elected representative.

The remarkable story of the political prominence of the west coast Jews has been told, and of the role their relatively small number played in that fledgling community. On the prairies the first Jew in public office was Moses Finkelstein, the son of an 1882 pioneer, who was elected a Winnipeg alderman in 1904. In 1910 S. Hart Green, also of Winnipeg, was elected to the Manitoba Legislature, the first Jew to serve in a provincial legislature since Henry Nathan, Jr., won his seat in British Columbia some forty years earlier.

Moses Finkelstein, Winnipeg alderman, 1905-1907.

BELOW LEFT
S. Hart Green, barrister, and the first Jew to be elected to the Manitoba Legislature, 1911-1914.

CENTRE
Max Steinkopf, the first Jewish barrister in the prairie provinces, served as Winnipeg school trustee, 1916-1919. A generation later, his son Maitland, achieved a cabinet position in a Manitoba government.

RIGHT
Rose Alcin, Winnipeg school trustee, 1920-21.

TOP LEFT
Mrs. S. Hart Green, Winnipeg school trustee, 1931-1932.

TOP RIGHT
Capt. William Tobias, member of the Manitoba Legislature, 1927-1932.

BOTTOM LEFT
A. A. Heaps, Winnipeg alderman, 1917-1926; member of Parliament, 1925-1940.

BOTTOM RIGHT
Morris Gray, Winnipeg school trustee, 1926-1930; alderman, 1930-1942; member of the Manitoba Legislature, 1942-1961.

Over the years, Jews have represented western constituencies in federal, provincial, and municipal government. British Columbia has recently been served by a Jewish premier, a provincial cabinet minister, and a member of the federal parliament. In Saskatchewan there have been Jewish mayors, members of councils and school boards, a senator, and members of the legislature and the cabinet. In Manitoba, eight Jews have served as members of the legislature, and two as members of the House of Commons; and in our time, five have been provincial cabinet ministers. In Winnipeg, seven Jews have served as aldermen, and six as members of the school board, among them two women: Rose Alcin (1920-1921) and Mrs. S. Hart Green (1931-1932). These elected representatives encompass a broad range of party affiliations and ideologies, from Conservative to Liberal to NDP; at one extreme is the lone Jewish communist holding public office in Winnipeg today.

While Jews of rival political parties have often run against each other in the same district, and the political infighting has always been heated, sharp, and divisive, most Jews tend to be broadly liberal in their outlook, no matter what party they represent. In the local arena the issues may be limited, but on the national scene lives are often at stake. The fate of many desperate people, of many nationalities, hung in the balance in the 1930's, when S. W. Jacobs, representing Cartier in Montreal, Sam Factor, representing Spadina in Toronto, and A. A. Heaps, from Winnipeg's North End, fought against harsh Canadian immigration barriers.

Jewish participation in political life was part of the journey outward into the mainstream community. Gradually Jewish electors ceased to cast their vote for a candidate simply because he was a Jew. The ethnic vote among Jews has given way to broad ideological support, or to decisions based on all the factors that motivate the general electorate.

John Blumberg, Winnipeg alderman, 1919-1956; chairman, Greater Winnipeg Transit Commission, 1956-1960; vice-chairman of Metro, 1960-1961.

BELOW
Harry Viner, mayor of Medicine Hat, 1953-1966.

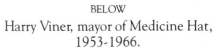

Portrait: A Man of His Time

In a community of outspoken individualists all pursuing the goal of a better world for themselves and for their people, one person might be singled out, both for his participation in a broad spectrum of the activities which shaped the Jewish community of Winnipeg and for the unswerving integrity with which he maintained his own position, even when it brought him into disagreement with his peers.

Joseph "Alter" Cherniack arrived in Winnipeg in 1905 at the age of twenty, with his radical fervour already in full blaze. He had repudiated the narrow traditionalism of his *yeshiveh* education to become a Socialist-

J. A. Cherniack (right) and Dr. Testnokow, who had arrived from Poland to deliver a series of lectures. Winnipeg, 1907.

Territorialist, a member of the Socialist Zionist movement in Russia. Militantly conscious of social inequities, he found the details of the difficult journey, with his mother and twelve-year-old sister, particularly offensive: the airless passage on a small ship from Finland to Liverpool, with men, women, and children crowded together in one undivided area; the converted cattle ship, with its primitive sanitation, which took them from Liverpool to Halifax; the segregation of men and women on board, separating families—and his inability to communicate with the crew to convey his protest; the degradation of people scrambling for food served en masse; the dirty tenement in Montreal where the family stayed a few days, and which quickly ate up their hoarded five dollars; the galling interview at the Baron de Hirsch Institute, to which he applied for pocket money and *matzo* for Passover, in deference to his mother's wishes, and despite his own secular antagonism to all such traditional observances. By contrast, his memoir notes with relief the cleanliness of the four little rooms his father had prepared for them on Stella Avenue, and the wonder of half a crate of eggs to celebrate the Passover.

Although he was a resolute agnostic, Cherniack took his father's place as a street sweeper on the Sabbath, in order to protect the older man's job. He himself worked as a watchmaker on Higgins Avenue, at twelve dollars a week, but earning a living was scarcely at the forefront of his attention. In 1906, just a year after his arrival in Winnipeg, he was sent to Boston as a delegate to a Socialist-Territorialist convention, and several years later he was again a delegate to the movement's convention in Cleveland. Quite without money, having paid another watchmaker to take his place at work, he met and deliberated with the foremost theoreticians of the movement, men whose views were to influence the shaping of Jewish institutions the world over —and who were penniless themselves. At this second conference, he recalls, he persuaded the renowned Dr. Nachum Syrkin to deliver a lecture in Winnipeg, and then had to travel back home to raise the money for a train ticket for the distinguished lecturer. Moreover, on the heralded day, Syrkin stepped off the train in a suit so crumpled and bedraggled that his hosts had to outfit him in a new one (it did not fit very well) before he entered the lecture hall.

Cherniack's zeal to change the world was matched by his hunger for education, for himself and for others. Having set his sights on a career in law, he was also one of the dedicated group of "radicals" who founded the I. L. Peretz School in 1914. Included in this group, among others, were Dr. B. Ginsburg, Berl and Bertha Miller, Moishe and Rose Alcin, and Cherniack's wife, the former Fanya Golden.

A vivid, forceful woman, Fanya Cherniack had been a member of the first Jewish theatre group in Winnipeg. As a founder of the women's organization, the *Muter Farein*, at the Peretz School, she was prominent for several decades in the operation of the school. She conducted a weekly

J. A. Cherniack and his long time friend and mentor, the philosopher and essayist, Dr. Chaim Zhitlovsky. Winnipeg, ca. 1925.

reading circle with other women, where Yiddish literature was read and discussed. Unlike their retiring sisters of earlier generations, many of these energetic young women had earned their own living as shop-girls, factory-workers, seamstresses, and they took their places as the equals of the men in the social and intellectual pursuits to which they were all dedicated. While Cherniack laboured against the barriers of an acquired language to earn first a B.A. at St. John's College and then a law degree, his wife worked as a seamstress to help support the family. He spoke later of the importance of her role in their life together, rejecting the traditional prayer of the pious Jew that his beloved wife might be allowed a place in heaven as his footstool: "In all [our] activities my wife accompanied me, hand in hand, and if I am allowed a place in heaven, my wife will sit next to me as an equal, not as a footstool below me."

By 1916 Cherniack and his friend M. J. Finkelstein were campaigning for a Jewish Congress, and when Congress elections took place in 1919, the greatest number of votes in Winnipeg were polled by Rabbi Kahanovitch, M. J. Finkelstein, and J. A. Cherniack. In addition to his work in the Congress, Cherniack was actively involved in JIAS (Jewish Immigrant Aid Society) and in the Jewish National Worker's Alliance. He was nominated as a candidate for school trustee in north Winnipeg in 1922, but great as his influence was by this time, he was not elected, nor did he ever achieve the popular accolade of being chosen for public office. Ironically, perhaps, this ambition was fulfilled in his children: his daughter served on the Winnipeg School Board, and his son became a cabinet minister in the government of Manitoba.

Cherniack continued to support the Zionist efforts toward a national homeland, but he insisted with even more vehemence on the importance of a vital Jewish life in the Diaspora. He became an eloquent speaker in English, and mingled freely in the community at large, but remained a devoted "Yiddishist," even more eloquent in Yiddish, and dedicated to the perpetuation of Yiddish culture.

Alter and Fanya Cherniack in their later years. Ca. 1960.

When fascism invaded Canada in the early 1930's, Cherniack was among the first to insist that immediate and direct action must be taken against this menace. Disagreeing with his own circle of friends, he became chairman of the militant Jewish Anti-Fascist League, which openly challenged the perpetrators of racist offences at a time when community leaders were still trying to use quiet diplomacy. He became the vice-president of the revitalized Western Canadian Jewish Congress in 1933, and attended the world Anti-Fascist Congress in Paris in 1937 as a delegate of the Jewish Anti-Fascist League.

Much of his most important work in the community was unknown to the public at large. Alert to every slur against Jews, whether careless or intentional, he wrote letter after letter to editors who had printed some slanderous cliché or to clergymen whose pulpit oratory had tapped a deep vein of traditional antisemitism. When Captain William Tobias brought an action against William Whittaker and the fascist *Canadian Nationalist* under the provisions of the Manitoba Defamation Act, it was Cherniack who prepared the brief, working tirelessly behind the scenes, and then arranged to have the prestigious firm of Andrews and Andrews plead the case in court.

A writer of great clarity and form as well as an effective speaker, he practised law until he was well past eighty. Six months after the death of his wife, he passed away, on June 27, 1972, at the age of eighty-six, among the last of a generation of extraordinary men and women.

THE SECOND IMMIGRATION: 1920-1939

9. INTO THE NATIONAL SCENE

From the beginning of the large-scale immigration of Jews from eastern Europe, the newcomers, once settled, turned to help those who came later, and each small group frequently became a kind of informal reception committee for arrivals from the same district. The tug of old associations was strong, and immigrant aid societies, springing up across the country, could count on a full measure of support.

The outbreak of World War I intensified the efforts of North American Jews on behalf of their European brothers. These new citizens of Canada and the United States knew only too well how grim living conditions were in those countries of eastern Europe from which they had so recently come, and war added an extra dimension of horror. War relief committees came into being within the first few months of the conflict, replacing immigrant aid as the prime concern. In November 1914, a Jewish Relief Committee was set up in Montreal, and in the spring of 1915 the Canadian Jewish Alliance, later known as the People's Relief Committee, was organized. Together they collected large amounts of cash, clothing, and other supplies.

In the west, all the Jewish organizations in Winnipeg, Saskatoon, Edmonton, Vancouver, and other cities and towns pooled their resources in a single agency, the Western Canada Relief Alliance, whose volunteer representatives visited every city, town, and hamlet. A canvassers' brigade of two hundred young people made regular rounds of Jewish homes in Winnipeg, and a specially convened meeting in 1916 of two hundred delegates from all over the west recommended that every Jew be taxed five cents a week for war relief. The tax was never enforced, but thousands of people made a regular voluntary weekly contribution. In Vancouver, several thousand dollars were raised in a tag day, when fifty ladies from the Workmen's Circle were joined by fifty volunteers from the Red Cross. For most of the war years, the money and goods collected by the efforts of all these groups were sent directly to local agencies in Poland, Romania, and the Balkan States, but by 1919 relief had begun to be channelled through a central organization, the Associated Jewish War Relief Societies of Canada.

A Community of Purpose

Meanwhile, strong support was gathering, mainly in Winnipeg, for a Jewish Congress, which would act as a unifying and co-ordinating body in all matters concerning Jews. The proposal was part of a broader movement among Jews the world over towards some common meeting ground, perhaps as a result of the wider perspectives brought about by war. An American Jewish Congress was founded in 1917, and in 1919 a *Comité des*

ABOVE
Fourth National Assembly, Canadian
Jewish Congress. Royal York Hotel,
Toronto, January 1939.

TOP
Western Canada conference for the
founding of the Canadian Jewish
Congress. Winnipeg, August 27,
1916.

Elections to Congress, December 24,
1944. Candidates ran as individuals
or as representatives of various
organizations: veterans, *lands-manshaften*, youth groups, political
groupings.

The 1919 founding convention, Canadian Jewish Congress, in Montreal.

Délégations Juives came into being in Paris, to speak specifically for Jewish war claims at the Peace Conference. It was this committee that evolved, in 1936, into the World Jewish Congress.

In western Canada, as mutual involvement in war work bound together hitherto isolated Jewish communities, the convening of a national congress was urged by the leaders of a wide spectrum of organizations, particularly at the grassroots level by the *landsmanshaften* and the Labour Zionist and Jewish trade union movements. On August 27, 1916, over two hundred delegates, including some from the remotest places, attended a western Jewish conference in Winnipeg, laying the ground for the establishment of a nation-wide Jewish organization.

In eastern Canada there was some resistance to the concept, especially in Montreal, where the Zionist Federation of Canada, considering itself the exclusive spokesman for Canadian Jewry, felt that its role as national leader and policy-maker would be threatened by a congress. But the increasing scale of war relief work and, as the war ended, the even greater task of rescuing war victims, made a central organization imperative. By this time, as well, antisemitism was on the rise in Canada, in the uneasy social conditions of the war's aftermath, so that a concerted effort seemed called for to promote a better understanding among all ethnic groups and religious bodies. These urgent considerations prevailed over calculated self-interest, and the 1918 Zionist convention reversed its opposition to the founding of a Canada-wide congress.

In January 1919, almost three years after the Winnipeg initiative, March 16, 1919 was set as the date for the first plenary session of a Canadian Jewish Congress, and Montreal as the place. On the proposed agenda were discussion of a national home for Jews in Palestine, equal rights for Canadian Jews, relief for Jewish war sufferers, and further Jewish immigration to Canada. All the Jewish communities in the Dominion were to be divided into districts based on population, and a delegate elected from each district. Every Canadian Jewish man or woman over eighteen, upon payment of ten cents, had the right to elect and be elected.

Simultaneously across Canada, from Halifax to Victoria, elections took place on March 2 and March 3. A total of 24,866 ballots was cast, and 209 delegates were elected. At Winnipeg's polling station in the Talmud Torah auditorium almost 3500 people made Chief Rabbi Kahanovitch their first choice. At the subsequent three-day conclave in Montreal, a cable was sent to Paris supporting the resolutions of the *Comité des*

Délégations Juives to the Versailles Peace Conference; and it was decided to proceed with the formation of the Jewish Immigrant Aid Society (JIAS), to urge the liberalization of Canada's immigration laws and to co-ordinate Jewish war relief activities across Canada. A number of standing committees were drawn up, to put all these plans into practice.

After this brave beginning, the Canadian Jewish Congress entered into a hiatus, and no further plenary sessions were held until 1934. It was only in the thirties, when Hitler was on the rise in Germany and antisemitic propaganda became widespread, that Congress fulfilled the potential which its early backers had foreseen. Beyond its specific functions of providing aid to immigrants and refugees and of combatting antisemitism, the Canadian Jewish Congress was to provide a face-to-face meeting place for Canada's Jews, and a public platform to debate the issues of the day. Across the thousands of miles of Canadian isolation, Congress eventually served to bind Jews together in a community of purpose, and to link them to Jews the world over. By that time, of course, World War II was imminent, and the strength of the organization would be taxed to its limit.

In the meantime, however, in the years following World War I, homeless Jews from Europe were clamouring for entry to Canada, and neither the long-standing Baron de Hirsch Institute nor the newly-created Canadian Jewish Congress had the capacity to deal with the problem. The Congress' arm, JIAS, and its related agencies, came into prominence to deal with the immigration pressures of the twenties, taking up all the available attention of the Jewish community.

The Baron de Hirsch Institute, Montreal, was officially opened June 17, 1891 as "a Free School for the poor children of the Jewish faith and a home for sheltering distressed immigrants and orphans."

Regina, ca. 1918. Delegates to the JIAS conference for the relief of war orphans pose at the railway station before their departure.

BOTTOM LEFT
The Saskatchewan and Alberta conference for the relief of war orphans. The banner reads: "Jews! Save our Future Generation!" Ca. 1918.

Western Canadian Jews contributed to the drive to aid the victims of pogroms in Russia. Jacob M. Schiff, a prominent American financier and philanthropist, was chairman of the International Russian Relief Fund.

Hands Across the Sea

A drastic change in the conditions of immigration had come about since those very early years when Macdonald's government, eager for population, had actively encouraged new settlers for western Canada. Now, as refugees from a broken Europe desperately sought admission to Canada and the United States as a matter of survival, the doors of these two countries were all but shut.

People here were in no mood to be generous to this flotsam of war. With the economy dislocated by the shift from wartime to peacetime industry, it was difficult to absorb the returning soldiers into the work force, and a shortage of housing compounded the problem. Unemployment rose, and there was widespread disillusionment. In the west the prices of all farm products dropped, including that of the mainstay of the western economy, wheat, and labour unrest culminated in the 1919 Winnipeg General Strike. As always in such difficult times, the alien was a visible target for suspicion and hostility.

The Canadian Immigration Act adopted in 1919 gave the government specific powers to regulate, control, curtail, or suspend admission of all immigrants it considered undesirable. A Privy Council order levelled the objection specifically at Doukhobors, Hutterites, and Mennonites, as former enemy aliens and "undesirable owing to their peculiar customs, habits, mode of living, and methods of holding property." By a further order-in-council, the amount of "landing money" required of each immigrant was raised to $250, an astronomical sum for a destitute refugee family. It did no good for papers like the Halifax *Morning Chronicle* to protest the short-sightedness of such a policy, or for William Lyon Macken-zie King, the new leader of the Liberal Party, to condemn such prejudice and inhumanity, in his election speeches against Sir Arthur Meighen's Conservatives. After the Liberals came to power in December 1921, immigration laws remained as restrictive as before.

Caught in the troubles of postwar adjustment, Canada did not seem able to accommodate more people. But for thousands of men, women, and children, among them many European Jews, with no other place to go, to be refused admission was tantamount to a death sentence.

In the chaos of war, a large number of Jews from eastern Europe had fled towards Siberia and Manchuria rather than towards the west. Some had landed in China and Japan and remained there for a time, seeking an opportunity to join relatives and friends in North America. While the usual port of entry into Canada for Europeans was still Halifax, by the middle of 1919 increasing numbers of Jewish would-be immigrants began arriving at Vancouver from across the Pacific. Most of them were bound for the United States, where the restrictions on immigration were as yet enforced less drastically, but almost all of those who declared Canada as their destination were detained and ordered deported.

The problems of all these refugees became the immediate concern of the Vancouver Jewish community. With Max M. Grossman acting as the attorney, an appeal had to be launched against each deportation order; and to release these exhausted travellers from detention while their cases were pending the government required that a bond of $500 to $1000 be posted for every individual. The local branch of the B'nai B'rith came to the rescue, putting up sizable amounts. Then accommodation had to be found for the refugees, sometimes only for a few days or a week, but often for as long as six months, while the committee worked tirelessly to obtain permission for the deportees to remain in Canada legally, or to have them admitted to the United States. It was a mammoth effort, and it brought the Vancouver Jewish community closer to the centre of organized Jewish activity in Canada.

The Jewish Immigrant Aid Society, which the first plenary session of Congress had created, was officially incorporated on August 13, 1922, although it had actually begun its work some time earlier, taking over from other agencies. In Winnipeg, a branch of the American-based HIAS, the Hebrew Immigrant Aid Society, had been in existence since 1912, but dormant during the war years. Now the organization sprang to life again in western Canada, under the JIAS banner, and joined in the complicated task of obtaining the admission of Jewish immigrants and then providing assistance towards their settlement. Many prominent Winnipeggers made the work their unpaid avocation, aiding new arrivals in Manitoba with loans, advice, and help in finding jobs and homes.

The desperation of the uprooted in those first years after World War I can scarcely be exaggerated. That it might be, in some sense, an obligation on the people of a more fortunate country to provide for the disaster victims of another country, that governments might accept this kind of responsibility — these ideas were not yet part of most people's thinking, as Canada and the United States closed in on themselves and their own problems. Particularly in eastern Europe, where the Russian Revolution added to the social chaos, dozens of localized "committees" sprang up, all attempting to deal with some particular part of a massive problem, all of them without money and appealing almost at random for support, none of them able to do much more than call attention to the human wreckage left behind by war. Early in 1920 the All-Ukrainian Relief Committee for Victims of Pogroms reported that over 100,000 Jews had been killed during the war and that there were close to 60,000 orphaned Jewish children left homeless in the Ukraine. Jews in Canada appealed to the Conservative government of Arthur Meighen to let some of these children in, and Mrs. Lillian Freiman of Ottawa raised $100,000 to back a plan to bring a

Kitchen supported by ORT for Jewish soldiers in the Polish army. Ca. 1920.

Jewish war orphans bound for western Canada. The children were issued warm clothing, but even music brought no smile to sombre faces. Ca. 1920.

thousand children to safety in Canada. The government finally allowed about 150 to enter.

During the winter of 1920-21, pressure on the ports of Halifax, Saint John, and Quebec was as intense as it was in Vancouver, and east coast JIAS representatives tried to act as a buffer between the rigid immigration bureaucracy and the human beings pleading to come in. In its first twelve months of operation, before its official incorporation, JIAS succeeded in having most of the detainees released; out of 1788, 232 were deported.

The immigration hall in any of these ports was purgatory for the detained immigrant, as he waited hopelessly for the signature on the paper that would grant him a new life, as he watched the hours pass on the clock and the days disappear on the wall calendar. Many people set out for Canada blindly, without visas, and were automatically barred until JIAS intervened. For those who had documents, a technical error or an omission could spell doom, and restrictive quotas shut the gate against many applicants with impeccable credentials. Compassionate workers from JIAS and other agencies tried to alleviate the waiting with some small kindness. In Saint John, A. L. Kaplansky, superintendent of the legal aid department of the Baron de Hirsch Institute, demanded kosher food for Jewish refugees detained at Passover, and after much objection the request was granted. When the *S. S. Saxonia* reached Halifax in October of 1921 it had a Jewish passenger list of 156, and every one of them was rejected and ordered deported until JIAS interceded. Forty-seven signed a letter of thanks to JIAS, almost incoherent in their gratitude:

ORT training shop for women workers in Vilna, Poland. These schools were set up to enable potential immigrants to learn a trade before embarking for America. Ca. 1921.

A fund-raising device for immigrant and war relief. Winnipeg, 1922.

No words or phrases can describe the feeling of the freed man towards his liberator.... We would ask you to accept the only means with which we can thank you, that is our blessings from the depths of our hearts which we hope will reach the gates of Heaven and be sanctioned by the Almighty.

Tirelessly, JIAS people cut through immigration red tape, reunited lost families, provided transportation, and arranged for shelter. They made sure there was someone to meet each newcomer at his destination in Canada, and they helped in the search for a job. In the west, the Jewish farmers of Saskatchewan and Alberta formed the Jewish Agricultural Association, to provide potential farmers with reliable information about agricultural opportunities on the prairies. During its first decade JIAS helped 41,873 Jewish immigrants into Canada. It obtained 8,329 entry permits from the Department of Immigration and Colonization, traced 1,889 relatives in Canada, supervised the serving of 49,986 meals to needy unemployed immigrants, and furnished 16,606 nights of shelter.

Jewish immigration into Canada dwindled between 1932 and 1935. Under the government of R. B. Bennett only the wives of Canadian residents and their children under eighteen were permitted to enter the country, and the work of JIAS was limited. But the western and eastern branches were active until about 1940, and the end of World War II once again brought the immigration services of Congress and JIAS into demand, when Canada reopened its doors to Europe's displaced persons.

The M. Kim Fur factory in the old Winnipeg Piano Building, Portage and Hargrave, 1922. The fur industry, in which many Jewish workers were employed, provided a number of seasonal and part-time jobs.

Rumblings

The Great Depression of the thirties followed a decade of economic and political unrest in Canada. Four elections had produced four unstable governments, and the stockmarket collapse of 1929 had been the final disaster in a cycle of boom and bust. It was as if the heartbeat of the entire country had stopped. The sawmills of British Columbia were silent. The fishermen of the Maritimes left the cod in the sea. Wheat from the prairies fell as low as forty cents a bushel. Without rain, Saskatchewan became a dust bowl, and destitute farmers lost their land to the banks, to the mortgage companies, or to the relentless wind. The depression affected all people, without favour. Jewish garment-workers, furriers, carpenters, electricians, like all their co-workers, either worked short time or were laid off indefinitely. Some small-town Jewish storekeepers who extended credit to hard-pressed farmers went out of business, and in the city small shop-keepers and corner grocers were no better off than some of their customers.

In Manitoba unemployment brought about a back-to-the-land movement, as some of the jobless sought an end to the humiliation of relief in their own acres of independence. A Jewish group of former farmers, organized by M. A. Gray, a leading political figure, and Mark Selchen, the editor of the *Israelite Press*, started the Vanguard Cooperative Colony near Winnipeg. But government grants proved inadequate, and the scheme faded out in disappointment.

Jewish tailors in the Paris Building, Winnipeg, ca. 1930. The needle trades, like the fur industry, operated on a part-time basis.

TOP
Winnipeg General Strike, 1919. Main Street, as the conflict neared a climax.

BOTTOM
Labour Zionists in Winnipeg join a May Day parade, 1932, demanding work in a
sign in both Yiddish and English.

TOP
With no work to be had in the cities, would-be homesteaders storm the land
office at Prince Albert, Saskatchewan. Ca. 1932.

BOTTOM
Riding the rods: a familiar depression scene at almost any railway terminal. Ca. 1933.

Swastika Over Canada

Fascism had proliferated in Europe's postwar disintegration, bringing Mussolini to the fore in Italy and Hitler in Germany. England had its fascist party in the followers of Sir Oswald Mosley, and the infection spread to Canada. Here, too, rival hate organizations found fertile ground in all the pent-up anger of the jobless and the deprived. They spread anti-Catholic tracts in predominantly Protestant areas, and anti-English tracts in predominantly French areas. They were indiscriminately anti-British, anti-"foreigner," anti-Mason, anti-government, anti-union, anti-employer, and they attracted many simple people looking for someone or something to blame for hard times. On the one hand these home-grown fascists raised the bugaboo that the "immigrants" were taking jobs away from "good Canadians," but on the other hand they fostered that deep, ingrained

The folly of antisemitism, as demonstrated in *Le Figaro*. Montreal, July 1933.

"GET OUT!"

"YOUR MOTHER WAS A JEWESS!"

Naziism in Winnipeg

The following quotations are taken from a Nazi paper published recently in Winnipeg:

"The Jew has not only stolen our business, he has stolen our Sabbath; through the literature and picture shows he controls, he has lowered the moral status of our people. His agents, the Communists, are trying to destroy our religion . . . etc., etc."

"Canadians must buy from Gentile Canadians . . ."

"Inoculation of Disease is a Jewish weapon against the Gentiles."

"No Depression for the Jews in Canada."

"The Nationalist Party is of the opinion that Hebrews or Jews, should not be permitted to absorb any more of the business than is 'represented by their percentage of the population . . . if the Nationalist Party ever gets into power in this country, we shall do our best to encourage their exodus to their spiritual home in Palestine . . ."

"The Jews, through the medium of the 'Protocals of the Learned Elders of Zion,' claim that they control the Press . . ."

"The second contingency, which we desire to avoid but must get prepared to meet, is that Nationalism shall come to power after a **violent struggle** following the collapse of the system.

"1. We must organize on a normal political basis for the ultimate capture of Parliamentary Power.

"2. We must organize to some extent on a military basis . . ."

All of the above are extracts from a so-called **"Official Organ of the Canadian Nationalist Party."**

We are not and need not be unduly alarmed about this. The average intelligent Anglo-Saxon is not likely to "fall" for such silly and vicious outbursts. Nevertheless, we must be on the lookout. We cannot simply ignore an attempt to foster such movements. It is with problems such as these that the Congress Committee is called upon to deal. There are larger problems that the Canadian Jewish Congress will have to deal with. For this we need your co-operation and assistance.

THE JEWISH CONGRESS COMMITTEE
OF MANITOBA.

Canadian hate literature, presented as patriotism. Ca. 1935.

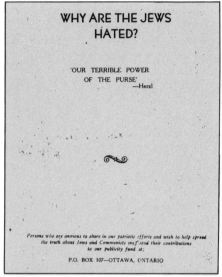

Canadian Jewish Congress appeal for aid to counter anti-Jewish propaganda. Ca. 1937.

Stamp distributed by the Jewish Anti-Fascist League of Winnipeg, 1938.

hostility to Jews harboured by many of those same immigrant groups. In particular, the half-million Germans living in Canada by the 1930's were inundated with a stream of racist propaganda pouring out from Hitler's Third Reich. In 1933, Fritz Kuhn of the German-American Bund sent an agent to organize Canadian branches of his organization. The leader of eastern Canadian fascism, Adrian Arcand, paraded the semi-military training of his uniformed followers, and his party boasted a membership of eighty thousand at its height.

The rallying point for western Canadian fascism was the discontent of a group of World War I veterans, hard hit by the Depression, who bitterly resented their poverty after their service to Canada. Like the National Socialists — the Nazis — of Germany, they preached an aggressive, racist super-patriotism and an opposition to all "foreigners," and they imitated the name and the style of their German model. The brown-shirted Canadian Nationalist Party was launched in Winnipeg, in September of 1933, by an old British soldier, William Whittaker, and his nineteen-year-old assistant, Jack Cole, and the group began to hold meetings not only in the hinterlands of Manitoba but in the North End of Winnipeg, deliberately inviting trouble in that explosive ethnic mix of immigrants and first-generation Canadians. Anti-fascist groups, determined not to let provocation go unanswered, mustered to oppose the Brownshirts. A series of clashes climaxed in a bloody riot in Market Square on June 5, 1934, described vividly by the Winnipeg *Free Press*:

> Knives flashed in the fast-waning sunlight, heavy clubs crashed against cap-protected skulls, and huge slabs of wood were torn from the stalls of market gardeners and used as battering rams against the tightly pressing wall of snarling humanity.

The violence and the subsequent court appearance of his battered followers served Whittaker's purposes equally well: he proclaimed the event "the first battle in the cause of Gentile economic freedom."

Striking Back

The *Free Press* under its great crusading editor, John W. Dafoe, steadily countered the Nazi inroads with editorial after hard-hitting editorial, but Whittaker's party continued its program of disruption, disseminating all the familiar antisemitic fabrications in its newspaper, the *Canadian Nationalist*. The fictions circulating in late nineteenth-century czarist Russia, about a Jewish "plot" to take over the world, had surfaced again in the tract, *The Protocols of the Elders of Zion*, which Henry Ford's *Dearborn Independent* had parroted; these now provided lurid reading matter in the *Nationalist*. Increasingly, civic authority itself was being challenged by the

Marcus Hyman, sponsor of the 1934 Manitoba Defamation Act, the first group libel law in Canada.

Americans
ON THE ALERT!

Hitler's agents are disseminating the poisonous virus of race-hatred and religious oppression in our country. At its last convention, the German-American Bund, official Nazi organization in the United States, issued a statement declaring that "our battle is the battle of all the hundred million Aryan (white gentile) citizens of these United States," and that this battle "will be won." Lovers of American democratic traditions must see to it that this will never happen here.

Lovers of Peace! Do you wish to stop Hitler aggression, the cancerous growth which menaces world-peace?

Do you wish to stem the onward march of Nazi militarism which has crushed Austria, overwhelmed the democracy of Czechoslovakia and is bringing us nearer and nearer to the brink of world disaster?

"We or They"

Free Men! Do you want to become the victims of Nazi propaganda? Shall Jews, Catholics, and Protestants, because of their religious faith, be persecuted as they are in Germany? Shall our religious leaders be imprisoned as were Niemuller and numerous other priests in Germany because they refuse to give up their faith and to subordinate religion to the State?

Workers! Do you want to be slaves of a system of forced labor at coolie wages? Do you want a government which forbids wage-increase and persecutes employers who raise wages?

Consumers! Do you know that under Hitler's "recovery" the consumption of meat, eggs, and fats, per capita, was lower in 1938 than in 1932—during the worst unemployment and depression period?

Women! Do you know that women in Germany today have no voice in the community, and that "woman is man's servant," according to the Nazi slogan? The hard-working, humiliated, undernourished, female workers are also compelled to bring more and more children into the world as cannon-fodder for Hitler's war program.

Mothers! Do you want your young boys and girls to be educated for war in our schools, as they are in Germany?

Do you know that boys and girls of 10 years of age are compelled to join the military camps of Hitler's youth army?

Taxpayers! Do you want your government to tax away 42% of the national income as Hitler does?

JOINT BOYCOTT COUNCIL
151 West 40th Street
New York City
PEnnsylvania 6-3864

JOINT BOYCOTT COUNCIL
151 West 40th Street
New York, N. Y.

I pledge myself to maintain the United Boycott Front against products made in Nazi-Germany.

Name_____

Address_____

For Humanity's Sake—

For the Sake of World Peace—

Boycott Nazi Germany!

BOYCOTT
NAZI GOODS AND SERVICES
Vol. III   JANUARY-FEBRUARY, 1939   Nos. 1-2

Carmack, *Christian Science Monitor*

The Answer to Race Persecution

THE NAZI MENACE TO THE AMERICAS	by Dr. Joseph Tenenbaum
WE CANNOT LOSE	by Bruce Barton
THE EXTORTIONISTS	by Georges Duhamel
RELIEF FOR HOLDERS OF GERMAN BONDS	by Dr. Max Winkler

LEFT
Advertisement of American Boycott Council, 1938.

RIGHT
Anti-fascist magazine published in the United States.

activities of this rabid fringe group, and moderates both in and out of government perceived the need for a carefully defined legal procedure by which such excesses could be controlled.

In February of 1934 the Trades and Labour Congress took steps to investigate the Nationalist party, and John Queen, who was the leader of the Independent Labour Party and the Mayor of Winnipeg, raised the issue in the Manitoba legislature. The following month a bill prohibiting group libel was introduced into the legislature by another Independent Labour Party member, Marcus Hyman. Born in Russia like many of his Jewish constituents, and the son of a rabbi, Hyman had taken an M.A. degree at Oxford and had been admitted to the bar at Gray's Inn, London. His bill, passed as the Manitoba Defamation Act, became the first group libel law in Canada. By its provisions, an injunction to cease publication can be obtained against the author or editor of any material that defames a racial or religious group or any member of that group, citing not personal injury but the "hatred, contempt, or ridicule" fostered by the offensive statement against the group as a whole. A further amendment, also sponsored by Hyman, made the publisher's or printer's name mandatory on all printed material, pamphlets, and handbills, to prevent convicted offenders from repeating the attack under another name.

Despite the legislation, Whittaker continued to print his message of hatred in his newspaper. Finally an article charging that Canadian Jews practised ritual murder — an accusation dating back to the Middle Ages — became the basis for a court case brought by a Jewish member of the Legislature. Captain William Tobias, a World War I holder of the Military Cross and a Conservative, took action against Whittaker and against his printers, and won the case. Whittaker was ordered to cease publication of such libels, and the court also granted Tobias $300 in costs.

This was not the end of the fascist movement, of course. From its base in Kitchener and Waterloo, Ontario, the *Deutsche Bund* (German League) began campaigning for members among Germans across Canada. The pro-Nazi, antisemitic paper *Der Courier* appeared in Regina, and the *Deutsche Zeitung*, the voice of the *Deutsche Bund*, began publication in Winnipeg. Later investigation revealed that the largest shareholder in the *Deutsche Zeitung* was the German consul in Winnipeg, and that the printer was also the printer of Whittaker's racist sheet.

While many people thought this brown-shirted posturing and violent rhetoric too alien to Canadian ways to be taken seriously, there was an increasing incidence of violence against Jews, and the community was deeply uneasy. Moreover, even as Hitler cast a longer and longer shadow across Europe, a strong undercurrent of sympathy for fascist doctrines developed in Canada and elsewhere in the western world, even among influential citizens. Initially, cautious Jewish leaders thought it best for Jews to maintain a low profile in the face of attack, but militant members of the community insisted on meeting fascism head-on.

It was in Winnipeg that an active Anti-Fascist League was created, to arouse public concern about the menace, and specifically to boycott German-made goods. Meetings were organized and well-known speakers brought in, and the League attracted many distinguished Jews and non-Jews alike. Although it proved far too aggressive for some elements in the community, it carried on its work with great effectiveness throughout this whole unhappy period.

An Uneasy Time

As the 1930's drew to an end and Hitler's aggression in Europe intensified, fascist activity in Canada became even more blatant than before. Adrian Arcand moved into Toronto from Quebec in the summer of 1937, sensing a receptive climate. In December of 1937, Quebec's *Le Jour* listed all the targets of Arcand's hate literature: free speech, some religious groups, various ethnic groups, unions, the Canadian constitution, constitutional

READ
THE
PROTOCOLS!

CANADA
FOR
CANADIANS!

THE CANADIAN NATIONALIST

THE LIGHT OF TRUTH

SERVIAM

"Speak the truth and bend the bow"

Vol. 2, No. 1.   January, 1938.   Price 5 Cents

THE CRUMBLING PILLARS

BRING LIBERTY AND PEACE TO MILLIONS!

Canadians! If you ignore this article, you will ignore your own death warrant at the hands of the Jews and communists as they have done in Spain and Russia!

THE PILLARS ARE CRUMBLING! The cunning plan of International Jewry as laid down in the Protocols of the Learned Elders of Zion, has slipped a gear and the astounding turn of events in the past year awoke the Jew to the fact that the stupendous game he has been playing for centuries is finally coming to an end.

The situation, in which the Jew figured he was holding the winning hand, has taken on a new aspect. The International Jew is beginning to sweat. The prospect of losing is bad enough, but what strikes real terror in his fanatical mind is the realization that no measures were taken in this subversive plan to meet the present day situation.

We read in Protocol 5: "For a time perhaps we might be successfully dealt with by a coalition of the Goyim of all the world: but from this danger we are secured by the discord existing among them whose roots are so deeply seated that they can never now be plucked up. We have set one against another the personal and national reckonings of the Goyim, religious and race hatreds, which we have fostered into a huge growth in the course of the past twenty centuries. THIS IS THE REASON WHY THERE IS NOT ONE STATE WHICH WOULD ANYWHERE RECEIVE SUPPORT IF IT WERE TO RAISE ITS ARM, FOR EVERY ONE OF THEM MUST BEAR IN MIND THAT ANY AGREEMENT AGAINST US WOULD BE UNPROFITABLE TO ITSELF. WE ARE TOO STRONG—THERE IS NO EVADING OUR POWER."

Protocol 7: "We must be in a position to respond to every act of opposition by war with the neighbors of that country which dares to oppose us; but if these neighbors should also venture to stand collectively together against us, then we must offer resistance by a universal war . . . ."

"In a word to sum up our system of keeping the governments of the Goyim in Europe in check, we shall show our strength to one of them by terrorist attempts, and to all, if we allow the possibility of a general rising against us, we shall respond with the guns of America or China or Japan."

But regardless of the above plan, Germany dared to raise an arm, and ever since Hitler threw the first wrench into the Jewish machinery, things have not gone so well for the Jew. Other countries, forgetting their Jew instigated religious and racial hatreds are raising their arms in support, and the repeated attempts to get Germany into another war have failed. It was only because the Jew was so cock-sure about the above quoted plan working, that he hollered loudly and firmly that Hitler wouldn't last a year. Hitler is still lasting and there will be much gnashing of teeth and tearing of hair (Jewish teeth and hair) but evidently Hitler will continue to last for a good many years.

As for the "terrorist methods" the plan seems to have worked the opposite way. In Spain for example, the show of Jewish communistic terror, has only become a terror to the communists themselves. In spite of the weeping and wailing of the "Jewrnalists" for their Democracy in Spain and the half hearted shouting that the so called Loyalists are winning, Franco has the situation well in hand, no one knows it better than the Jew.

The idea of answering a general rising against the Jews with the guns of America, China or Japan has been the most miserable failure of all. Japan has become National and realizing that the Jewish Soviet was Sovietizing China in order to use the some odd 450,000,000 Chinese as an International Army to subdue any Fascist rising, has proceeded to nip the plan in its early stages. That is why the Jew is so interested in boycotting Japan. That is why he is trying to bring up some "incident" so as to throw the rest of the world into a "universal war".

During the past few years anti-Jew parties have risen in every country of the world, no exception being made of Russia, where we learn from the "Yiddish Morning Journal", Oct. 7th, N. Y., "Anti-Semitism is on the increase"

These parties are increasing in size and power every day, and with Germany, Italy, Japan, Portugal, Brazil, Cuba and Spain hanging out a National banner, the situation, by the end of 1937 had a very serious outlook for the Jew. He has found it isn't so easy to start a revolution or a universal war as it was in the past. To crown this black year for International Jewry, Roumania decided to throw off the Jewish shackles. Now the fat is really in the fire.

Such countries as Poland, Bulgaria, Hungary, Austria, Denmark, France, CONT'D ON PAGE 6

"For Jerusalem is ruined, and Judah is fallen: because their tongue and their doings are against the Lord, to provoke the eyes of his glory." Isaiah 3: 8.

   ALWAYS BUY GENTILE!

The pro-Hitler, anti-Jewish, anti-liberal *Canadian Nationalist*, published in Winnipeg until 1939.

government itself—all were attacked with an inflammatory exaltation of race superiority. Since this material was being distributed by mail, the Canadian Jewish Congress appealed to the Postmaster General. A special investigator was appointed, and batches of hate literature from Germany were discovered in Arcand's post office box, but despite briefs from Congress to Prime Minister Mackenzie King no significant action was taken.

The Duplessis government in Quebec was silent. *Le Jour* demanded that the "fascist gangsters" be stopped, and the provincial Liberals openly took a strong stand against an acquiescent government; but Arcand, undisturbed, declared that 1938 would be the year of the National Socialist Party, and that it would spread across Canada.

By 1938 Nazi propaganda in Saskatchewan had reached such alarming proportions that responsible veterans' groups and patriotic societies sent letters of protest to the Minister of Justice in Ottawa. In Manitoba the militaristic ranks of the German *Bund* swelled, and they clashed verbally and sometimes even physically with the members of the Jewish Anti-Fascist League.

With the war against Hitler by this time inevitable, the Canadian Jewish Congress had fully joined the preliminary battle against Hitler's representatives in Canada. The Actions Committee of the Central Division of Congress organized a systematic nationwide campaign against the sale of German-made goods, proclaiming, with an optimism that now seems naive, "The Anti-Nazi Boycott Is Hastening Hitler's Downfall!" At the Fourth Plenary Session of Congress, held in Toronto in January of 1939, a display of hate literature in circulation in Canada provided graphic evidence of the extent of the fascist penetration.

The march of Hitler towards the domination of Europe had produced an unparalleled floodtide of desperate human beings looking in vain for sanctuary anywhere. A conference on "the refugee problem" was called by U.S. President Franklin Delano Roosevelt in July 1938, at the scenic little town of Evian-les-Bains, in the French Alps; only the Dominican Republic undertook to admit a substantial number of Jews. After "Crystal Night" in Germany, November 10-11, 1938, when Jewish homes, businesses and synagogues were systematically put to the torch and broken glass littered the streets, the doom of German Jews was sealed.

The United Kingdom admitted some 65,000 refugees, although Jewish immigration to the British mandate of Palestine was tightly restricted. In the United States the quotas on immigration remained virtually unchanged, but at President Roosevelt's direction visitor's permits were extended to alleviate the situation. In Canada the government of Mackenzie King held fast to its closed immigration policy; in January 1939, the Secretary of State, Fernand Rinfret, speaking in Montreal, declared: "Despite all sentiments of humanity, so long as Canada has an unemployment problem there will be no 'open door' for potential refugees here."

Finally, on September 10, 1939, Canada declared war, and the face of the enemy was officially identified at last.

Twilight of an Era

The Canadian Jewish Congress was ready with a unified agency for assistance, both at home and abroad, for the victims of war and persecution. By the end of the thirties a number of organizations, such as the Canadian Committee for Refugees, the Organization for Rehabilitation through Training (ORT), the Joint Distribution Committee, the Jewish People's Relief, and the Federation of Polish Jews, were engaged in overseas relief work, and a host of women's groups and fraternal organizations had undertaken similar projects. To act as co-ordinating body for all these efforts, the Congress established the United Jewish Refugee and War Relief Agencies in 1939, and the assistance program accelerated steadily throughout the war years. Immigration, of course, was virtually halted, but the Congress continued to aid the sporadic groups of people who could be brought to safety in Canada. Among the thousands of former German citizens whom the British government rounded up as "enemy aliens" and sent to internment camps in Canada, there were, ironically, a large number of Jewish refugees from Germany. The Congress was permitted to provide a welfare program for the Jewish internees, and eventually succeeded in having them released and given legal immigrant status. After Poland fell, a small group of rabbis and Talmudic students escaped and reached Japan, in 1941. Eighty permits were obtained for their immigration to Canada, and twenty-seven people made the journey immediately. The rest were caught in Japan by Pearl Harbor, and transported to internment in Shanghai. Their entry permits were renewed in 1946, and they finally reached Canada.

In 1943 the Canadian Jewish Congress took up the case of five hundred Jewish refugees in Spain, Portugal, and North Africa who had fled across the Pyrenees. Congress agencies guaranteed that the refugees would not become a public charge, and a Portuguese ship, under international safe conduct, crossed the Atlantic three times to bring the group to Canada. The first and last journeys were made without incident, but on the second attempt the ship was stopped by a German submarine. The refugees on board were forced into lifeboats and held there during an entire bleak Atlantic night, then permitted to return to the ship and continue on their way. In the panic to board the lifeboats, three people, including a baby girl, lost their lives.

A particularly intensive program provided help for a number of Jewish refugee farmers who arrived in 1939 and early 1940. In Winnipeg B. Sheps and M. A. Gray headed farm establishment committees that placed Jewish farmers on land near the city. The International Colonization Association sent three farm families to the colony in Edenbridge, providing improved 160-acre farms and some loans for livestock and equipment; because it was too late in the season for seeding, the Jewish farmers from the surrounding countryside arrived with horses, tractors, and farm machinery, and in one day put in the first crop for these families. In the years that followed, 204 Jewish farm families from Belgium, Germany, Austria, Hungary, Poland, Czechoslovakia, Romania, and Yugoslavia were placed on land across Canada, some brought under the auspices of the C.P.R. and others by the C.N.R. Nineteen families settled in Manitoba, four in British Columbia, three in Saskatchewan, one in Alberta, and the majority in eastern Canada.

The greatest demands on the Jewish community and its institutions were still to come. In the chaos of Europe after the war, they would have to labour tirelessly to bring out war orphans and to rescue and reunite families. Through representatives in Europe, JIAS and Congress would conduct anguished searches for the survivors of the Holocaust. The Central Local Index in Paris, working with the Red Cross and other agencies, would track down every rumour about survivors, in the hope that a lost family or even a single, wandering individual might be discovered and restored to relatives. World War II made the immigration work of Congress and JIAS more than ever a heartbreaking imperative.

Immigrants arriving at Quebec City, on the S. S. *Beaverbrae*, June, 1948.

TOP
In the immigration hall. Ca. 1948.

BOTTOM
The National Council of Jewish Women held classes for Jewish
newcomers from Europe. Ca. 1950.

People of Peace Go to War

Jewish service in the Canadian armed forces dates back to the Boer War, when there were some Jewish officers and men among the Canadian volunteer contingent with the British forces in South Africa. During World War I, almost 38% of the Jewish males in Canada who were over twenty-one and British subjects were enlisted in the armed services, and the highest rank attained by a Jewish officer in the Canadian military forces was that of lieutenant-colonel. In World War II, 16,883 Jewish men and women served in the Canadian Army, Navy, and Air Force. In all the armed forces of the Allied Nations in the struggle against Nazi Germany, an estimated 1,500,000 Jews were in service during the years 1939-1945.

Jews are traditionally a peaceful people but, as the surprising military exploits of the state of Israel have demonstrated, they can be very tough in defense of what they hold dear. As Jewish-Canadian soldiers took up arms at the outbreak of the second World War, they were deeply aware of a special commitment to the destruction of Hitlerism. Although free people everywhere were imperilled by Nazi territorial demands and Nazi racist philosophy, Jews were the immediate victims when Hitler's armies overran a country. First Austria's Jews and then Czechoslovakia's came under the power of the German dictator, and with the fall of Poland another three-and-a-half million Jews were taken captive. Canada's Jews went to war in 1939 knowing perhaps better than any other people the horror of the enemy and the need for his destruction.

LEFT
Aaron Pascal, of Winnipeg, in Cairo, 1918.

RIGHT
Recruiting for the Jewish Battalion. Winnipeg, 1917.

BOTTOM
Benjamin Grossman of Victoria, on patrol with the British Imperial Army in
the Libyan desert. North Africa, 1916.

AN APPEAL
JEWISH YOUNG MEN!
*The time has come for the Jews
to restore their ancient home*
You can do your bit by joining
THE JEWISH BATTALION
· 907 MAIN ST.

Four members of the Jewish Legion, 1914-18.

Tableau at a Victory Ball at the Royal Alexandra Hotel, Winnipeg. Ca. 1919.

Jewish dead in an overseas cemetery.
About 1,500,000 Jews were in the
armed forces of the Allied Nations
during the years 1939-1945.

THE THIRD IMMIGRATION: 1945 ONWARD

10. THE VALLEY OF THE SHADOW

The central trauma for Jews of the present generation is the Holocaust, the mass murder by concentration camp and gas chamber carried out by the Nazis during World War II. Persecution is a familiar theme in the long Jewish history; what happened in Europe has reminded many Jews of the peculiarly fragile tolerance with which — at best — they have generally been regarded, and they have responded with a reaffirmation of their identity as Jews. But the very scale of the Nazi campaign, and the thoroughness of its documentation, pose a disturbing problem for thoughtful Jews and non-Jews alike: given this evidence of evil, how is one to maintain a belief in the essential decency of human beings, and of an innate order in the world? Possibly the question itself, in

THE JEWISH BADGE

TOP LEFT
English Jew, 1275, wearing distinctive badge as required by the *Statutum de Judaismo*: tabula of yellow cloth, six fingers long and three fingers wide.

TOP RIGHT
"The yellow fop": sixteenth-century woodcut of a Prague Jew with the obligatory identification.

BOTTOM LEFT
Jewish market-woman of Worms, Germany, sixteenth century. Most frequently yellow, the circular badge was first introduced in thirteenth-century France.

BOTTOM RIGHT
"Jew": the yellow Star of David introduced in Germany by the Nazis on Sept. 1, 1941, and subsequently prescribed for Jews in all occupied territories.

its very despair, may represent a small step forward in the efforts of human beings to achieve humanity. It may be necessary to tell and retell the pain of the Holocaust, not to perpetuate guilt, but to further our understanding.

The historical facts are available enough: Hitler's accession to power in 1933, his successive demands for more and more territory, annexing the Saar and the Rhineland, then Austria, then Czechoslovakia; the capitulation of British Prime Minister Neville Chamberlain to these demands at Munich in September 1938; the Russo-German Pact in August 1939; and finally the attack on Poland in September 1939, which triggered the Allied declaration of war. While these events were shaping, the Nuremberg Laws within Germany systematically deprived Jews of their civil rights, of their homes and property, of their livelihood, of their lives. A limited number of Jews managed to get out; for most there was no avenue of escape. No effective protest was made by any government, and tight immigration policies in the free world remained largely unchanged. After the outbreak of war, Hitler's "Final Solution" was put into practice: the wholesale deportation of Jews to Poland, beginning in October 1941; the death camps, the gas chambers, the policy of genocide, of total annihilation of all Jews under German domination. It was not until the war ended, too late for most of Europe's Jews, that the long-delayed work of rescue could proceed.

Canada's record in this humanitarian task is, on a per capita basis, better than that of any other country except Israel. In the two decades between 1940 and 1960 Canada admitted almost seventy thousand Jewish immigrants, most of them refugees. Boys and girls who scarcely remembered a home, men and women whose entire families had been wiped out, came to begin life again, in a return to normalcy even more miraculous than mere survival. Now integrated, functioning citizens of communities across Canada, these survivors of horror have added their indomitable vitality to the Canadian scene. It is in their stories, perhaps, that the nature of the Holocaust may be perceived.

A Vanished World

Poland before World War II was a thriving centre of Jewish culture, concentrated in a number of major cities. One of these was Lodz, the heart of the Polish textile industry, where the Jewish community had grown with the rise of the textile factories. Before 1800, Jews from the neighbouring small towns had begun to flock into Lodz, seeking employment at the looms, in small shops and larger mills, often owned by Jews. By 1939, out of a general population of about 700,000, Lodz had over 200,000 Jews: as many as 50,000 were employed as weavers, and a large number as tradesmen, merchants, and professionals, in all the diversified occupations of a large, industrialized city. The rich Jewish cultural and religious life

GHETTO CHILDREN

included a well-organized educational system, a Yiddish theatre, and a daily and periodical press.

When the Nazis arrived in 1939, Lodz suffered the fate of virtually every other Jewish community at their mercy: obliteration. A ghetto was set up in 1940, and the entire Jewish population herded into a systematically more and more restricted area, under steadily increasing deprivations. Additional Jews from Germany were crammed in, and the entire group subjected to a coldly scientific process of dehumanization. In the end, the surviving remnant was dispersed to forced labour and extermination camps.

One of the survivors was Peretz Weizman, now rabbi of the B'nay Abraham Synagogue in Winnipeg. He brought with him a full set of the posters and newspapers by which the inhabitants of the Lodz ghetto received their instructions from their German masters, a record of entrapment all the more horrifying because of its initial appearance of concern for the welfare of the victims. The story of Lodz is told here in Weizman's words and in a selection of the Lodz posters and photographs, as a memorial to all the other communities that perished, and to the men, women, and children who died at Belzec, Treblinka, Maidanek, Auschwitz, Bergen-Belsen, Dachau, Chelmno, Buchenwald, Sobibor, and many other unnamed charnel-houses.

Peretz Weizman was born in Lodz in 1920, one of a family of six children. His father, Shmuel, was a wholesaler of chemicals and pharmaceuticals and a prominent member of the community. The rabbi remembers Lodz with bittersweet pride:

"Life was good for my family; we felt secure. Besides our comfortable home, the community itself was very warm, very Jewish. We had Jewish schools, Jewish colleges, everything that a community needs culturally and spiritually. We had our own welfare institutions, not supported by the government, and these did immeasurable good for the people. Religious life was very much a part of the city. Lodz was a fortress of Chassidism, and I was a follower of the great *Gerer Rebbe*.

"When the Germans came in, the city was annexed to Germany, and all remnants of Polish existence were completely erased. The names of the streets were changed, the name of the city was changed completely. It became Litzmannstadt, after the general who conquered Lodz.

"First they started by taking Jews to labour camps. The Germans used to come into a restaurant or any public meeting place and take ten Jews. People we knew just disappeared, and we found out later what happened to them. You never knew when your own turn would come.

"Then came the order that all Jewish people were to be moved into a ghetto, which was in the poorest slum area of Lodz. Many didn't want to leave their homes, many committed suicide, many were shot as they were being taken from the most beautiful parts of the city. But finally, in May of

Home of the Israel Kalman Poznanski family, textile manufacturers, in Lodz, Poland.

Piotrokowski Street in Lodz, where many Jewish businesses were located, before the turn of the century.

Building the ghetto wall, on Piotrokowski Street. Lodz, 1941.

Jews of the Lodz ghetto being marched to the railway station for "the Final Solution."

1940, the ghetto was closed and we had no more connection with the outside world. I lived in the Lodz ghetto to 1944. All the members of my family were taken away from there, one by one. My father and mother — all my family — died at Auschwitz. I was the only one of a family of twenty-five who survived. In 1944 I was deported to Hasag concentration camp. We were eventually liberated, in 1945, by the Russians....

"The German government appointed a Jew by the name of Chaim Mordecai Rumkowski as head administrator of the Lodz ghetto, to organize the Jewish community — to be responsible for its behaviour. Instead of dealing with the Jewish people directly, the *gauleiters* would manipulate the ghetto through Rumkowski. He was a naive man — I'm not condemning him — he probably did what he thought best.

"We existed and tried to lead decent lives in intolerable and inhuman conditions that cannot be described in any language. I think that this is the most heroic part of the Jewish nature — striving to maintain and preserve the image of a living human being, while surrounded by death and degradation. In spite of starvation, and the thousands of people who died daily, we tried to keep our physical and cultural and moral standards as high as was humanly possible, and it wasn't easy. We operated schools in secret, without permission of the Germans, so that the morale of our children could be kept up. We observed the day of rest, the holy Sabbath, and the holidays, so that our religion might sustain us. We organized a Jewish press in the ghetto, to tell the people how to get the most out of life, such as it was. We told them how to protect themselves, and how to maintain their human dignity and the image of God, and how to be full of hope when there was really very little to hope for. There were children born in the

A Jew in prayer shawl and phylacteries, with a neat row of Jewish dead, amuses soldiers of the Third Reich.

ghetto who didn't know what an egg looked or tasted like; children who never saw an apple or a lemon, children who never enjoyed a drop of milk. We tried our best to organize our lives in such a way that each day would count, and hoped and prayed that it would last.

"The irony of it was, they gave us the right to have our own money, and they gave us a Star of David badge. The Star of David didn't mean then what it signifies today. In those hopeless days we had to wear it on our jackets or coats to show that we were Jews; it was intended to be a symbol of shame or of death. Thank God, today the Star of David is a symbol of pride and of life.

"I'm not bitter about those years of pain. I don't say that we should forget — we should never forget. I surely cannot say that we should forgive. How can I ask someone to forgive his tormentors for something that has been lost forever? I can forgive someone for the hurt that he caused me, and for life's treasures that someone has taken away from me: I can say to myself, 'Forgive.' I am in no position to ask somebody else to forgive, to say, 'Forgive for the death of your father, for the death of your mother, for the death of your brother, for the wrongs they did to your sister.'

Women and children of the Lodz ghetto asembled for deportation; in the background, box cars. Note the boy with the yellow Star of David.

"If the world had paid attention, then our world would have been different. It is true that many non-Jewish people showed great moments of selfless generosity by helping to save the lives of Jews, when they knew they risked certain death if they were discovered in the act. We will never forget the Danish people — their generosity, their courage, their great effort to save a segment of humanity will be woven into the fabric of our history. But these brave people were only too few. It's sad to say that those good people who extended a helping hand indirectly accused those who did not even lift a finger. And those who did the heroic thing, the righteous thing, who showed the great heights that humanity can reach, are inscribed in golden letters in the annals of Jewish life forever."

Six lamps burn perpetually at the B'nay Abraham Synagogue on Winnipeg's Enniskillen Avenue, a memorial to six million victims of the Nazis. The congregation had at first planned to erect the commemorative tablet at the synagogue's cemetery, but they placed it instead on one wall of the sanctuary itself, where the Sabbath and the holidays are celebrated, where the Bar Mitzvahs and the weddings take place. The dead, Rabbi Weizman teaches, must live forever in the memory of the living.

Members of the Weizman family in their own home in the Lodz ghetto. Three wear the yellow patch. The only survivor of a family of twenty-five was Peretz Weizman, second from the right, back row. Ca. 1940.

ABOVE
Peretz Weizman in 1947, just before he came to Canada.

LEFT
Memorial to the six million Jews who perished in the death camps. Rabbi Peretz Weizman at the plaque in his synagogue, the B'nay Abraham, in Winnipeg's North End. 1978.

LODZ GHETTO POSTERS

After the closure of the Lodz ghetto in 1941, official instructions were conveyed to the Jewish inhabitants by means of posted notices, signed by Mordecai Chaim Rumkowski, the Jewish "elder" appointed by the Nazis. These posters, covering every phase of daily life, begin innocently enough, with an apparent regard for the people's welfare, but end with the fatal deportation orders. The sequence, sampled here, affords graphic evidence of the progressive dehumanization of the Jewish citizens of Lodz by the Nazis.

Bulletin No. 285. All men in the ghetto are to register on specific days for forced labour, according to their years of birth. Those who fail to do so will lose their ration cards and face severe punishment. June 27, 1941.

Air Raid Bulletin No. 1. Notice to the ghetto dwellers on protecting themselves in the event of an air raid. All attics must be cleared, all double windows removed; pails of water and boxes of sand must be available, with other means of fighting fires. Special courses will be announced for air-raid wardens and sanitary squads. May 21, 1941.

Bekanntmachung Nr. 289

Bezugnehmend auf mein neues Arbeitsprogramm laut Getto-Zeitung Nr. 13 vom 20. Juni 1941 müssen sich

ALLE FRAUEN

im Alter von **17** bis **40** Jahren einschl., *die Unterstützung beziehen*, **registrieren.**

(Ausgenommen sind die Frauen, die Kinder bis zum Alter von 14 J. einschl. haben.)

Alle anderen Frauen dieser Jahrgänge müssen sich laut nachstehender Reihenfolge auf dem Hofe meiner

Arbeits-Einsatz Abteilung,
Telegrafenstr. 13 (Lutomierska)

registrieren und zwar:

		die Jahrgänge	
Montag,	den 7.7.1941		1923 und 1924
Dienstag,	„ 8.7.	„ „	1921 , 1922
Mittwoch,	„ 9.7.	„ „	1919 „ 1920
Donnerstag,	„ 10.7.	„ „	1916, 1917 und 1918
Freitag,	„ 11.7.	„ „	1914 und 1915
Sonntag,	„ 13.7.	„ „	1911, 1912 und 1913
Montag,	„ 14.7.	„ „	1907, 1908, 1909 und 1910
Dienstag,	„ 15.7.	„ „	1901, 1902, 1903, 1904, 1905 und 1906

Registriert wird

von 8 Uhr früh bis 17 (5 Uhr) nachmittags.

Diejenigen, die nicht erscheinen, werden sofort das Recht auf Unterstützung verlieren und werden ausserdem **noch bestraft.**

Personalausweis (Pass) muss mitgebracht werden.

Litzmannstadt-Getto, den 4. Juli 1941. (—) **CH. RUMKOWSKI** Der Aelteste der Juden in Litzmannstadt.

Bekanntmachung
für die Neueingesiedelten im Getto!

BETR.:

ANKAUF

von Pelzmänteln, Pelzkragen und Füchsen aller Art.

Nachdem das Tragen von:

PELZEN, PELZKRAGEN und **FÜCHSEN**

aller Art im Getto verboten ist, fordere ich hiermit ALLE Neueingesiedelten auf, dieses PELZWERK in meiner

BANK, Bleicherweg 7 *zum Kauf anzubieten.*

Der Ankauf findet in der Zeit vom:

Sonntag, den 16. November 1941 bis einschl. **Sonntag, den 7. Dezember 1941** statt.

Um Andrang zu vermeiden, bitte ich, rechtzeitig mit dem Verkauf zu beginnen und nicht bis zum letzten Tage zu warten.
Die Angebotenen Pelzstücke werden in der Bank von meinen Vertrauensleuten geschätzt und dortselbst bezahlt.

(—) **CH. RUMKOWSKI** Der Aelteste der Juden in Litzmannstadt.

Litzmannstadt-Getto, d. 2. November 1941.

באקאנטמאכונג
די ניי־אנגעקומענע אין געטא

בנוגע דעם איינקויף פון פוטערמאנטלען,
פוטערנע קראגנס אוו אלערליי פיקסן.

צוליב דעם, וואס דאס טראגן אין געטא
פוטערס,
פוטערנע קראגנס או
אלערליי פיקסן
אין פארווערט,

פאדער איך אויף דערמיט אלע ני־אנגעקומענע,
אז זי זאלן אנבאטן זייערע זאכן
מיין באנק אויף ציעשעלסקא. 7

דער איינקויף קומט פאר אין דער צײַט פון:

זונטאג, דעם 16־טן נאוועמבער 1941
בי זונטאג, דעם 7־טן דעצעמבער 1941
איינשליסליך.

כדי צו פארמיידן א געדראנג, בעט איך רעכטצײַטיק אנצוהײבן
דעם פארקויף או נישט ווארטן ביזן לעצטן טאג.

אנגעבאטענע פיסעכ, שטיק וועלן נשאטאט ווערן אין דער באנק דורך מיינע
טרייטע־מענטשן אן אויפן ארט ארט באצאלט.

(—) מרדכי חיים רומקאװסקי
דער עלטסטער פון די יידן אין ליצמאנשטאט.
ליצמאנשטאט־געטא, דעם 2־טן נאוועמבער 1941

באקאנטמאכונג נר. 345.

וועגן
לעבנסמיטל־צוטייל.

דערמיט מאך איך באקאנט,
אז אויפן קופאן נר. **25**
פון דער לעבנסמיטל־קארט
וועגן
זונטאג או,
ד. 14־טן דעצעמבער 1941.

אין מינע קאלאניאל־ און ברויט־פינקטן אריסגעגעבן ווערן אין
יעדע פערזאן דער ווייטערדיקער לעבנסמיטל־צטייל:

100	גראם	ווייצנמעל,
100	„	קארנמעל,
50	„	גרויפן,
250	„	ווייסן צוקער,
200	„	ברוינעם צוקער,
150	„	אייל,
50	„	האניק,
5(	„	מארמאלאדע,
1	„	זאלץ,
5Ö	„	קאווע,
20	„	טיי־סאדע,
5	„	הירשארו־זאלץ,
200	„	וואש־פולווער,
200	„	סאדע,
1	ליטער	עסיק אין
2	שטיקל זייף „ריך".

די דאזיקע ראציע באטרעפט

2.85
מארק.

א חוץ דעם באקומט יעדע פאמיליע,
אויפן סמך פון דער גרינציג־לעגיטימאציע,
פון זונטאג אן ד. 14־טן דעצעמבער 1941.

אין מינע קאלאניאל־ און ברויט־פינקטן
1 בייטעלע קרישטאל־סאכארין
פאר **30** פעניג.

בי דער נעלעגנהייט מאך איך אויפמערקזאם, אז דער קופאן
נר. 41 אויף לעבנסמיטל־צטייל פון 25־טן נאיועמבער 1941, א.
גילטיק נאר ביז פרײַטאג, ד. 19־טן דעצעמבער 1941 איינשלי־ב׳

(—) מרדכי חיים רומקאװסקי
ליצמאנשטאט־געטא.
דעם 11־טן דעצעמבער 1941
דער עלטסטער פון די יידן אין ליצמאנשטאט.

Bulletin No. 289. All women between the ages of seventeen and forty must register for work, again by age and under the same threats of punishment for failure to comply. July 4, 1941.

TOP RIGHT

Newcomers to the ghetto are notified that the wearing of furs is prohibited and that all valuables must be turned over to the authorities for evaluation and sale. November 2, 1941.

RIGHT

Bulletin No. 345. Rationing in the ghetto: the allocation per person of flour, sugar, tea, soap and other necessities, plus one 30-pfennig packet of saccharine per family, available at authorized distribution points. Dec. 11, 1941.

באקאנטמאכונג נר. 371

ארויסשיקן

וועגן

דערמיט מאך איך באקאנט, אז אויף
דער פאראָרדענונג פון דער מאכט

קומט די **ארויסשיקונג**
ווייטער פאר.

איך פאָדער דעריבער אויף די צום ארויסשיקן באשטימטע
פערזאָנען, אז נאכן דערהאלטן די אױפפאָדערינג וועגן
ארויסשיקן, זאָלן זיי

צום טערמין
אומבאדינגט פינקטלעך
זיך צושטעלן

אין דעם אנגעגעבענעם טרער-פונקט,

אײ קעגנפאל
וועלן זיי ארויסגעשיקט ווערן
אָן וועלכן עס איז באגאַזש.

(–) **מרדכי חיים רומקאוסקי**

ליצמאַנשטאַט-געטאָ.
דער עלטסטער פון די יידן אין ליצמאַנשטאַט.
דעם 22-סן מערץ 1942

Bulletin No. 371. Deportation by names. The
specified list of persons must present themselves
punctually at the railway terminal or be deported
without any baggage whatsoever. March 22, 1942.

AUFRUF

an die Leiter, Arbeiter und Angestellten
der Wäsche- und Kleiderabteilungen.

Die Leiter, Arbeiter und Angestellten der nach-
stehend genannten **Wäsche- und Kleiderabteilungen:**

Franzstrasse 13-15,
Franzstrasse 85,
Cranachstrasse 19,
Mühlgasse 25,
Matrosengasse 10,
und **Matrosengasse 14,**

stellen sich <u>heute geschlossen</u> mit ihren
Familienangehörigen im

Sammelpunkt: Franzstrasse 13

zum Abtransport.

Litzmannstadt-Getto,
-n 14. August 1944.

(-) **Ch. Rumkowski**
Der Aelteste der Juden in Litzmannstadt

אויפרוף

צו די לייטער, ארבייטער און באאמטע
פון די וועש- און קליידער-אפטיילן.

די לייטער. ארבייטער און באאמטע פון די
ווייטער- אָנגעגעבענע

וועש- און קליידער-אפטיילן:

פראנצישקאנער 13-15,
פראנצישקאנער 85,
זשידאָחסקע-גאס 19,
מלינאַרסקע 25,
דוואָרסקע 10,
אי דװאָרסקע 14,

שטעלן זיך ה"ינט צוזאמען מיט זיערע פאמיליע-
מיטגלידער, אין זאמלפונקט אויף

פראנצישקאנער 13

צום אפפאר.

(–) מרדכי חיים רומקאוסקי

Deportation by specific trades — the last stages.
Supervisors and workers in the designated laundry and
clothing divisions to appear, together with their
families, today, at 13 Franzstrasse, for deportation.
Aug. 14, 1944.

"I Don't Want to Wander Any More"

Eva and Paul Berger live in a trim stucco-and-siding house on a tidy street of green lawns and flower beds in Winnipeg's West Kildonan, the continuation of the old North End. They have two daughters, one recently married, and a son still in school. Paul is employed in a sportswear factory.

The Bergers came to their quiet suburban life out of a background scarcely comprehensible to their present neighbours. Both were born in Poland, Paul in the city which the Russians called Lvov and the Jews called Lemberg, and Eva Rothbard in Siedlice, a small town in central Poland. Eva's father was a cattle dealer, and she had two sisters, one older and one younger. In September 1942, when it became clear that the German army would take over Siedlice, Rothbard paid a professional forger to make false identification papers for the two older girls; at thirteen, the youngest was not required to carry papers. Before the documents were ready, the Nazis surrounded the town, the family was ambushed, and the parents and the eldest daughter were killed. The two younger girls managed to hide in the countryside until Eva could claim her false documents.

At sixteen, armed with her new identity as "Sofia Pokora, Roman Catholic," Eva took a job as nursemaid to a Polish family in Domanice, a village about twenty kilometres from Siedlice. Her employers only found out that she was Jewish after the war was over; Eva does not know to this day what their reaction would have been, had they discovered her secret.

The Russian counter-offensive swept the Germans out of Siedlice late in 1944. Eva and her sister worked that winter in a Russian hospital, and they were joined in Siedlice by their mother's youngest sister, Luba. They also heard from a cousin, Henrik Czernowicz, but then lost touch again. One morning in May 1945, another aunt appeared—their father's young sister, Miriam, who had been liberated by the Russians after ten months in Maidanek and two years in Auschwitz. Rejoicing in this reunion, Eva and her two aunts decided on impulse to look for Jewish soldiers among the Russian-led Polish troops who were newly arrived in town, and to ask if anyone had heard of Henrik Czernowicz.

Paul Berger in Polish tank corps uniform, at war's end, 1946.

At this point, the young women's path crossed that of Paul Berger, whose own arduous odyssey had led to a street corner in Siedlice on that May morning.

Paul had assumed adult responsibilities in a harsh world very early. In 1936, he says, as a youngster of thirteen, he worked in a Lvov bicycle factory owned by a man named Grosskopf.

"We operated an assembly line ten to twelve hours a day, making bicycle wheels. Every six minutes, a wheel. If I didn't make a wheel, the whole line stopped. I was earning two *zlotas*, or fifty cents a week. . . . My father, who worked in a brewery, broke his back in an accident, and the family needed money, so I decided to ask for a raise. Instead of giving me a

ABOVE

French passport issued to Eva Rothbard Berger in 1949, on her immigration to Canada.

TOP

Forged certificate, in German and Polish, identifying fifteen-year-old Eva Rothbard as "Sofia Pokora, Roman Catholic."

raise, Grosskopf fired me. Conditions were so bad, the workers still on the job decided to go on strike — they sat in the factory and didn't move. The boss had the police surround the plant. They shut off the water and cut off the electricity, and tried to starve the strikers out. This was Poland in the summer of 1936.

"Things went from bad to worse. In 1939 the war started, and after the Russo-German pact the part of Lvov where I lived was occupied by the Russians. I went to work in a garage as an apprentice, at the age of sixteen. Then the Russians started forcibly relocating people — doctors, lawyers, city officials, businessmen. Finally they got down to ordinary working people. With a Berger on their list, they came for my father, but he was out, so they took me.

"I was shipped off to a forced labour camp — a Russian *gulag* — in the tundra region near Siberia. None of us there knew anything about wood-cutting, but we had to cut five cords between two people every day. There was never enough food, but if we made our quota of wood we could get an extra piece of bread. Men were killed by falling trees or died of starvation. We were packed two hundred men to a bunker, just like sardines in a can.

"There was a garage in the camp where the men worked without the supervision of the Russian guards. Because I had some experience with cars, I tried to get a job as a mechanic in the garage. They were desperate for someone, so they took me. I worked to win little extras: I chopped wood for the camp cook and he gave me a bowl of soup; I sharpened a knife on the garage grindstone for the camp baker and got a piece of fresh bread. That's how I survived.

"One day the truck delivering flour to the bakery broke down. The baker needed that load of flour badly, and I managed to fix the truck. The baker was so grateful he gave me a whole loaf of hot bread. I broke off a piece and gulped it down, and then I tucked the rest under my arm to keep it warm. I was on my way back to the garage when an old man like a skeleton came up to me — he must have smelled the fresh bread. He was starving, and he babbled that he would give me all the gold I wanted for a piece of bread. Suddenly I recognized in this skeleton my old boss at the bicycle factory back in Lvov, the man who had fired me. 'Mr. Grosskopf,' I

Berger (in helmet) with his commanding officer and friend, Lt.-Col. Alexander Malutin (fur hat), and the colonel's adjutant, beside a captured German Opal.

LEFT
Paul Berger as a driver in the Polish tank corps organized by the Russians.

said, 'don't you recognize me?' I had changed, I guess, and he didn't know me. I couldn't stay mad at him, so I gave him the rest of my warm loaf of bread and ran away. He staggered off, and I never saw him again."

When Germany attacked Russia in 1941, the Russians released all the Polish prisoners. The eighteen-year-old Berger was drafted into the armoured tank corps of the Polish army organized by the Russians. There his ingenuity and his skill as a mechanic caught the attention of the Russian brigade commander, Lt. Colonel Alexander Malutin, who was later promoted to general. The colonel, Berger says, was very good to him, treating him like a son, and he served as Malutin's tank driver for three and a half years, during the long campaigns from Smolensk, Kiev, and Berdichev, through Rovna to Warsaw, and finally to Danzig in May 1945.

In all the turmoil of occupation and liberation, right-wing Polish guerillas were active across the country, not against the Germans but against the Russians, and incidentally against the remaining Jews. Berger's brigade was sent to Siedlice, where the guerillas were concentrated in that spring of 1945, to bring the district under control. Berger recalls that he was standing on a crosswalk, directing the tangled traffic, when three girls came up to him with questions about their cousin. He had no information, but offered to make inquiries. Identifying himself as a Jew, he asked if the girls were Jewish and where they lived, and whether there were any other Jews left in town. That evening he came to visit, bringing two friends with him, Alex Spinak and Max Sokol.

Six months later, on October 2, 1945, in Warsaw, where the young people had gone in an effort to reconstruct their lives, twenty-two-year-old Paul and eighteen-year-old Eva were married in a double ceremony together with Alex Spinak and Eva's aunt Miriam. Amid the ruins of the city they had found a synagogue that had somehow survived, and a wedding canopy, and a rabbi named Rabinovitch. Their *ketubahs* had to be written by hand, and there was some difficulty in rounding up ten Jewish men for the requisite *minyan*. General Malutin was present at the ceremony.

The Spinaks, like the Bergers, eventually settled in Winnipeg. Max Sokol later married Eva's aunt Luba in Germany, and they now live in Paris.

Henrik Czernowicz turned up in Denmark. Eva's younger sister elected to go to Russia, hoping to escape the antisemitism of Poland and to benefit by the free higher education the Russian system provided. But before the Bergers made their way to the freedom of the new world, Paul returned once more to his birthplace:

"After I was demobilized in 1946 I went back to my home, although I knew there was nothing to come home for. The place I remembered drew me back like a magnet. Maybe it was my bad luck, being dragged off to that labour camp, but it was my good luck too, because I survived. My parents had been killed, I found out. The fascists had pushed my father from the fifth floor of the apartment building we lived in, and one sister was killed when they bombed the city. I don't know what happened to their bodies.

Marriage contract of Eva Rothbard and Paul Berger, handwritten in Hebrew by Rabbi Shlomo Rabinovitch. The wedding took place on October 2, 1945, in a Warsaw synagogue that had somehow survived.

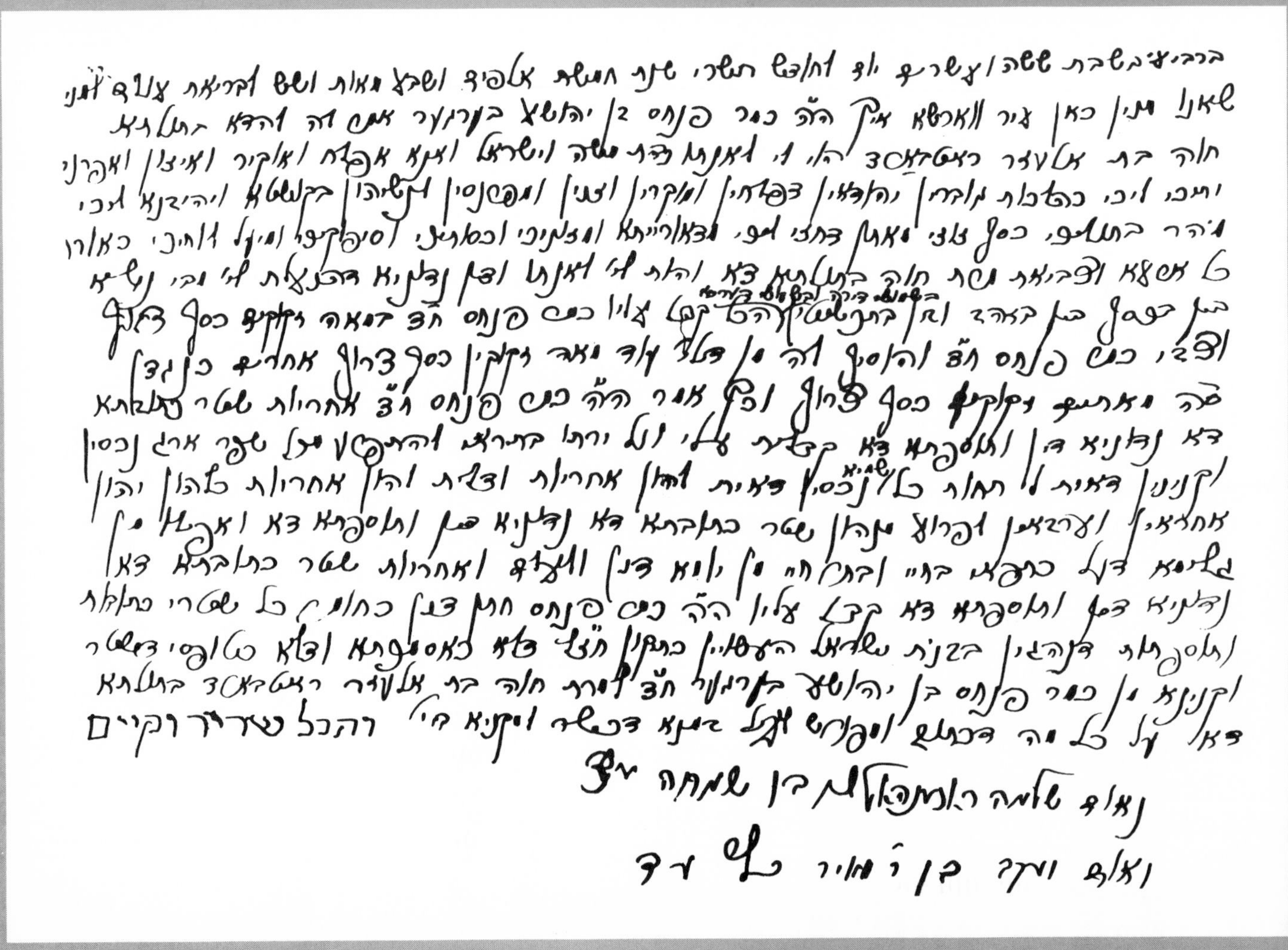

"There were sand pits in our city where the Nazis buried our dead, and when they couldn't dispose of the bodies fast enough they used to cremate them. The Nazis were efficient, too. They extracted the bones and made bone meal; and from human fat, they made soap.

"The Germans hadn't destroyed the apartment, but strangers were living there. The wedding pictures of my mother and father had been taken out of their frames and replaced by pictures of Lenin and Stalin. The furniture was there, but they wouldn't let me in to see the rest of the apartment. They were afraid I would ask for everything back. It wasn't mine for the asking any more. I saw what had became of Lvov, and I just turned back and went on to Warsaw. . . .

"Eva and I escaped to Czechoslovakia through the mountains, and then to Austria, through the Russian zone to the American zone. In Vienna we asked for help from an American agency and from there we went to South Germany. From Germany we got to France, and from France we came to Canada. We crossed eight borders without a document, and without money.

"I was happy to be in Canada because it's a free country. And I said, 'That's it! I don't want to wander any more.' You know, from 1939 to 1949 I never slept in a bed—I was always on the move. When I came here I realized that I could live like a free man, that I could come and go as I pleased. You can work, you can go to a school, you can go to a church, you can go to a synagogue, and nobody bothers you. You can raise a family, knowing that there is a life ahead for them. I say, that's paradise, and I'm happy here. I don't want anything else."

Eva and Paul Berger, with son Lindsay, February 15, 1977. Missing from this photo are daughters Yvette and Sharon.

A Gift of Life

Winnipeg's highly regarded Manitoba Theatre Centre was the first of the regional theatre centres in Canada, and the first on the continent. As the moving spirit behind the development of this professional enterprise, John Hirsch is something of a legend in Winnipeg today. He has since gone on to direct at Stratford, Ontario, and at the Guthrie Theatre in Minneapolis, at the Lincoln Centre Repertory Theatre, the New York City Opera, and on Broadway. Hirsch directed Chekhov's *The Seagull* at the New National Theatre of Israel, and *The Dybbuk* at Los Angeles' Mark Taper Auditorium, and he served as Director of Drama for the Canadian Broadcasting Corporation. Quite an achievement for "a rather anemic Jewish orphan from Hungary," as he describes himself.

In his continuing love affair with his adopted country, Hirsch is intensely aware of how unlikely it once seemed that the Jewish orphan would have any future at all, and therefore, of what his gift of life has meant:

"One of the most important events in my early life was my choice of a second country. Some immigrants feel towards their adopted country as parents do towards their adopted children. They can say, 'I love you more because I chose you.' This makes for an element of passion and determination in the relationship that is seldom present between ordinary parents and their children. For me, the adopted home turned out to be Winnipeg.

Six war orphans, brought to Canada by the Canadian Jewish Congress, 1947. Left to right: David Erlich, Anton Deutch, Ernest Green, Lazlo Greenspan, Eugene Josef and John Hirsch. The social worker is Thelma Tessler Edwards.

Out of my deep and urgent need for roots I became a 'Winnipegger,' a 'North Ender,' before I knew where I was, before I learned English, before I had any idea of the size of this huge country. I wanted to be part of something in a hurry. This was the place that had chosen me and I, in turn, chose it. Here there was space; here there was room; here different nationalities were living together reasonably and in peace — a tremendous change for a Hungarian war orphan. Here in Winnipeg Jews and Ukrainians were neighbours and didn't kill each other.

"I was born May 1, 1930, in a small town in Hungary called Siofok, on the shore of Lake Balaton, which is the largest lake in central Europe. My family consisted of my father, mother, grandfather, a brother who was two years younger than I, and also a great many aunts and uncles and nephews and nieces who all lived in a very, very large house with a courtyard in the middle of it. We must have been around twenty-five all together.

"My grandfather was a marvellous, gentle man, an old man when I got to know him. He was a member of the provincial legislature and on the board of the Bank, a very respected, well-known person in the community and in the province as well. He had a licence to sell stamps and tobacco, and that was a rare thing for a Jew. And to be a member of the legislature was even rarer at the time, although Hungary, at the beginning of the century, had a fairly liberal attitude towards Jews — Jews were engaged in the professions and could own land. Quite a different picture from the one in eastern Europe, in Russia and Poland.

The young John Hirsch conducts a children's theatre class. Ca. 1953.

"The whole family were great Hungarian patriots. For example, we never spoke Yiddish at home — we didn't even know that language existed. My father was an officer in the Hungarian army during the first World War. He was wounded, and every time there was a parade in town he marched right in the forefront of it. And then, when the second World War came — in fact, even before that — we were looked on as foreigners and strangers and not as Hungarians, even though our family went back, as far as I know, for hundreds of years.

"We didn't have an orthodox home, but a 'liberal' one — that's what it was called in Hungary. My grandfather prayed every morning, and he used a prayer shawl, but he was not what you would call an orthodox Jew. It was a kosher household, but my father was not beyond taking me to his friends who were peasant farmers, and there we ate sausages and all kinds of things that we were not supposed to eat at home. Saturdays we had to go to the synagogue, and I went to a Jewish school. It was a kind of split family, really. Though my grandmother was born in Hungary, she spoke Hungarian as little as possible. She spoke German, and all her newspapers and books came from Germany. Her people were not very Jewish but really Viennese and very proud of it. Their whole background was German. Schiller and Beethoven and Mozart were their gods, not the Jehovah who was my grandfather's God.

"When the Germans officially occupied Hungary, all the rightist elements in the country, that had been kept in check before this, took over the government, and all the laws in effect in Germany against the Jews were brought into force in Hungary too. Whole communities were rounded up and sent to camps in Hungary. Other people were shipped away in cattle cars to Poland and various extermination camps.

"For a while my family thought that we would be exempted somehow from all the horror. When our relatives began to come from Germany and Austria, fleeing the Nazis, they told us what was happening. People arrived from Poland who had seen concentration camps, who had seen or heard of gas chambers — they fled to Hungary and they warned us to leave. My grandfather wouldn't hear of it; he was a Hungarian, and his whole family was Hungarian, and nobody would do anything to him or to his children or to his grandchildren. When your family has lived in a place for hundreds of years, you can't really imagine that suddenly your neighbours will turn against you and murder you.

"One day an old friend of the family, who had been a maid in grandmother's house, came and took me away from home. I was thirteen at the time and just Bar Mitzvah. I had been going to school in Budapest — a Jewish high school, because Jews were not allowed to go to the public schools — but I had been forced to come back to Siofok. The Germans were there, and it was quite clear by then that they were going to deport us, but we didn't know where.

"I remember it was very early in the morning, and the train was leaving around 6:30. Most of the people in the house were still asleep so there was no way of saying goodbye to everyone. My father was up, and he ran to the baker and bought two rolls which my mother stuck into my pockets. I remember they were still hot. My mother and father kissed me goodbye, and that was the last I saw of them.

"My grandfather, who was eighty-five at the time, was also sent away somewhere to hide. We finally got back together in the ghetto in Budapest and lived there for six months, during the time when the Russians were besieging the city. About 300,000 people were herded into the ghetto, in an area really built for about 30,000. Around thirty of us, I remember, lived in a tiny room. There was no light, there was no water, and there was no food. During the day we were allowed to go out into the streets for an hour or two. I used to take a big kitchen knife and a basket and look for dead horses, so that we could cut some meat off the carcasses that were lying in the street.

"The ghetto was unbelievable. Now I think it was unbelievable; then it was just the ghetto, the world I lived in. Corpses were piled up all winter like cordwood — twenty people this way and twenty people that way — and maybe a hundred piles like this in the centre of the ghetto. When we went once a week to the soup kitchen, which was run by the Swiss Red Cross, we had to pass by those corpses.

"No news came into the ghetto, but the rumours that people were being taken to Auschwitz turned out to be true. I didn't know it then, but after the war I found out that my mother and my brother and all our family were gassed, and then burned in the ovens in Auschwitz. My father, who was taken away to Germany, survived all the way through the war, but just at the end, during the course of a march, he couldn't walk any longer, and they shot him by the wayside. And that was it.

"It was a miracle that some did survive — that I survived, at any rate. My grandfather starved to death at the end of the siege of Budapest. There was just no food, and in a kind of delirium he kept saying, 'If you could just get me a piece of white bread!' That's all he wanted. I had to take care of him, and at one time I also looked after an eight-month-old baby until it was finally smuggled out of the ghetto.

"When the Russians came and liberated the city, the Germans ran away, and then we could go back and pick up whatever pieces were left of our lives. I climbed up on top of a train and travelled to southern Hungary, where conditions were better at the time, and stayed there a while. Then I started to walk back towards my birthplace, nurtured by this really insane kind of hope — insane because I knew that nobody was going to come back — that I would find my mother and my father, that everybody would be there. So I walked miles and miles, for weeks, following the Russians who were chasing the Germans out, and sleeping in the fields and in barns and in villages. And I began to live this crazy dream, some kind of vague unbelievable hope—being only fifteen years old at the time—that at home I would find my mother, my father, my brother, and the whole family sitting under the trees as they did in the summer time, and we would all have dinner, and then I would go to sleep in my bed. Well, that never came.

"Finally I came to the canal that had its mouth at the lake where my town was. I remember the tall grasses and the weeds. It was a lovely day, and this delusion was becoming more real in my mind, that in another hour I would be home, the same home that I had had before. And as I was walking along the canal, I remember somebody shouting across it, "Jew, you've come home, hey?" I was only a very scrawny, very miserable fifteen-year-old, and I just ran from then on, like someone crazed, until I got to our house.

"My father's name was still on the front of the big iron gates leading into the courtyard, but the windows were all broken. I walked into the courtyard, and it was filled with mountains and mountains of furniture, because our house, the biggest one in town with the biggest courtyard, had been used as a kind of storage place for all the Jews' furniture. I could hardly get through the door, but I did, and again there was furniture, and in my parents' bedroom all their books were dumped in a heap.

"I remember walking into my parents' room, where I had sometimes slept as a small child, sitting on top of these books and crying for what must have been twenty-four hours. Sitting there, it dawned on me slowly that no one would be coming home again.

"After a while, some sort of normalcy was restored in Hungary. I went to live with an aunt and uncle. I tried to go back to school, but it was no use. I was totally disturbed, dislocated, very wild, doing things that were not really acceptable in a home. I wanted to go to Israel then, and at the first opportunity I left Hungary. I was in Germany for six months, living in a former concentration camp which was a gathering place for orphans. You couldn't go directly to Israel from Hungary, you had to go to Germany and to these camps. Then a group of us went off to France, and some got on the ship *Exodus 47* that went to Israel. I wandered around in Paris, living on tomatoes and sleeping on the benches on the Boulevard Strasbourg, until I managed to get some false documents which got me into an orphanage outside of Paris.

"Every week I would go to a different embassy and ask whether they could use a sixteen-year-old Hungarian-Jewish orphan, and I put down my name on all the lists there were. Every time you applied for a visa to a country you had to undergo a medical examination, and they always took your blood. When you're starving you can't really afford the pint of red blood that they take from you, so I had to time these visits to the embassies pretty judiciously, because you could keel over after you had two tests in one week. I discovered that I was too young to emigrate to Brazil; Argentina was interested only in lumberjacks; Mexico needed dental technicians; the United States rejected me because I was underweight.

"The Canadian Jewish Congress was looking for Jewish orphans who could be brought to Canada, so I came under their auspices in the fall of 1947. When I was asked whether I wanted to go to Vancouver, or Montreal, or Toronto, or Halifax, I asked for a map of Canada. I didn't know where Winnipeg was or what Winnipeg was. Just because it was in the middle of the continent, I pointed to it and I said, 'That's where I want to go. It looks safe.' So there I was in Canada at the age of sixteen, feeling like a growing plant plucked from its soil, roots in mid-air, desperately searching for a handful of earth—a home.

John Hirsch today, with friends.

"I reached Winnipeg and went to live with the Shacks — Mr. and Mrs. Shack and their daughter Sybil, the most exceptional people I have ever come across in my life. I didn't know it then, although I could feel it, but now, years later, I realize that I was placed in the home of extraordinary human beings. They really put me back together and they did it with the only glue that can put human beings together, with love and concern, and this love and concern lasted and I hope will last as long as we live. I think it has something to do with being Jewish, that a total stranger, coming from nowhere, could be accepted with as much love as I was. Although I really wasn't very Jewish at all—I didn't speak Yiddish and I didn't share their Russian-Polish background. I had a marvellous family when I was a child, but I found an equally marvellous family when I came here.

"A couple of weeks after I arrived in Winnipeg, I got a job as an office boy at an insurance firm. I didn't speak English, and it was difficult for me to learn the business, not knowing the language. I went to night-school right away and did learn English, and by spring I knew enough to begin private lessons in mathematics, English, and history. At the end of the summer I went to St. Johns High School and passed Grade 12, and then I went on to the University. By working on Saturdays, during Christmas and Easter, and always during the summer holidays, I put myself through school and then university.

"While I was at university I began to write poetry and short stories, which were published in the *Manitoban*, the campus newspaper. I also became involved in the Winnipeg Little Theatre—painting scenery, acting in tiny bit parts, designing—whatever came up. I graduated with a B.A. Honours in English literature and philosophy, and then went to work with the Winnipeg Little Theatre. That was just after the war. I was around twenty-two and I became the Theatre's first paid director and general manager.

"Around that time, James Duncan started Rainbow Stage and we teamed up, producing musical comedies. Then television came to Winnipeg, and I became the C.B.C.'s first producer. For three years I put on educational programs, baseball games, hobby shows, drama, literary programs—you name it—I did them all. Then I went to Toronto, and from there to the Central School of Speech and Drama in London, England, and back to Winnipeg to start Theatre 77. Finally, we combined with the Winnipeg Little Theatre to form the Manitoba Theatre Centre. That's how things got started for me....

"I feel myself very Jewish because my whole life has been shaped and formed by the fact that I was born a Jew. It's not the only influence in my life, but a very important one. I have been enriched by Jewish traditions. The idea of suffering is very much part of my Jewishness, and the idea that life must be lived here and now, not in another world, not after death. My sense of social responsibility, that I am here not only for myself, for what I can do for myself, but for what I can do for others, comes from a very strongly Jewish strain in me. That's why I have started theatres, involved myself in community affairs, all my life.

"My experience in Winnipeg, in Canada, with the Canadian Jewish Congress, and more specifically with the Shacks, has taught me the real meaning of Judaism, that it is inherently a service, a fellowship, a bond, a caring and loving for fellow human beings."

John Hirsch directing *The Dybbuk* at the Mark Taper Theatre, Los Angeles, 1975. Sketch by Sylvia Drake.

AFTERWORD

The most recent newcomers to the Jewish community of Canada come, once again, from Russia, escaping Soviet repression just as the Jews of 1882 had fled czarist inhumanity. For Russia's Jews, the Revolution had never quite fulfilled its lofty initial promise of common brotherhood and equality for all men. Given equal rights by law with their fellow Russians, Jews still found that under duress they were the first to be attacked, that the age-old antisemitism could be revived at any time.

The events of the recent past confirm the unhappy pattern. When the Nazis invaded the U.S.S.R. in 1941, breaking the Russo-German pact, and the U.S.S.R. had to make a sudden about-face in policy, the Soviet government used a number of Russian-Jewish luminaries in its calculated rapprochement with the west. Itzik Fefer, the Russian-Yiddish poet, and Solomon Mikhoels, the actor and director of the Jewish State Theatre then in existence in Moscow, were sent to assure audiences in the United States and Canada that the U.S.S.R. was truly anti-fascist, and to show Jewish audiences in particular the goodwill of the Russian people. When the war ended, and Nazism was no longer a threat, the Stalinist regime reverted to form. Mikhoels and Fefer were liquidated, along with the prominent novelist and playwright, David Bergelson, and other Jewish intellectuals: as exponents of Jewish culture, they were accused of "harbouring nationalist tendencies." Jewish schools, publishing houses, and newspapers were shut down, and the Jewish State Theatre closed. A particularly vicious Stalinist invention was the so-called "Doctors' Plot" of 1952 — the charge that prominent physicians, most of them Jews, were plotting to kill Soviet leaders — and a savage campaign of trials and executions ensued. The death of Stalin and the execution of Lavrenti Beria, the dreaded head of the Russian secret police, brought the campaign to an end, and all the survivors were, rather belatedly, exonerated. While racism is officially illegal in Soviet Russia, editorials in its controlled press are frequently antisemitic; and although official pronouncements stress the variety of nationalities within the federal state, Russian culture is monolithic, and Soviet domination has proved as destructive to Jewish identity as czarist persecution was to Jewish lives.

In the past few years, Russia has grudgingly permitted the departure of some of the Jews clamouring to be set free. About 140,000 are known to have left the Soviet Union between 1961 and 1976, to settle in Israel, Canada, Australia, the United States, and other western countries. The Canadian immigrants are once again the prime concern of the Jewish Immigrant Aid Society, but since many of them come under private auspices and are provided for by their families here, their exact number is not known. In the larger cities, those who require help in their adjustment are assisted by Jewish Child and Family Services.

249

Sarina and Michael Abramovitch are among the limited number of Russian Jews who have been able to leave the Soviet Union in the past few years to make a new home in Canada. They were married in Lvov, where their daughter, Regina, was born, and they came — coincidentally — to Regina, Sask., in 1975. A son, Norman William, is Canadian-born, and the Abramovitches have now been joined by Sarina's father. Michael practises his profession as an engineer.

There are some significant differences between the Russian Jews who came to Canada in 1882 and those who came in the 1960's and 1970's. The settlers of the earlier immigration period were consciously Jewish, whether they arrived with all their religious faith and traditional life-style intact, or had already adopted, with equal intensity, the ideology of a "modern," secular Judaism. The Yiddish language held them together, and the Yiddish press, theatre, and literature continued to evolve for several decades in the new world. By contrast, in Russia since the Revolution the religious and cultural institutions that shaped the earlier generations of Jews have withered. The Russian Jew of today rarely has any knowledge of Yiddish; he probably has no Hebrew at all, and only a distant memory of Jewish customs and traditions. In Canada he finds the vigorous Jewish community of his Canadian cousins as unfamiliar as Canadian society as a whole.

For these newcomers, adjustment presents a complex challenge. Most of them are very well-educated, and there are a large number of skilled tradesmen and professionals among them—doctors, dentists, nurses, academics, engineers—but to use their training in Canada they require a high degree of fluency in English and a familiarity with Canadian social customs. Before re-entering their profession, for example, the medical practitioners must overcome the major hurdle of the qualifying examinations in English, to verify their professional competence. The children must make new friends and adjust to a new school system; many parents choose to send their children to a Jewish parochial school, undoubtedly for its intimacy and close community ties. Parents and children alike find themselves rediscovering their identity as Jews even as they define their relationship to an open social order.

Jews cannot thrive in a repressive society; this is the fundamental truth that has been reaffirmed by the latest Jewish exodus from Russia. An authoritarian system feels threatened by the attempt to assert the dignity and importance of the individual—precisely the thrust of Jewish culture and tradition. Markedly, the Soviets attempt a rigorous control of their intellectuals, and Jews are prominent among the writers, artists, scientists, and academics who lead in the battle for self-determination, as a people and as individuals. It is to escape the stifling of the spirit that the latest Jewish immigrants from Russia have come to Canada.

The Journey Continues

Canada is enriched by a mix of many of the world's races, creeds, and languages. Most Canadians are immigrants or the descendants of immigrants, who landed on these shores fearing the unknown, but hoping that their new life would be better than the old one they had left behind. So it was for the Selkirk Settlers in 1811 and the Icelanders in 1874, who came to Canada because their homelands were too poor to sustain them; so it was for the Jews in 1882, who fled the poverty and mindless hatreds of nineteenth-century eastern Europe; and so it was for the survivors of the twentieth-century Holocaust.

During the vigorous pioneering days, when western Canada welcomed large numbers of immigrants from many lands and many cultures, newcomers were free to continue their own traditions, to worship in their own way, and to transmit their values to their children in schools and other institutions. In this open climate the Jewish immigrants gladly developed their own characteristic social patterns, side by side with their neighbours, and all prospered even as their common Canadian bond grew stronger. The establishment of the state of Israel has added a new dimension to the lives of most Canadian Jews, the same link with a homeland that enriches all the various ethnic groups in our pluralistic society.

Some 305,000 Jews now live here, little more than 1.3% of the entire population. About 40,000 Jews live in western Canada, from Thunder Bay to Victoria. As a group they consciously cherish their heritage. Their communal, cultural, educational, and religious institutions are still flourishing and expanding. Many children, grandchildren, and great-grand children of the pioneers still attend the various Jewish schools, and the community centres are filled to capacity with the sights and sounds of all ages crowding into their programs.

Nevertheless, there are differences. The Yiddish language spoken by the Jews of eastern Europe is falling into disuse. No longer expressive of today's generations, it now has meaning only for a diminishing number of people, for whom the memory of Yiddish spoken, of Yiddish read, of Yiddish sung, is part of a nostalgic past, but no more. Yiddish has, however, left an indelible mark on North American English, in vocabulary, in idiom, in syntax. As for Yiddish literature, the stories of Sholem Aleichem, I. L. Peretz and Isaac Bashevis Singer are now enjoyed in English translation — in effect a minority culture is being expressed in the majority language. As people visit back and forth in increasing numbers, Hebrew, the language of Biblical times and of modern-day Israel, is gaining in use.

Perhaps most important of all, Canadian Jews have moved into the mainstream of society. As strong as all the forces are that make of Jews a cohesive, inward-seeking people, the forces outward are equally strong. In their desire to become an integral part of the bountiful land they inhabit, Canada's Jews participate vigorously in the economic, political, and cultural life of the general community. Out of the unlimited energy of the Jewish immigrant has developed a rich and continuing contribution to the many-faceted pattern of Canada today. Though the pioneer generations have passed into history, the story that has been told in these pages continues its endless unfolding.

BIBLIOGRAPHY

BOOKS

Abrahams, Israel. *Jewish Life in the Middle Ages.* New York, 1958.

American Jewish Historical Society. *Preserving and Understanding Your Local Jewish Heritage.* Waltham, Mass., 1968.

Belkin, Simon. *Through Narrow Gates.* Montreal, 1966.

Betcherman, Lita Rose. *The Swastika and the Maple Leaf.* Toronto, 1978.

Caiserman, H. M. "Anti-Semitism in Canada." *Universal Jewish Encyclopedia,* Vol. I.

Caplan, Frank, and Norman Sheffe. "The Jews." In *Many Cultures, Many Heritages.* Ed. Norman Sheffe. Toronto, 1975.

Chiel, Arthur A. *The Jews in Manitoba: A Social History.* Toronto, 1961.

Comas, Juan. *Racial Myths.* Paris, 1951.

Dimont, Max I. *Indestructible Jews.* New York, 1971.

Dimont, Max I. *Jews, God and History.* Toronto, 1965.

Dobroszycki, Lujan, and Barbara Kirshenblatt-Gimblett. *Image Before My Eyes.* New York, 1977.

Fishman, Shikel, ed. *Studies on Polish Jewry, 1919-1939.* New York, 1974.

Frumkin, Jacob, Gregor Aronson, and Alexis Goldenweiser, eds. *Russian Jewry 1860-1917.* Translated by Mirra Ginsburg. London, 1966.

American Committee of the Yiddish Encyclopedia. *General Encyclopedia.* 5 vols. Paris and New York, 1934-1944.

Gibbon, John Murray. *Canadian Mosaic: The Making of a Northern Nation.* Toronto, 1938.

Gibson, Dale, and Lee Gibson. *Substantial Justice.* Winnipeg, 1972.

Grayzel, Solomon. *A History of the Contemporary Jews.* New York, 1960.

Hart, Daniel Arthur, ed. *The Jew in Canada.* Toronto and Montreal, 1926.

Hoffer, Clara, and F. H. Kahn. *Land of Hope.* Saskatoon, 1960.

Howe, Irving. "Introduction." *Jewish American Stories.* Ed. Irving Howe. New York, 1977.

Howe, Irving. *World of our Fathers.* New York, 1976.

Howe, Irving, and Eliezer Greenberg, eds. *A Treasury of Yiddish Stories.* New York, 1958.

Howe, Irving, and Eliezer Greenberg, eds. *Voices From the Yiddish.* New York, 1975.

Hubman, Franz, Miriam Hubman, and Lionel Kochan. *The Jewish Family Album.* Toronto, 1975.

Institute of Jewish Affairs and World Jewish Congress. *The Jewish Communities of the World.* 3rd revised edition. New York, 1971.

Kage, Joseph. *With Faith and Thanksgiving.* Montreal, 1962.

Lavender, Abraham D. *A Coat of Many Colors: Jewish Subcommunities in the United States.* Westport, Conn., 1977.

Leonoff, Cyril Edel. *Pioneers, Pedlars, and Prayer Shawls.* Victoria, 1978.

Madison, Charles A. *Yiddish Literature: Its Scope and Major Writers.* New York, 1968.

Marcus, Jacob R. *The Jew in the Medieval World.* Cleveland, 1960.

Marcus, Jacob R. *Early American Jewry.* Philadelphia, 1951.

Meltzer, Milton. *World of our Fathers: The Jews of Eastern Europe.* New York, 1974.

Metzker, Isaac. *A Bintel Brief.* New York, 1971.

Rhinewine, Abraham, and Isadore Goldstick. *Looking Back a Century.* Toronto, 1932.

Ricker, John C., John T. Saywell, and Elliot E. Rose. *The Modern Era.* Toronto, 1960.

Rome, David, ed. *Canadian Jews in World War II.* 2 vols. Montreal, 1948.

Rosenberg, Louis. *Canada's Jews: A Social and Economic Study of the Jews in Canada.* Montreal, 1939.

Rosenberg, Louis. *Canadian Jewish Population Studies.* Montreal, 1960.

Roth, Cecil, and Geoffrey Wigoder, eds. *The New Standard Jewish Encyclopedia.* Garden City, New York, 1970.

Roth, Leon. *Jewish Thought as a Factor in Civilization.* Paris, 1954.

Rubens, Alfred. *A History of Jewish Costume.* London, 1973.

Sack, B. G. *History of the Jews in Canada.* Montreal, 1965.

Samuel, Maurice. *Prince of the Ghetto.* New York, 1948.

Samuel, Maurice. *The World of Sholem Aleichem.* New York, 1943.

Shirer, William L. *The Rise and Fall of the Third Reich.* New York, 1960.

Singer, I. J. *The Brothers Ashkenazi.* New York, 1936.

Vaugeois, Denis. *Les Juifs et la Nouvelle-France.* Trois-Rivières, P.Q., 1968.

Wiesel, Elie. *The Jews of Silence: A Firsthand Report on Jews in Russia.* New York, 1972.

Wigoder, Geoffrey, ed. *Jewish Art and Civilization.* 2 vols. Jerusalem, 1972.

Wolff, Martin. "The Jews of Canada." In *The American Jewish Year Book,* 27 (Sept. 19, 1925 to Sept. 8, 1926). Philadelphia, 1925.

Zbrowski, Mark, and Elizabeth Herzog. *Life Is with People: the Jewish Little Town of Eastern Europe.* New York, 1952.

PERIODICALS AND MISCELLANEOUS PAPERS

Abella, Irving, and Harold Troper. "The Line Must Be Drawn Somewhere: Canada and Jewish Refugees, 1933-1939." *Canadian Historical Review,* LX, No. 2 (June, 1979).

Arnold, Abraham J. "The Life and Times of Jewish Pioneers in Western Canada." *A Selection of Papers Presented in 1969-70.* Jewish Historical Society of Western Canada.

Arnold, Abraham J. "Jewish Immigration to Western Canada." *Jewish Historical Society of Canada Journal,* 1, No. 2 (Fall, 1977).

Arnold, Abraham J. "The Prairies." *Viewpoints,* VII, Nos. 3 and 4 (1973).

Canadian Jewish Congress. Boycott Committee Bulletins. 1939.

Canadian Jewish Congress. "Fifty Years of Service, 1919-1969." 1970.

Cam, Elizabeth (Malkin). "Jews in University Life in Manitoba." *A Selection of Papers Presented in 1969-70.* Jewish Historical Society of Western Canada.

Cherniack, J. A., Q.C. "Reminiscences of 40 Years of Jewish Community Life." *A Selection of Papers Presented in 1969-70.* Jewish Historical Society of Western Canada.

Cherniack, J. A., Q.C. Collected papers, 1905-1970. Jewish Historical Society of Western Canada.

Chiel, Arthur. "Jews of Manitoba Revisited." *A Selection of Papers Presented in 1969-70.* Jewish Historical Society of Western Canada.

Crowe, Harry. "No Place to Hide: The Fortieth Anniversary of the Evian Conference." *Middle East Focus,* I, No. 4 (November, 1978).

"The Federenko Case." *Manitoba Reports,* 20 (1910).

Feingold, Henry L. "Who Shall Bear Guilt for the Holocaust: The Human Dilemma." *American Jewish Quarterly,* LXVIII, No. 3 (March, 1979).

Gale, Harry. "The Jewish Labour Movement in Winnipeg." *A Selection of Papers Presented in 1968-69.* Jewish Historical Society of Western Canada.

Ginsburg, Dr. J. B. Collected papers, 1913-1962. Jewish Historical Society of Western Canada.

Greeley, Andrew M. "After Ellis Island: In Praise of Ethnic Chauvinism." *Harper's,* Nov., 1978.

"A Half Century of Jewish Education, 1914-1964." I. L. Peretz Folk School, Winnipeg.

Hayes, Saul. "A View of Canadian Jewish History." *Viewpoints,* VII, Nos. 3 and 4 (1973).

Hayes, Saul. "Jewish Refugees in Canada." *Canadian Jewish Year Book,* 1941.

Henderson Directory, 1880, 1881.

Hershfield, D. C. (Sheppy). "Growing Up in North Winnipeg." *A Selection of Papers Presented in 1969-70.* Jewish Historical Society of Western Canada.

Herstein, Harvey H. "Jewish Religious Leadership in Winnipeg, 1900-1963." *Canadian Jewish Historical Society Journal,* 2, No. 1 (Spring, 1978).

Herstein, Harvey H. "The Growth of the Winnipeg Jewish Community and the Evolution of its Educational Institutions." *Transactions of the Manitoba Historical Society,* 1965-66.

Hoffer, Israel. "Recollections." *Saskatchewan History,* V., No. 1 (Winter, 1952).

"Jewish Communities: Regina, Saskatoon, Edmonton, Calgary, Fort William, Vancouver." *Israelite Press* [Winnipeg] Jubilee Edition, May, 1932.

"Jewish Parliamentary . . . Jewish Civic Representatives." *Israelite Press* [Winnipeg] Jubilee Edition, May, 1932.

Jewish Radical School, Winnipeg. Reports and programs, 1914, 1915, 1916.

"Jewish Welfare . . . Jewish Community Institutions." *Israelite Press* [Winnipeg] Jubilee Edition, May, 1932.

"The Jews in America." *Fortune Survey,* April, 1939.

Kage, Joseph. "This War Our Job: A Report on Jewish Immigration and Immigrant Adjustment in Canada for 1952." Jewish Immigrant Aid Society of Canada.

Kampf, Avram. "The Jewish Experience in Art of the Twentieth Century." Catalogue, Art Gallery, Mount Saint Vincent University, Halifax, Dec. 1976-Jan. 1977.

Klenman, Allan. "The Emanu-El of Victoria, Vancouver Island: a Short History of the Beginnings of Congregation Emanu-El." Congregation Emanu-El bulletin, n.d.

Laing, F. W., and W. Kaye Lamb. "Fire Companies of Old Victoria." *British Columbia Historical Quarterly,* X, No. 1 (January, 1946).

Manitoba Daily Free Press, May 22, 1882 to July 7, 1882.

News of the YIVO. Nos. 140-7 (1978). YIVO Institute for Jewish Research.

Rivkin, Ann. "British Columbia." *Viewpoints,* VII, Nos. 3 and 4 (1973).

Rosenberg, Louis. "The Canadian Jewish Congress 1919-1969: Fifty Years of Organized Jewish Community Life." *A Selection of Papers Presented in 1968-69.* The Jewish Historical Society of Western Canada.

Rosenberg, Louis. "Jews in Agriculture in Western Canada." *Israelite Press* [Winnipeg] Jubilee Edition, May, 1932.

"Russian Jewish Immigration to Canada." JIAS *Information Bulletins,* Sept. 8, 1976, No. 396; Nov. 15, 1977, No. 416.

Selchen, S. M. "The Western Canadian Jewish Settlement." *Israelite Press* [Winnipeg] Jubilee Edition, May, 1932.

Silcox, Claris Edwin. "Canadian Post-Mortem on Refugees." An Address, March, 1939, Canadian National Committee on Refugees, Toronto.

I. L. Peretz Folk School, Winnipeg. Souvenir books, 1916, 1918, 1920, 1921, 1922, 1925, 1929.

"The Voice of Canadian Jewry at Home and Abroad." Canadian Jewish Congress, April, 1962.

"Why Is Anti-Semitism?" *Fortune Survey,* April, 1939.

Wilder, H. E. "History of the Jews in Canada." *Israelite Press* [Winnipeg] Jubilee Edition, May, 1932.

Wilder, H. E. "Jewish Students in the Liberal Professions." *Israelite Press* [Winnipeg] Jubilee Edition, May, 1932.

Winnipeg Hebrew School (Talmud Torah). *Golden Jubilee Journal,* 1905-1957.

INDEX